Creative Evaluation

Creative Evaluation

Second Edition

Michael Quinn Patton

SAGE PUBLICATIONS
The Publishers of Professional Social Science
Newbury Park   Beverly Hills   London   New Delhi

For information address:

SAGE Publications, Inc.
2111 West Hillcrest Drive
Newbury Park, California 91320

SAGE Publications Inc.   SAGE Publications Ltd.
275 South Beverly Drive   28 Banner Street
Beverly Hills   London EC1Y 8QE
California 90212   England

SAGE PUBLICATIONS India Pvt. Ltd.
M-32 Market
Greater Kailash I
New Delhi 110 048 India

Printed in the United States of America

Library of Congress Cataloging-in-Publication Data

Patton, Michael Quinn.
    Creative evaluation.

    Bibliography: p.
    1. Evaluation research (Social action programs)
I. Title.
H62.P3215   1987   361.6′1′068   87-13197
ISBN 0-8039-3056-9

Contents

To
The American Evaluation Association

Preface

The author of a rather pretentious book entitled *Thoughts* once asked well-known British actor and playwright Samuel Foote if he had read it. "No, I'm waiting for the second volume," Foote replied. Since no second volume was planned or expected, the author was baffled and asked why. "Because I have heard that second thoughts are best," said Foote.

This revised edition contains my second—and updated—thoughts about creative evaluation. The opportunity for second thoughts is occasioned in part by an unfortunate fate that befell the original. Due to the vagaries of international mail, my final revisions and corrections for the original edition never reached the publisher from Trinidad, where the book was written. As a result the published original left a few things to be desired. This revised volume corrects those earlier deficiencies while updating and refining the substance of the book.

I've pulled together in this book many of the ideas, techniques, and approaches that I find are central to my own evaluation practice. I was never taught these things in formal courses and so had to pick them up through trial-and-error experimentation over years and miles of evaluation activity. Much of the book is about how to work creatively with decision makers and information users throughout an evaluation process by using a variety of conceptual approaches, focusing techniques, communication skills, and teaching devices.

It's no longer sufficient to produce a technically defensible and methodologically rigorous final report if one cares about the use of evaluation findings to improve programs. Where *actual use* of evaluation findings for program decision making and improvement is the goal, evaluators will often find that they need communication, facilitation, and consulting skills that go well beyond the usual content of most methodologically oriented evaluation and social science training programs. This book is an effort to enlarge the curriculum and expand the goals of such training programs in order to enlarge the creative repertoire of professional evaluators, thereby making it possible for them to be more genuinely situationally responsive, utilization-focused, and methodologically flexible.

Part I establishes a framework for creative evaluation. The three chapters in Part I discuss the need for creativity in evaluation, barriers to creative evaluation practice, and a vision of what greater creativity in evaluation might mean. The chapters in Part II deal with various creative approaches and techniques as applied to program evaluation. There are chapters on using metaphors; conceptual creativity and flexibility; flowcharting for insight and simplicity; storythinking; picturethinking; matrix thinking; simulation games and experiential exercises; illustrative methods; and humor in the evaluation process. While there is a logical flow to the sequencing of Parts I and II, understanding later chapters does not depend on having read earlier chapters. Each chapter in the book is self-contained. The chapters can thus be read in any order.

The book is *not* a "how to" book. Such a book would be a basic contradiction of the fundamental perspective presented throughout these pages—that creative evaluation is situational and that individual creativity is a matter of professional style and personal definition. A set of standard operating instructions on how to be creative would be counterproductive to the goal of stimulating both individual and situational creativity in evaluation. This book contains some things to think about and try, not a set of rules to follow.

* * *

This book is dedicated to the American Evaluation Association. In 1985 the members of the Evaluation Research Society and the Evaluation Network approved a merger to form the AEA. The officers and boards of the two predecessor organizations worked diligently to establish evaluation as a credible, respected, and useful field of professional practice. When the original edition of *Creative Evaluation* appeared in 1981 the future of evaluation was uncertain. When I returned to the United States in 1982 after two years in the Caribbean I found many colleagues asserting that evaluation was just a passing fad, well on the way to obscurity. The professional leadership was in the throes of very difficult and often bogged-down merger discussions. A kind of gloom hung over the field.

But in the last two years I have sensed a new enthusiasm. The gloom has lifted. There is no longer any question about the survival of evaluation as an important field of professional practice. It now even appears likely that we'll all survive the Reagan years. With the merger accomplished and the AEA a reality, the professional leadership is able to devote full attention to strengthening the profession. And stronger we are clearly becoming. We have learned a great deal about how to conduct useful evaluations and we are putting that learning into practice. Our expertise is valued as never before. The future has never looked brighter for program evaluators. I am therefore particularly pleased to dedicate this book to the new American Evaluation Association and its prosperous future. My thanks to the officers and members of AEA for their support of my own evaluation work and for all they have taught me about creative evaluation.

My thanks also to Margaret Y. Russell, who diligently and painstakingly typed this manuscript. She worked under the usual impossibly tight deadline, and did so with patience, good humor, and great competence.

PART I: The Creative Imperative
in the Practice of Evaluation

"Creativity is in the EYE of the beholder."

The Ten Commandments
of Evaluation

(1) Thou shalt have no other gods before evaluation—not planning, not policy analysis, not applied social science, *certainly not* basic research or theory or sociology or psychology or any other *ology* or *ism* because the fields of research are confused enough already and if evaluators don't put evaluation first, then who will?

(2) Thou shalt not worship any idols or other graven images whether they be rock stars, politicians, TV personalities, big-name academics, or any other stakeholders because stakeholders put their pants or skirts on one leg at a time just like evaluators, so if evaluators start worshipping stakeholders, then stakeholders will get to thinking they're better than evaluators and they won't accord us the proper respect—which, if you have noticed, is already in pretty damn short supply.

(3) Thou shalt not take the name of evaluation in vain. (If you can't say something nice, don't say anything at all, unless of course you're writing a final evaluation report—then give 'em hell.)

(4) Remember the day your report is due, to keep it holy. Six days (metaphorically) you may gather your data, but the seventh day is set aside to report and apply findings. (There is no day of rest for evaluators.)

(5) Honor your stakeholders and data providers, so that you may continue to find more work to do.

(6) Thou shalt not kill. (Remind stakeholders often of this commandment—especially as it applies to bearers of bad news.)

(7) Thou shalt not commit adultery with stakeholder spouses. (This tends to threaten validity, reliability, objectivity, and your life. If you fail to heed this commandment, and get caught, refer the offended stakeholder back to commandment 6.)

(8) Thou shalt not steal other evaluators' contracts—data maybe, but never contracts.

(9) Thou shalt not bear false witness against thy neighbor. (In other words, don't fudge the data. It's not nice.)

(10) Thou shalt not covet thy stakeholder's house or thy stakeholder's spouse, or servant, or ox, or donkey, or anything that belongs to your stakeholders, including especially thy stakeholder's stake, which if you coveted it and actually got it would make you the stakeholder rather than the evaluator, which just goes to show you the trouble that can come of this coveting business to begin with—so don't.

CHAPTER 1: *The Source of the Creative Imperative*

> *Human salvation lies in the*
> *hands of the creatively maladjusted.*

Martin Luther King, Jr.

A Setting

The scene is a coffee shop in Memphis, site of the 1980 annual professional evaluation meetings. Some colleagues are trying to help me define creativity as it might apply to evaluation. But one of them takes exception to the task: "With everything else we're asked to be as evaluators, surely you're not going to ask us to be creative too? Give us a break."

Even a cursory review of the various sessions at the meetings supported his point that the demands being made on evaluators were already awesome. We were admonished by presenters to be technically competent, politically neutral, methodologically rigorous, politically sophisticated, theoretically sound, politically connected, ethnically pure, methodologically open, client oriented, cost conscious, professional, independent (not just morally and politically, but also financially—thus advice on how to start your own consulting practice), epistemologically grounded (whatever that means), and conscientiously prompt in paying annual dues to the professional evaluation association.

We were also told to follow the scriptural mandate to "go forth, be fruitful and multiple"—*multiple* methods, *multiple* audiences, *multiple* funding sources, *multiple* perspectives, *multiple* paradigms, *multiple* roles, and *multiple* solutions to *multiple* problems.

With everything else evaluators are supposed to be, it may indeed seem to be going a bit far to ask that creativity be added to the list. But perhaps, just perhaps, creativity would *lighten* the burden evaluators are called on to bear rather than make it heavier. This book explores that possibility. In fact, I shall argue in this book that creativity may have become the sine qua non of evaluation. *How else but by being creative could we possibly be and do all the things we're supposed to be and do?*

The call to be creative is implicit in the call to play multiple roles and exemplify multiple virtues in a multitude of demanding situations while all the time being responsive and useful to such diverse stakeholders as program staff, program participants, funders, administrators, politicians, fellow professionals, and the general public. From this perspective, creativity isn't just an optional extra to be added on after all the other good-scout criteria for evaluators have been mastered. Creativity is a source from which the other virtues and competencies can draw energy and direction.

Creativity might just make evaluations *easy* to do, "easy" as meant by Salvador Dali in his reply to an admirer who asked, "Is it hard to paint a picture?" "No," the great artist is said to have replied, "It's either easy or impossible."

THE PROFESSIONAL PRACTICE OF EVALUATION

This book presents some ways of thinking about and doing program evaluation. As the title indicates, the emphasis is on *creative* ways of thinking about and doing evaluation. Creative evaluation is not some new model of evaluation. It is not meant to supplant or compete with major approaches in the profession. Rather, I shall argue here that creativity is an inherent demand of effective evaluation practice in general.

The practice of evaluation involves the systematic collection of information about the activities, characteristics, and outcomes of programs for use by specific people to reduce uncertainties, improve effectiveness, and make decisions with regard to what those programs are doing and affecting. This definition of evaluation emphasizes (1) the systematic collection of information about (2) a broad range of topics (3) for use by specific people (4) for a variety of purposes. This broad definition focuses on gathering data that are meant to be—and actually are—used for program improvement and decision making.

The practice of evaluation is to be conducted in accordance with stated professional standards. The standards are necessarily broad principles meant to provide guidance in a wide variety of evaluation situations. The standards specify what constitutes excellence as well as minimally acceptable professional behavior.

It will be my contention in this chapter that the standards implicitly constitute a mandate to be creative. To support that assertion it is necessary to begin by examining the standards, for those standards of conduct and excellence are the source of the creative imperative in evaluation.

Standards of Excellence in Evaluation

A major function of a profession is to establish standards of excellence for practitioners.

> Because every "scientific" discipline deals with a subject matter that is different in some key respects from that of other disciplines, each discipline must develop at least some methodological standards that are to a significant degree unique to that discipline. No discipline can rely solely on a straight-forward application of a general philosophy-of-science doctrine. (Beardsley, 1980, p. 39)

Until relatively recently, evaluators looked to their respective disciplines for guidance regarding standards. Psychologists looked to psychology, educators to education, economists to economics, and so on. Moreover, in the infancy of the profession, methods discussions dominated evaluators' concerns about quality and excellence. Evaluators were primarily concerned about technical adequacy, validity, reliability, measurability, and generalizability. "Good" evaluation research was judged by the same basic research standards as "good" science, which typically meant a preference for quantitative measurement, experimental designs, and statistical analysis. Evaluators followed the methodological rules, norms, and standards of basic research.

But over time, program evaluation has emerged as significantly different from basic research. Research is aimed at truth. Evaluation is aimed at action. Researchers produce knowledge for the sake of knowledge. Evaluators produce information meant to affect policymaking and improve program effectiveness.

Program evaluation has emerged as a specialized field of interdisciplinary professional practice quite distinct from other fields of research. Evaluation draws on all social science fields of inquiry, but is quite distinct from and cuts across traditional disciplines. As a specialized profession, evaluation needs its own set of standards to guide professional practice. The most important effort in this regard to date has been the work of Dan Stufflebeam and the Joint Committee on Standards for Educational Evaluation (1981). While originally developed with educational evaluations in mind, these standards have proved to be generally applicable across all kinds of evaluations.

The standards call for evaluations that have four primary characteristics:

UTILITY

FEASIBILITY

PROPRIETY

ACCURACY

Stufflebeam said of the standards:

> I think it is interesting that the Joint Committee decided on that particular order. Their rationale is that an evaluation should not be done at all if there is no prospect for its being useful to some audience. Second, it should not be done if it is not feasible to conduct it in political terms, or practicality terms, or cost effectiveness terms. Third, they do not think it should be done if we cannot demonstrate that it will be conducted fairly and ethically. Finally, if we can demonstrate that an evaluation will have utility, will be feasible and will be proper in its conduct then they said we could turn to the difficult matters of the technical adequacy of the evaluation, and they have included an extensive set of standards in this area. (Stufflebeam, 1980, p. 90)

The standards—utility, feasibility, propriety, and accuracy—capture the essence of evaluation as a distinct field of professional practice. The articulation of priorities in the statement of evaluation standards represents a cohesive philosophy for evaluation practitioners and professionals. This philosophy has profound implications for the practice of evaluation. In comparison to the traditional practices of the social and behavioral sciences, implementation of a *utility-focused, feasibility-conscious, propriety-oriented, and accuracy-based approach to program evaluation* requires special skills, commitments, and sensitivities:

- commitment to making a difference
- taking personal responsibility for how an evaluation is used
- skill in helping nonresearchers formulate meaningful and important evaluation questions that are researchable
- political sensitivity and diplomatic sophistication
- interpersonal communication skills
- a large repertoire of diverse methods
- group facilitation skills
- skill in writing for and speaking to a variety of audiences with very different levels of research sophistication
- creativity

I intend this list to be merely suggestive, not exhaustive. The purpose of this list is to call attention to the shifts in emphasis that have occurred as evaluation has developed and matured.

The context for creative evaluation includes several developments. First, methods decisions no longer dominate the evaluation decision-making process or judgments about the quality of an evaluator. Concerns have broadened to include the usefulness of the evaluation, the practicalities of actually implementing an evaluation process, and the politics of evaluation practice. Second, there has been a marked shift away from the dominance of quantitative and experimental methods toward a paradigm of choices emphasizing multiple methods, both qualitative and quantitative, and matching evaluation methods to specific evaluation situations and stakeholder questions. Third, evaluation has developed beyond a narrow focus on whether a program has attained its goals to encompass a broad array of questions, purposes, approaches, models, and uses. Fourth, a large evaluation literature has blossomed to explore and support the many new facets of evaluation practice since the publication of the seminal *Handbook of Evaluation Research* (Guttentag & Struening, 1975). Fifth, the American Evaluation Association has developed into a professional organization devoted to and capable of supporting diverse evaluator needs and interests. Sixth, the accumulation of practical evaluation experience over the last 20 years has led to both increased sophistication about and exploration of many new arenas of evaluation activity. Seventh, users of evaluation have become more demanding and less tolerant of evaluations that are overly academic, irrelevant to their needs, and/or wasteful of time and resources. Eighth, evaluation training programs have emerged to provide the skills, sensitivities, and understandings necessary to engage in effective evaluation practice. Ninth, evaluators have lived through and learned from both the tremendous expansion of social programs in the sixties and the retrenchment of government services in the eighties, and in so doing have found that the profession of evaluation has not only survived but has matured. And, finally, in that maturation, evaluators lost their innocence and discovered the real world of special interests, competing stakeholders, and decision making that is seldom purely "data-based," "rational," and "logical" in ideal textbook terms.

These developments and the corresponding articulation of evaluation standards are the sources of the mandate to be creative. That mandate derives directly from the need for evaluators to be situationally responsive in adapting their evaluation practices to fit the interests of specific stakeholders, the constraints of political realities, the frustrations of too little money, and the demands for high-impact evaluations. The next section examines the creative mandate embedded in being situationally responsive and flexible.

Situational Responsiveness

The philosophical perspective that undergirds creative evaluation is the recognition that *there is no one best way to conduct an evaluation*. This insight is critical.

Every evaluation situation is unique. A successful evaluation (one that is useful, practical, ethical, and accurate) emerges from the special characteristics and conditions of a particular situation—a mixture of people, politics, history, context, resources, constraints, values, needs, interests, and chance. Despite the rather common sensible nature of these observations, there are a host of subtleties and nuances implicit in this shift in perspective—a shift from evaluation judged by a single, standard, and universal criterion (methodological rigor) to situational evaluation where decision criteria are multiple, flexible, and diverse. This shift in perspective places new demands on evaluators.

Situational responsiveness requires that an evaluator be "active-reactive-adaptive." This is the phrase I used in *Utilization-Focused Evaluation* (Patton, 1986) to try to capture the dynamic nature of the evaluation consultative process in working with primary information users. The evaluator actively solicits information about program contingencies, organizational dynamics, environmental uncertainties, and decision-maker goals in order to focus the evaluation on questions of real interest to primary information users. The evaluator reacts to the information obtained to work with stakeholders in designing a useful, practical, and accurate evaluation. As new information emerges in the process of designing or conducting the evaluation, the evaluator adapts to that new information or to a changed and changing situation. In short, situational responsiveness means being active, reactive, and adaptive.

Creativity is essential to situational responsiveness. If one is being genuinely active, reactive, and adaptive in responding to the special and unique people, circumstances, and factors in any particular evaluation, one cannot simply borrow an old design and make it fit this unique, new situation. Each evaluation situation becomes unique, and leads to a unique evaluation creation.

There are a large number of factors and variables to take into account in being situationally responsive. One important situational variable is the number of stakeholders to be dealt with in the evaluation. Some evaluations have a single client—one decision maker—to whom the evaluator is responsible. Other evaluations involve a large number of diverse stakeholders from many different constituencies.

Evaluations have many different purposes. The classic distinction between formative evaluation, aimed primarily at program improvement, in contrast to summative evaluation, aimed at making fundamental judgments about program success, calls attention to two very different kinds of evaluation situations. But the formative-summative distinction only begins to illuminate the diversity of purposes evaluation may serve. There are political purposes, for example, to highlight a program, to try to kill a program, to build support for a program, or merely to provide for public accountability.

There are variations in the program itself that will affect the evaluation. New programs are different from old programs. Large programs are different from small programs. Programs that take place at multiple sites are different from single-site programs. National programs are different from local programs. Programs with only one funding source differ from those with multiple funding sources to which they are accountable. Some programs have very simple and unidimensional treatments, while others have complex and multidimensional treatments. Some treatments and programs are highly standardized and routine; others are very individualized and nonroutine.

Programs also differ in how they are conceptualized. Some programs have very clear and specific goals, while for many others goals are vague and general. Some programs have very detailed implementation plans; others are very fluid with minimal planning. Some programs have operating management information systems; others collect almost no data. Some programs are designed to test a model or theory; other programs simply operate in response to some need or want. Some programs have very clear points of intake and exit for clients; in others it is very difficult to tell when a client is in or out of the program, and client participation may be ongoing, sporadic, or both.

Staffs also differ tremendously from one program to another. A staff experiencing its very first evaluation will be quite different from one that has gone through many other evaluation exercises, either positive or negative. Professional staffs are different from programs relying heavily on volunteers. The organization of the staff can affect the program and the evaluation. A very hierarchical staff arrangement will require a different working relationship than will one that is horizontal and egalitarian in organization and working relationships.

The evaluation situation itself varies in as many ways as programs vary. Some evaluations have very short time lines; others can go on for quite a long period of time, or may even be ongoing. Internal evaluators are often called on to operate quite differently from their external counterparts. The resources available for evaluation will greatly affect what can be done. The evaluators' prior experiences, discipline, credibility, and confidence will all affect the evaluation.

These preceding paragraphs are only a few illustrations of the many variables and factors that affect evaluations and evaluators. Situational evaluation means that evaluators have to be prepared to deal with a lot of different people and situations. It is this great variation that makes each evaluation a unique creation. Being situationally responsive and creative in dealing with these myriad variables and factors is no easy task. It was recognition of precisely this challenge that led evaluators in attendance at the 1978 Evaluation Network meetings in Aspen to adopt Jim Hennes's lament as their official slogan and bumper sticker:

> Evaluators do IT under difficult circumstances.

No One Best Way

> Nothing is more dangerous than an idea when it is the only one you have.
> —Emile Chartier, French Philosopher

Evaluation students are frequently asked to analyze a program and determine the single best evaluation design. There is an assumption in many methods courses that there is such a thing as the single best design. This seems to follow logically from the premise of much scientific thinking that for every problem there is a single best answer. However, the implication of the previous section describing the many variables to be taken into consideration in any given evaluation means that there can be neither a single best way to proceed nor a single best design.

What constitutes "the best" depends on the criteria one chooses for any given situation. The criterion of methodological rigor will lead in many cases to a design that is different from focusing on the criterion of utility. Serving some stakeholder interests over others (an inevitability) will mean that different stakeholder groups will have different perceptions about the "goodness" of the evaluation.

In his best-selling book on creativity, Roger von Oech, founder and president of Creative Think, identifies the search for "the one right answer" as the number one barrier to creative thinking and problem solving.

> Much of our educational system is geared toward teaching people *the one right answer*. By the time the average person finishes college, he or she will have taken over 2,600 tests, quizzes, and exams. . . . Thus, the "right" answer approach becomes deeply engrained in our thinking. This may be fine for some mathematical problems where there is in fact only one right answer. The difficulty is that most of life doesn't present itself in this way. Life is ambiguous; there are many right answers—all depending on what you are looking for. But if you think there is only one right answer, then you will stop looking as soon as you find one. (von Oech, 1983, p. 21)

There is a certain freedom that comes with realizing that there is truly no one right answer. Understood at the deepest level, this precept means that one can give up the burden of having to come up with the *right* design or the *right* analysis or the *right* findings. The design, the analysis, and the findings will all depend on the situation, including the evaluator's perception of the situation, the stakeholders' perceptions of the situation, and the unique interplay between the evaluator's and stakeholders' interactions concerning their respective perceptions.

Rather than having to be faithful to some model or paradigm, the evaluator can be faithful to the situation—and in so being, can be creative. At the simplest level, then, creative evaluation means nothing more than matching evaluations to unique situations where it is understood that the evaluator himself or herself is part of both the situation *and* the uniqueness.

A Paradigm of Choices

To be situationally responsive it is necessary to consider a variety of factors and weigh a number of evaluation alternatives in matching the evaluation to the situation. Various options (always more than one) will have to be considered, often in collaboration with intended users and stakeholders.

While this all sounds very reasonable and straightforward, there is substantial evidence to suggest that *genuine* situational responsiveness is quite difficult in practice. The evidence from social and behavioral science is that in any area of decision making, when faced with complex choices and multiple variables, we fall back on a set of rules and standard operating procedures that *predetermine* what we will do, effectively short-circuiting situational adaptability. This means, quite simply, that most of the time we are operating on preprogrammed mental tapes. The programs on those tapes come from the scientific paradigm in which we have been trained, usually including the idea that there is a single best solution and a single right answer.

A paradigm tells a scientist how to operate in the face of a new situation. Faced with some decision about what to do in the face of uncertainty, the scientist unconsciously turns to paradigmatic rules for guidance. This may help explain why so many evaluators who have genuinely embraced the philosophy of situational evaluation find that the approaches in which they are trained and with which they are most comfortable *just happen* to be particularly appropriate in each new situation they confront—time after time after time.

A paradigm is a worldview, a general perspective, a way of breaking down the complexity of the real world. As such, paradigms are deeply embedded in the socialization of adherents and practitioners: paradigms tell them what is important, legitimate, and reasonable. Paradigms are also normative, telling the practitioner what to do without the necessity of long existential or epistemological consideration. But it is this aspect of paradigms that constitutes both their strength and their weakness: Their strength is that it makes action possible; their weakness is that the very reason for action is hidden in the unquestioned assumptions of the paradigm.

Paradigms make it possible for researchers to engage in "normal science," the nitty-gritty, standard operating procedure work of filling in the details and testing the specific hypotheses of major theories. You will notice that there isn't a lot of room for creativity in Kuhn's description of normal science.

Scientists work from models acquired through education and through subsequent exposure to the literature often without quite knowing or needing to know what characteristics have given these models the status of community paradigms. . . . That scientists do not usually ask or debate what makes a particular problem or solution legitimate tempts us to suppose that, at least intuitively, they know the answer. But it may only indicate that neither the question nor the answer is felt to be relevant to their research. Paradigms may be prior to, more binding, and more complete than any set of rules for research that could be unequivocally abstracted from them. (Kuhn, 1970, p. 46)

The practice of "normal science" within any of the major disciplines is quite different from the practice of creative evaluation. Creative evaluation is a paradigm of choices. It recognizes a broad range of viable research methods and approaches. Creative evaluation involves situational responsiveness, methodological flexibility, conscious matching of evaluation approaches to the needs and interests of those with whom one is working, and sensitivity to the unique constraints and possibilities of particular circumstances. Creative evaluation is a problem-solving approach that emphasizes adaptation to changes and changing conditions, as opposed to a technical approach, which attempts to mold and define conditions to fit preconceived models of how things should be done.

Creative evaluation involves overcoming what Brightman and Noble (1979) have identified as "the ineffective education of decision scientists." They portray typical decision scientists (a generic term for evaluators, policy analysts, planners, and so on) as

hopelessly naive and intellectually arrogant. Naive because they believe that problem solving begins and ends with analysis, and arrogant because they opt for mathematical rigor over results. They are products of their training. Decision science departments appear to have been more effective at training technocrats to deal with structured problems than problem solvers to deal with ill-structured ones. (Brightman & Noble, 1979, p. 150)

An Example of a Paradigm Shift

This chapter has already presented one example of a paradigm shift in discussing the implications of the standards for evaluation—a shift from a single, universal criterion in judging evaluation quality (methodological rigor) to multiple and situational criteria. There is another recent paradigm shift, however, that is highly relevant to evaluation in general and to the perspective in this book in particular. That paradigm shift involves the work of the "public choice" school of economics.

In 1986 George Mason University professor James Buchanan was awarded the Nobel Prize in Economics for his "public choice doctrine," which uses the economic idea of self-interest to analyze the behavior of politicians and bureaucrats in policymaking. The traditional economic paradigm was based on an optimization assumption in which economists theorized that policymakers always attempted to find the best policy package to reach certain specified targets of government policy. This paradigm assumed, first of all, that there would be a great deal of information available. Second, it assumed that government officials would have access to this information. Third, it assumed that people in government would have incentives to follow the optimal policy.

The optimization model, like the earlier maximization model that it replaced, was very logical and rational, and assumed logic and rationality on the part of decision makers and policymakers. The public choice school of economics, however, points out that decision makers and policymakers have vested interests, conflicts of interest, and self-interests like all other human beings. Those personal interests affect their decisions. The public choice school analyzes the behavior of politicians and public administrators under the assumptions that, as human beings, they have limited information and use that limited information to serve the interests of their own groups based upon their own perceptions of costs and benefits. It is particularly noteworthy for evaluators, I think, that part of the inspiration for the public choice school was the observation from experience that policymakers very seldom followed the advice of economists in anything like pure form. Likewise, the standards for evaluation grew out of the observation, based upon a great deal of experience, that decision makers and stakeholders seldom follow evaluators' advice and recommendations in anything like pure form.

The public choice school of economics calls on economists to analyze the individual perspectives and situations of the people involved in making policies. Situational evaluation makes the same demand on evaluators.

Part of that demand is avoiding Type III errors. Ian Mitroff (1978) described Type III errors as solving the wrong problem when you should have solved the right problem. Type I and Type II errors involve falsely accepting or rejecting an hypothesis. The error of the third kind involves inadequate problem formulation rather than inadequate problem solving.

> To get away from the Type III error you have to examine how a problem changes as you vary the paradigm for conceptualizing it. . . . I see an emerging notion of managerial (and social science) rationality. We need new methods for solving what I call ill-structured problems. Most of the methodology that we have is for working on well-structured problems, but all the fundamental problems . . . are ill-structured. (Mitroff, 1978, pp. 130-131)

To understand the enormous challenge of moving beyond traditional paradigms to situational evaluation, and the creativity required to be situationally flexible, it will be instructive to review evidence about how humans typically make decisions and deal with complexity.

BARRIERS TO CREATIVE PROBLEM-SOLVING

Experimental evidence shows that human information processing appears to be severely limited by memory capacity. Short-term memory is highly limited, long-term memory presents serious problems of access, and moving items from short-term memory to long-term memory is a problematic process fraught with error. Given these limitations, information scientist Michael Inbar asked this fundamental question:

> In view of the extremely stringent constraints which limit man's information-processing capability, how does he solve problems of more than trivial complexity? For despite the theoretical impossibility, he does play chess in real time, and sometimes very well. Moreover, he behaves adaptively in the countlessly more complex situations he confronts daily. Shopping, for instance, is routinely done in minutes or hours, despite the number of choices to be made which far exceed the twenty options available at the beginning of a game of chess. (Inbar, 1979, p. 59)

The problem of playing games has received a good deal of attention in the decision-making literature. The literature makes a critical distinction between the "comprehensive decision model" and the "noncomprehensive decision model." A comprehensive decision model requires considering *every possible solution* to a problem. Thus in an evaluation situation with just 20 variables to consider concerning program characteristics, stakeholder interests, organizational dynamics, political factors, and so on, a comprehensive approach to situational evaluation would require consideration of the possibility that a given situation fits any one of 8,000 to 3,200,000 possibilities (the permutations and combinations of 20 variables each with a minimum of three categories). A computer program designed to test that many possibilities (10!) would require several hours of supercomputer time to run. A comprehensive examination of *all* the possible moves in a game of chess 10^{120} has yet to be undertaken even by the most powerful computers. Practical limitations mean that we cannot function without some kinds of *noncomprehensive* search procedures that provide us with shortcuts in decision making. This has significant implications for the quality of the resulting decisions and problem solutions.

> One thing appears to be clear. Except, perhaps, for some simple laboratory tasks involving at most a couple of dichotomous or trichotomous choices, man cannot and does not solve problems by anything resembling the comprehensive strategy. This fact has an immediate implication if we note that no other strategy can guarantee that a chosen course of action is the best path to a goal. Quite clearly, if one does not generate and inspect the whole decision tree of a problem, the solution, or another solution may have been overlooked. It follows that whatever alternative strategy man actually follows, he cannot be sure of the quality of his decision for his own purposes. Whatever the noncomprehensive strategy which is used, it must amount to a sampling of the problem space. Under these conditions, and without some knowledge of the decision-making strategy and of the nature of the problem, the probability of having found the correct solution, or a good solution, is an open question. Insofar as most people do not have such conscious knowledge the objective quality of any decision which cannot readily be validated is unassessable, including by and for oneself. From these considerations it appears that the usual belief that in decisionmaking there is always some possibility of making a mistake, is probably grossly misleading. In truth, the situation is more likely to be the other way around. On a priori grounds it would seem that for any nontrivial problem, it is an *error-free decision which is accidental.* (Inbar, 1979, p. 59)

The ideal of rational decision making requires making comprehensive searches and then selecting the option that maximizes, or at least optimizes, attainment of the desired outcome(s). The impossibility of comprehensive searches means that most decision making is "satisficing" (Simon, 1957) rather than maximizing or even optimizing. Maximizing means picking the best of all possible alternatives; satisficing means picking the first solution that appears to provide a reasonable solution to the problem. Such a solution is "satisfactory" rather than ideal, thus the term *satisficing*. Because of the complexity of most decisions and the limitations of our human decision making powers, most decision making processes are aimed at satisficing. In order to satisfice, however, one still has to have a process for finding at least "satisfactory" solutions and for recognizing such solutions when they appear in the course of a noncomprehensive search. That is where human heuristics come in.

Human Heuristics

It turns out that in order to make even trivial decisions we rely on *heuristics*, a term that refers to all noncomprehensive decision strategies, for example, rules of thumb, standard operating procedures, tricks of the trade, and in some respects even scientific paradigms. "Whether man is aware of the fact or not, (heuristics) turn out to be the only strategy available to him for nearly all the problems he confronts" (Inbar, 1979, p. 61).

Observations in both experimental and nonexperimental settings are making it possible for researchers to describe and classify certain common human heuristics. Some of these are particularly salient as limitations on our ability to do situationally creative evaluations.

One of the most common heuristics is the "representativeness" strategy of problem solving. It is used when confronted with such questions as the following:

> "What is the probability that object A belongs to class B? What is the probability that event A originates from process B? What is the probability that process B will generate event A?" (Tversky & Kahneman, 1974, p. 1124)

In program evaluation the relevant questions would be of the following types: What is the probability that these people are genuinely interested in evaluation? What is the probability that this evaluation is just being done because it is required? What is the probability that a goals-based approach (or responsive evaluation or utilization-focused evaluation) will generate relevant information that is used for program improvement? Answering any of these questions would involve proba-bility estimates of where the program or situation falls along a number of situational dimensions (for example, nature of the program, purpose of the evaluation, and so on). Inbar notes that there are powerful statistical problem-solving algorithms available to assist in making such needs estimates. But the representativeness heuristic is almost always used instead.

> In most cases people do not have either the time, the information, or the knowledge required for applying the algorithms. What happens then? That is, how do people, including statistically sophisticated scientists, solve everyday problems of the type illustrated above? The empirical evidence is that they rely on a simple heuristic, the essence of which is that judgments of likelihood are reduced to judgments of similarity. (Inbar, 1979, p. 82)

Inbar presents a great deal of evidence documenting the prevalence of the representativeness heuristic, including its routine operation among sophisticated researchers. Basically, what appears to happen is that upon entering a new situation, we make sense out of that situation (that is, categorize and label it) by focusing on those aspects of the situation that are most familiar to us and those elements of the situation that are most similar to our previous experiences. We thus *force* the new problem or situation to be "representative" of things we already know, selectively ignoring information and evidence that is unfamiliar or that doesn't fit our stereotypes developed through past experiences. This can result in systematic judgmental errors about the problem or situation.

Many of the exercises and techniques presented in this book are aimed at helping people (both evaluators and decision makers) move beyond their usual reliance on the representativeness heuristic. Creative evaluation opens up the possibility of defining situations as new and looking for new solutions to fit the situation at hand, so that we need not automatically become limited by and victims of our past experiences.

Lest we have doubts about decisions reached and judgments made by applying the representativeness heuristic, there is always the "confidence" heuristic to ward off such doubts. The confidence heuristic operates as we obtain more and more information about a situation or problem. The more information we obtain, the more confident we are about our judgments. But experimental evidence shows that "the level of accuracy does not vary significantly with increased information" (Inbar, 1979, p. 85). We tend to force new information to fit initial judgments while steadily increasing our confidence in those judgments.

Another heuristic that could readily affect our ability to engage in a creative situational evaluation process is the "availability" heuristic. It is used where memory is needed in an analysis. Things that have happened to us often or information that we come across frequently is more readily available for retrieval than less common information. We thus carry into new situations probability estimates about the likelihood of a new situation falling into a certain category based on our previously available experiences with that category. A sociologically trained evaluator is likely to have available a large repertoire of cases where a survey was the "appropriate" evaluation method. This increases the probability of defining a new situation as one appropriate for the conduct of a survey.

The availability heuristic is the epitome of the satisficing approach to decision making, the tendency to settle for the first solution that seems to offer a minimal solution to a problem. By contrast, creative evaluation assumes that there is always more than one way of doing things. While generating multiple possibilities does not mean conducting a comprehensive search for the ultimate solution, it does mean moving beyond the narrow limitations of single-solution satisficing.

Finally, for our purposes, there is the "anchoring" heuristic. This problem-solving strategy explains the tendency to be conservative in moving away from an established position. When people make an estimate of the likelihood of occurrence of some new event, that estimate is *anchored* in whatever previous estimates are available to that person. In evaluation this heuristic is seen most readily in goal-setting, budgeting, and data analysis exercises. Goals and budgets are basically set incrementally, not on the basis of all available information, including new information that might involve major deviations from past levels. In a similar vein, decision makers and evaluators may be operating by this heuristic when they tend to give most credence to data that fit expectations (prior probability estimates) and to ignore or explain away findings that do not conform to expectations. The anchoring heuristic is especially likely to be manifest at the data analysis and interpretation stages of evaluation. Thus *creativity is not something that is just applied at the beginning of an evaluation, then back to business as usual. Creative approaches are needed throughout the evaluation process— from beginning to end, conceptualization to utilization.*

Heuristic Awareness

The real difficulty posed by the human reliance on paradigms and heuristics for problem-solving and decision making is not so much their existence but our general lack of awareness of their existence. Autonomic thinking systems and conditioned reflexes are barriers to creative evaluation. It is difficult to be attuned and responsive to the uniqueness of each new situation when our programmed heuristics and scientific paradigms are controlling the analytical process, screening unfamiliar data, anchoring the new situation within the narrow parameters of our past experience, and making available to us primarily those approaches we have used most often in other situations. Inbar summarizes the limitations on creative human decision making quite succinctly:

> As a rule, man can only satisfice, not maximize, attends to a few cues at one time, cannot order preferences well, and engages in analytical problem-solving only as a last resort, and even then reverts to his habitual mode of decision-making at the first opportunity. (Inbar, 1979, p. 115)

> The overwhelming evidence is that man develops stable rules which are relatively easy to model. While decisions may be discretionary in terms of role prerogatives, the fact is they become rapidly stereotyped . . . , very predictable, and can be modeled with a surprising degree of accuracy— whether the decision-makers themselves or the people who are in complementary role sets, are aware of the fact or not. (Inbar, 1979, p. 112)

We are usually not aware of our paradigms and heuristics. We are typically not conscious that what we perceive to be discretionary judgments are really predictable routines. We are more like the mouse who *"chooses"* to like cheese or the bear who *"chooses"* to like honey than we generally care to admit. The difference is that they act primarily on instinct, whereas we act out our socialization patterns.

Fortunately, the same human nature that makes us such easy prey for falling into patterns holds the potential for our release from those patterns. It is not easy, it is not usual, but it is possible to become aware of our paradigms and heuristics and in that awareness take control of our decision processes, thereby releasing our creative potential. The scientists who have done the most work in experiments on heuristics hold out the hope that we need not be limited in our analyses by the confining patterns of our heuristic approaches.

> People are rarely aware of the basis of their impressions and they have little deliberate control over the processes by which these impressions are formed. However, *they can learn to identify the heuristic processes that determine their impressions, and to make appropriate allowances for the biases to which they are liable.* (Tversky & Kahneman, 1974, pp. 1124-1125)

There is other evidence that we can move beyond simple heuristics as our sole mode of response to problem solving and decision making. Bryson and Delbecq (1979) have reviewed some 15 years of work on "contingency approaches" to planning. The contingency approach to project planning is equivalent to what I have called the situational approach to evaluation. The contingency approach requires adapting decision making choices based on a variety of organizational structure and process dimensions. The ideology has existed in planning for a long time. The difficulty has been getting planners actually to behave that way. Bryson and Delbecq ran planning simulations where they found that it was possible to get planners to behave contingently if given the choice and the instructions to do so. Contingency behaviors, however, were used in conjunction with some standard planning heuristics. The authors noted that the training of planners needs considerable revision to equip students with the skills needed for thinking and acting in accordance with situational contingencies. Especially needed, they believe, are communications, group process, political, listening, and negotiating skills.

For me, learning to be truly active-reactive-adaptive as evaluators, learning to think situationally and contingently, and learning to take into account the biases introduced by our heuristics and paradigms means learning to be creative. New brain pathways can emerge within the existing brain structures. The existing brain structures and pathways are the location of our paradigms and heuristics. Creative pathways work around and between these existing pathways, sometimes touching them, sometimes connecting them, but ultimately carving out a new, different, and unique channel rather than making existing channels deeper. The starting point is awareness that you have the option of creating new pathways; you don't have to just follow along the old ruts, making them deeper and deeper. Rudolf Flesch put it more eloquently:

> Creative thinking may mean simply the realization that there's no particular virtue in doing things the way they've always been done.

Creative Thinking

Creative evaluation is likely to require a bit of creative thinking. This section emphasizes the *thinking* part of creative thinking. What does it mean to think?

I no more have a definitive definition of thinking than I have a definitive definition of creativity (the subject of the next chapter). But we can examine some of the characteristics of thinking. First, when I use the term *thinking*, I am referring to *conscious* activity in the mind. "Unconscious thinking is a contradiction in terms," asserts evaluation sage Halcolm. Becoming aware of one's heuristics implies consciously thinking about one's own problem-solving and decision-making patterns.

Second, thinking is the expenditure of mental energy. It is neurological exertion. It is work.

A good many very thoughtful people have commented on what they perceive as a basic human aversion to consciousness and the work of thinking. These commentators on thinking have arrived at the conclusion that as a species (referring here to the human species in general, not the subspecies known as evaluators) we don't do much thinking, don't like to think, and aren't really very good at it despite the fact that the ability to think characterizes and distinguishes us as a species. There are various estimates of how much we actually use our gray matter—the kinder guesses suggesting we may occasionally attain as much as 20% of our potential. Thomas Edison is reputed to have been sufficiently skeptical about our willingness to think that he had the following sign posted in every room of the Edison Laboratories:

THERE IS NO EXPEDIENT TO WHICH A
MAN WILL NOT GO TO AVOID THINKING.

Henry Ford, another great inventor, was no less impressed with the willingness of people to think. He said, "Thinking is the hardest work there is, which is probably the reason why so few engage in it." Nor are we even credited with being aware of or willing to admit our slovenly ways when it comes to thinking. Jane Taylor penned a thoughtful rhyme to point out our basic thoughtlessness.

Though man a thinking being is defined,
Few use the grand prerogative of mind.
How few think justly of the thinking few!
How many never think who think they do!

Third, and last, there are different kinds of thinking. The term *thinking* includes such complex and interrelated processes as questioning, gathering information, analyzing, synthesizing, arranging, integrating, criticizing, taking things apart, making linkages, adapting, modifying, combining, interpreting, substituting, conceptualizing, generalizing, abstracting, creating and . . . well, thinking. Different thinkers have emphasized all of these processes at one time or another.

One of the more important distinctions in work on creative thinking is the difference between *convergent thinking* and *divergent thinking*. Divergent thinking involves approaching a problem by branching out to generate multiple possibilities. Convergent thinking narrows those possibilities to find the most appropriate solution. The combination and sequence of divergence then convergence is central to what John Couper (1984) has called "imaginaction."

Another important insight from work on creativity is the value of *not* thinking too hard about a problem at times but rather allowing for a period of idea incubation. Following immersion in a problem or idea, relax and let it be for a while. Let it incubate in the back of the mind (Rossiter, 1984).

For our purposes one other distinction made by people who study thinking is especially important. This is the distinction between "critical" thinking and "creative" thinking. The critical thinker assumes a stance of doubt and skepticism. Things have to be proven; faulty logic, slippery linkages, tautological theories, and unsupported deductions are the targets of the critical mind. The critical thinker studies details and looks beyond appearances to find out what is really happening. Evaluators are trained to be rigorous and unyielding in critically thinking about and analyzing programs. Indeed, critical thinking is the foundation upon which evaluation is built.

The problem this poses is empirical evidence that critical thinkers tend *not* to be very creative. The creative mind generates new possibilities, the critical mind analyzes those possibilities looking for loopholes and imperfections. In summarizing these findings, Barry F. Anderson warns that the centrality of doubt in critical thinking can lead to a narrow, skeptical focus that hampers the creative ability to come up with new ideas or new insights.

> Just as creative thinkers want to be creative, critical thinkers, it seems, want to be critical, or at least to be certain.
>
> Yet the critical attitude and the creative attitude seem to be poles apart. . . . On the one hand, there are those who are always telling you why ideas won't work but who never seem able to come up with alternatives of their own; and, on the other hand, there are those who are constantly coming up with ideas but seem unable to tell the good from the bad.

There are people in whom both attitudes are developed to a high degree . . . , but even these people say they assume only one of these attitudes at a time. When new ideas are needed, they put on their creative caps, and when ideas need to be evaluated, they put on their critical caps. (Anderson, 1980, p. 66)

The profession of evaluation could not have emerged without a solid grounding in critical analysis. The integrity of the profession rests firmly on the quality of critical thinking exhibited by its practitioners. Yet it is just possible that in focusing on the critical side of our profession we have neglected the creative imperative of our work. As the nature of professional practice has changed through the emergent emphasis on utilization-focused, feasibility-conscious, propriety-oriented, and accuracy-based evaluation, it may be increasingly necessary to better balance our thinking repertoire, making sure we give ample attention to both critical fundamentals *and* creative capabilities. While our past has been rooted in the quality of our critical analyses, our future may depend on the realization of our creative potential. This book is dedicated to that end.

CHAPTER 2: *Creative Evaluation Professionals*

The Prophet says, "Physician, heal thyself."

To the evaluator he says, "Evaluator, study and judge thyself."

Yet there is reason to believe that evaluators are no better at judging themselves than physicians are at healing themselves. Just as physicians have gained well deserved reputations as terrible patients so evaluators have seemed to excel at resisting evaluation. They each prefer their own ignorance to that of another. Thus do both physicians and evaluators manifest their awareness of the uncertainties and limitations in the practice of their respective crafts.

from Halcolm's Evaluation Treatises

Creative evaluation requires creative evaluators. Creative evaluation is not an abstract process that just happens. Individual evaluators and decision makers make it happen. While later chapters discuss a variety of ways to structure situations in such a way that creative alternatives are more likely to emerge and take hold, creative evaluators still have to be there to set up the situation, facilitate the process, and then recognize creative outcomes as they emerge from the process. Creative evaluation requires creative evaluators.

The first chapter focused on the creative imperative inherent in an evaluation practice that meets the standards of utility, feasibility, propriety, and accuracy. This chapter focuses on the creative potential of the professionals who practice evaluation. This chapter also takes up the problem of defining creativity.

THE PERSONAL NATURE OF CREATIVITY

The great end of life is not knowledge but action.

Thomas Henry Huxley

Creativity is an individual and highly personal matter. This chapter is aimed at helping you, the reader, decide how you want to approach the issue of your own creative potential—and, consequently, how you want to (and will) approach this book. At the same time, this chapter represents an approach to helping clients, decision makers, and other participants in an evaluation process decide how they will approach any particular evaluation process. We will be operating, then, at two levels. First, there is the issue of your own personal engagement in evaluation as a creative evaluator. Second, there is the question of how to engage others in that process, that is, how to encourage and provide opportunities for the personal engagement of the people with whom you work.

The Invitation

In opening a teaching or consulting session, I like to invite participants to shift from a passive to an active stance. Correspondingly, I want to shift responsibility for what they get out of the session from me to them. This is a delicate undertaking. Coming on too strong can annoy, frighten, or turn people off; being too vague may mean that they miss the invitation. The "invitation" is to define the situation as one ripe with learning possibilities in which the individual can release, test, and realize his or her own creative and analytical capabilities.

The following invitation is a transcription of an actual workshop session. It is the kind of introduction that might be used in a session with program staff at the beginning of an evaluation process, or with evaluation trainees, or with a group of professional evaluators in a formal workshop. While any given invitation will vary, depending on the situation and the people involved, the invitation that follows illustrates the basic framework I hope to establish.

OPENING WORKSHOP COMMENTS

"Today's session focuses on program evaluation. Evaluation is a process of studying something, making observations, drawing interpretations, and then making judgments on the basis of those observations and interpretations. Of course, we all observe and evaluate things all the time. We are basically a highly judgmental species. The problem is that we're usually not very systematic or deliberate in making observations, and we're not aware of the criteria we use or the standards we apply in making judgments.

"In fact, the evidence is that most of the time we walk around in a fog. We're really not very aware of what's going on around us. We're selective in our perceptions, sloppy in our communications, lazy in our observations, and highly biased in our judgments. We still manage relatively well because for most of what we have to do we operate on preprogrammed tapes. Through the marvels of human socialization we avoid having to think about what we're doing and why. We rely on habits, patterns, and being too busy most of the time to worry about the fact that we're simply behaving according to expectations, habits, and socialization patterns.

"You've all heard that we typically use less than 20% of our thinking potential. You've heard me say that we get through most days in a fog, not much tuned in to the fine points of what we're experiencing. The real challenge of program evaluation is to lift the fog, turn on the lights, and take a close look at what's going on in comparison to what we think should be going on. That means not just taking a quick look around, but really *seeing*. It means opening up all of our senses to the data and the stimuli that make up our environments. It means turning on consciousness, becoming aware, concentrating, focusing—getting the electricity in the brain really crackling.

"In doing this you may find out some things about human service programs that you didn't know before. You may find that you can generate solutions to problems you didn't even know existed before you took a careful look around. Those are the programmatic and professional outcomes of the evaluation process: increased knowledge, more effective action, and improved service to program clients.

"There are also some personal outcomes of this process. You have the opportunity to test and develop your own observational skills; you can find out some things about your own thinking patterns, how you draw interpretations, and how you make judgments. Every successful evaluation in which I've participated has allowed me to learn things about myself while I learn things about a program. One of the most common reactions I hear from participants in an evaluation process concerns their own personal learning.

"I invite you to begin right now to actively enter into this situation to observe, to study, to question, to analyze, and to energize your thinking circuits. Evaluation rests on the hope and holds out the promise that we can know about the world we live in and act on that world to shape it more in the form we want it to take.

"To begin this process of deliberate evaluation I want to ask you to think about your expectations when you came here this morning. On a scale of 1 to 10, where 1 represents 'getting nothing out of this session' and 10 represents 'getting a tremendous amount out of this session,' I want you to rate what your expectations were before we began. I'm not going to collect your ratings, but I do want you to write it down in order to crystallize the rating and force yourself to make a judgment [Pause for writing.]

"Now I want to invite you to reasses your level of expectations, not based on your perception of me, but based on your own determination and commitment to learn from this process. Think about that commitment for a moment, then I'll ask you to write down a number from 1 to 10 representing what you intend to get out of this process because of your own commitment to actively engage in observing, analyzing, creating, and thinking.

"By way of helping focus your decision and commitment, let me read to you some thoughts from philosopher J. Krishnamurti about learning and knowledge. Then I'll ask you to write down for yourself your new rating. You can then keep both ratings until the end of the session, when I'll ask you to rate what you actually got out of the session. Here's Krishnamurti:

> Do you know what it means to learn? When you are really learning you are learning throughout your life and there is no one special teacher to learn from. Then everything teaches you—a dead leaf, a bird in flight, a smell, a tear, the rich and the poor, those who are crying, the smile of a

woman, the haughtiness of a man. You learn from everything, therefore, there is no guide, no philosopher, no guru. Life itself is your teacher, and you are in a state of constant learning. (Krishnamurti, 1964, p. 14)

Self-knowledge comes when you observe yourself in your relationship with your fellow-students and your teachers, with all the people around you; it comes when you observe the manner of another, his gestures, the way he wears his clothes, the way he talks, his contempt or flattery and your response; it comes when you watch everything in you and about you and see yourself as you see your face in the mirror. . . . Now, if you can look into the mirror of relationship exactly as you look into the ordinary mirror, then there is no end to self-knowledge. It is like entering a fathomless ocean which has no shore. Most of us want to reach an end, we want to be able to say, "I have arrived at self-knowledge and I am happy," but it is not like that at all . . . ; if you can just observe what you are and move with it, then you will find that it is possible to go infinitely far. Then there is no end to the journey, and that is the mystery, the beauty of it. (Krishnamurti, 1964, pp. 50-51)

*   *   *

That's the invitation for a workshop experience, but the same principle applies in reading this book. The materials in this book cannot, and are not meant to, *make* you creative. The materials in this book provide an opportunity and a stimulus for you to make some decisions about your own capacity for being a creative evaluator. The next section invites you to consider some areas for expanding your own creative potential.

Baseline Assessment

In the first chapter I argued that creative evaluators would need a repertoire of skills, sensitivities, analytical approaches, attitudes, and capabilities that are quite different from those required in the traditional conduct of social science research. This section asks you to conduct a baseline assessment of your own professional strengths and weaknesses so that you can decide where you want to focus your efforts to realize your creative potential. This section invites you to apply to yourself the evaluation techniques of needs assessment, goals clarification, and priority setting. The assessment questions that follow can be applied individually, or individuals might share their personal assessments in a group. I recommend writing out answers, not necessarily all at one sitting, but taking the time to do a serious baseline assessment of yourself.

(1) On Thinking. Creative evaluators are aware of how traditional paradigms and heuristics limit their perceptions. Out of what scientific paradigm(s) have you tended to operate? What heuristics do you rely on in problem solving and decision making? Take some time to reflect on a recent evaluation situation or problem-solving experience and analyze your own thought patterns. How did you define the situation? What categories of past experience seemed to direct your thinking? How might your initial analysis of the situation have biased your analysis? Thinking back now, what are some other ways of thinking about that situation that might have led you to proceed in a different fashion? In short, how do you typically think through things in an evaluation or problem-solving situation?

(2) On Skills. Creative evaluators are capable of using a variety of methods; they have a large repertoire of communication and group process techniques they can use; and they are skilled in matching methods or techniques to unique situations.

In what research methods are you strong? In what methods are you weak? To what extent are you skilled in both experimental and naturalistic designs, in both quantitative and qualitative data gathering techniques, and in conducting both statistical and content analyses of data? How can you expand your repertoire of research methods?

What are your strengths and weaknesses in communications? What is your repertoire of communications capabilities? Verbal communications? Written? Media? One-to-one? Group? Scientific? Political? Inspirational? Directive? Nondirective? Simple? Complex? Sensitive? Succinct? Diplomatic? How would you describe yourself as a professional communicator? (All evaluators are, you know.)

How skilled are you in working with groups? Inventory your repertoire of group process and facilitation techniques. How many of those do you use? To what extent is your work with groups patterned and routine? In what ways do those patterns and routines limit your flexibility and effectiveness?

How skilled are you at recognizing the nuances of situations? How skilled are you at recognizing the nuances of situations in which you find yourself? Consider the following in making your assessment:

It takes at least 15 years of hard work for even the most talented individuals to become world-class chess masters: what they seem to learn is a repertoire for recognizing types of situations or scripts, or intuitive sensibilities and understanding about how these situations will likely unfold. Simon (1978) estimates a differential repertoire of 50,000 situation recognitions at the world class level in chess. There is also some increase in overall long-range strategic planning ability—beginners typically are hard pressed to go beyond one move deep; world class players often do 3, or sometimes 5, in calculating alternative reactions to their moves. . . . Data from experienced and highly successful chess players, poker players, and tennis players suggest the theory that one further learning from experience is the capacity to diagnose not just specific game situations but to model ("psych-out") different opponents. It is also likely that experienced players have developed more efficient scanning and the ability to discard unnecessary information and to have a ball park, intuitive sense of where to devote attention. (Etheredge, 1979, p. 40)

How skilled as an evaluator do you want to become? A world-class player? A recreational amateur? How hard are you prepared to work to increase your skills? How much time are you willing to devote to skill development?

(3) On Philosophy. What are your beliefs about evaluation? To what extent do you share the philosophy and priorities expressed by the Evaluation Standards—that evaluations should be useful, practical, ethical, and accurate? What is your philosophy about the purpose, function, role, and potential of program evaluation? Or of evaluators? In what areas is your evaluation philosophy well-developed? In what areas weak or ambiguous? What is your stance with respect to evaluators as change agents? Scientists? Political activists? Servants of the powers that be? Independent observers? Businesspersons? Professionals?

(4) On Feelings. What are your feelings about yourself as an evaluator? How committed are you to your own professional development? Personal growth? Realizing your creative potential? What are your hopes? What are your fears? What risks are you willing to take? Where do you want to be in these areas in five years? Ten years?

How in touch with your feelings are you? To what extent are your feelings part of the data you use in working with decision makers? How sensitive are you to group processes, climate, ambiance, and dynamics? To what extent do you monitor your feelings as you work so that you're aware of cues about rapport? Empathy? Tension? Anxiety? Pressure? Stress? Caring? Fear? Commitment? Openness?

How sensitive are you to the feelings of others along these dimensions?

To what extent and in what ways are you able to use information about the feelings of others to release creative energy? Do you trust your feelings? Suppress them? Manipulate them? Experience them?

Dilemmas of Evaluation Practice

The questions in the previous section were aimed at addressing what Fritz Steele (1975) calls "the existential dilemmas" of being a professional consultant. Steele is the consultant's consultant. He trains professional consultants in a variety of fields, particularly management consulting specialists. He has observed that there is a real tension between long-term development of personal potential and short-term performance.

> The dilemma of performance and learning means that if you always strive to perform tasks to the highest level of performance of which you are capable, you will tend to choose to do those things which you can do well already. Over a period of time this will result in relatively little learning of new skills, since those areas in which you could learn have been avoided in favor of those areas where you are already capable. This dilemma often seems to be experienced in the moment where the choice is between looking smooth and competent (by doing something well) or looking clumsy and incompetent (by trying something with which you do not have facility, and indeed cannot predict the outcome very well). (Steele, 1975, p. 14)

Steele suggests that the consultant who specializes in a particular skill runs the risk of being a technician who is increasingly stale and obsolete as the profession develops beyond that consultant's specialty. On the other hand, the consultant who is always trying new things may not be able to deliver sufficient quality of performance to build a stable clientele. The answer, he suggests, lies in properly balancing professional practice of well-developed skills with a conscious openness to new opportunities for learning. A consultant "must mix projects with potential for high learning with high-performance projects if he wants to grow" (Steele, 1975, p. 15).

Steele also describes other existential dilemmas that can limit personal and professional development. All of these are applicable to evaluators. There is the dilemma of how open to be in new situations: Openness invites new possibilities but risks getting caught off guard, while entering a new situation with a predetermined (closed) framework limits possibilities but increases having some control and something to offer.

Another dilemma is how to find a balance between action and reflection. Action for consultants usually involves helping clients take time for reflection, but when do the consultants take time for reflection and processing personal experiences? This "action-processing dilemma" results, Steele believes, from the "emotional seductiveness of the action side of the coin" (Steele, 1975, p. 19). There is always the temptation to move on to the new action without fully processing what occurred in a finished project, getting feedback from clients, reviewing notes, and discussing the experience analytically with colleagues. Taking the time to evaluate an evaluation process, reviewing a consulting experience, or follow-up utilization of a study's findings are ways to continue learning. Steele warns that "the less energy you put into processing activities, the lower the probability that you will learn very much that is new from your doing" (Steele, 1975, p. 19).

The dilemmas identified by Steele are not so much to be resolved as managed. Becoming a creative evaluator is not some end state to be ultimately attained, once and for all, but rather a process of continually pushing against the limits of our experience. Thus while the first chapter emphasized the importance of creative evaluation to the future development of our profession, this chapter is focusing on the importance of creative development to the personal and professional futures of individual evaluators. *Creative evaluation requires creative evaluators.*

For those of you who are interested in a normative point of reference to assist you in assessing your creativity, I suggest using a self-assessment instrument developed by Princeton Creative Research (Raudsepp, 1981). The 100-item instrument is based on several years of research aimed at determining the behavioral and attitudinal correlates of creativity among various professionals: writers, artists, technical professionals, business executives, and scientists. The 100 items yield a scale that varies from –17 to 240, which is normatively divided to yield five categories from "not creative" to "exceptionally creative." However, from my point of view, generating a score that puts you in one of the five categories is of less interest than examining the weightings of the individual items and thinking about what your self-assessment reveals about heuristic routines you could change to become more creative. An item analysis aimed at revealing characteristics you share, or do not share, with creative people may help you identify some personal patterns that you want to change, call your attention to others that you want to strengthen and nurture, or lead you to value some characteristics that you've previously regarded as problems. Used in this way the focus is on what you can learn from your responses to the test items, thereby avoiding concern about a low score or elation over a high score.

Creativity: Heredity or Environment?

Creative minds always have been known to survive any kind of bad training.

Anna Freud

I don't know where I first came across this Anna Freud quote. I know that I really liked it from the very first time I saw it. It's such a hopeful, such an optimistic, sentiment.

But look at it more closely. It seems to imply that creativity is innate. You either have it, in which case your creative mind can survive a bad environment, or you don't have it, in which case it probably doesn't matter whether your training is good or bad—you just don't have it. This question of heredity versus environment matters to us here mainly because it may determine how you approach your own learning *and* how effective you are in working creatively with evaluation groups.

First there is the question of your own creativity. If you believe that creativity is innate and somehow embedded in the genes, then all you need test is whether you happen to have the "right" kind of genes— whether you're one of the lucky (or unlucky) ones with creative potential.

If, on the other hand, you believe that creativity is learned (that is, a function of environment), then all you need add to that axiomatic position when doing evaluation work is the logical corollary that *you* can learn to be more creative. You can become aware of, control, expand, and creatively adapt your own heuristics.

I happen to have it on very good authority that the heredity versus environment question is absolutely and irrefutably unresolveable at this point in time. It may be one, it may be the other; it's probably a combination of the two. No one knows for sure what the balance is. For purposes of this book, I invite you to consider the possibility that everyone has unrealized creative potential.

Your belief about the creative potential of people can affect your skill and effectiveness in working with others. *It is pretty difficult to lead a group of people through an evaluation process aimed at stimulating and releasing their creativity if you don't believe they have any creative potential to release.* Like the canine's instinctive ability to sense fear in human beings, decision makers and information users have a sixth sense that tells them when they're being conned.

I admit that with some groups it is hard to believe that there is any creative potential to be released. Lewis Carroll has prescribed an exercise that can be helpful in expanding one's capacity to believe in the creativity of another, or even to believe in one's own creative potential. It is an exercise prescribed for Alice by the Queen of Hearts.

"There's no use trying," Alice said: "one can't believe impossible things."

"I daresay you haven't had much practice," said the Queen. "When I was your age, I always did it for half-an-hour a day. Why, sometimes I've believed as many as six impossible things before breakfast."

PREREQUISITES FOR CREATIVE DEVELOPMENT

This section attempts to pull together in capsule form a variety of writings and research on learning, creativity, and evaluation as a statement of prerequisites for personal engagement in the process of realizing creative potential as an evaluator. As another self-assessment tool, this listing is meant as yet a further invitation to examine actively your own assumptions about professional growth as those assumptions apply to the practice of creative evaluation.

(1) Recognition that there is something to be learned. In 1899, Charles H. Duell, director of the U.S. Patent Office, announced: "Everything that can be invented has been invented." There was nothing left to learn for Duell.

Learning is more likely to take place when there is recognition that there is something to be learned. Etheredge (1980) comments that a major barrier to "government learning" is failure to recognize the need to know something.

No one probably learns well when the agenda, role and incentive systems provided by the environment . . . , say there is no problem. That is, one condition which applies to many people in many jobs in Washington is that they see no important problems to solve or learn about. The job is routine, the individual feels his sole responsibility and appropriate role is just to do the job. The surrounding organizational identity, culture, and norms legitimate the status quo. The interest groups, Congress, and bureaucratic superiors are either satisfied with, or indifferent to his work. (Etheredge, 1980, pp. 57-58)

The self-assessment questions listed earlier in this chapter were partly aimed at helping you decide if there is something still to be learned.

(2) Recognizing a need for and the importance of creative evaluation approaches. This book is not concerned with evaluation learning in general but rather with learning to be more creative in evaluation practice. The first chapter presented the basis for the claim that evaluators need to be more creative. Evaluators increasingly find themselves in situations where standard operating procedures simply are not appropriate. Then, too, decision makers are increasingly less likely to accept normal science as a relevant solution to their specific evaluation concerns, that is, evaluators may find that more sophisticated decision makers simply won't let evaluators have their way in imposing old practices on new situations. Eric Hoffer observed, "The most gifted members of the human species are at their creative best when they cannot have their way." We may be forced to be creative.

(3) Believing that learning to be more creative is possible. This prerequisite was addressed in the section on heredity versus environment. Self-fulfilling prophecies seem to be particularly powerful where creativity is concerned. If you're convinced that you aren't the creative type, you probably won't be, and vice versa. If you act toward the groups you work with as if they're incapable of creative thought, you'll probably confirm your good judgment; they won't be creative.

(4) Commitment to put time, energy, and resources into the creative process. Many people harbor a misconception that creativity just happens. Psychiatrist Albert Rothenberg (1979) has studied creative thinking among scientists, artists, writers, and philosophers. He believes that most important creative thinking occurs as a conscious and deliberate effort. It isn't just a matter of inspiration, dreaming, or some other unconscious process. People who are inspired prepare themselves for inspiration; creative ideas come from doing creative work. Clarence Day put it quite succinctly: "Creation is work."

(5) Willingness to take risks. Management consultant Fritz Steele (1975), in discussing the existential dilemmas of consulting, concludes that the major barrier to growth and learning is a concern for personal security. "A consultant should look carefully at the experiences in which he typically finds himself involved, and he should widen his range of

experiences to include those at which he is not greatly practiced" (Steele, 1975, p. 29). If you want to stretch your creative capacity, you've got to put yourself in situations that provide opportunities for—or demand—creative evaluation approaches.

The willingness to take risks depends on the other prerequisites: recognition that there is something to be learned; recognizing a need for and the importance of creative evaluation approaches; believing that learning to be more creative is possible; and a commitment to put time, energy, and resources into the creative process.

At base, these prerequisites may assume what Krishnamurti (1964) calls a kind of "creative discontent." Creative discontent is the feeling that things are not quite what they should be, that we can do better, use more of ourselves, realize more of our potential, and become more effective as persons and as professionals even as we aim to help make programs more effective.

> Do you know what it means to be discontented? It is very difficult to understand discontent, because most of us canalize discontent in a certain direction and thereby smother it. That is, our only concern is to establish ourselves in a secure position with well-established interests and prestige, so as not to be disturbed. It happens in homes and in schools too. The teachers don't want to be disturbed, and that is why they follow the old routine; because the moment one is really discontented and begins to inquire, to question, there is bound to be disturbance. But it is not only through real discontent that one has initiative. . . .
>
> *Creativeness has its roots in the initiative which comes into being only when there is deep discontent.*
>
> If you can be in revolt while you are young, and as you grow older keep your discontent alive with the vitality of joy and great affection, then that flame of discontent will have an extraordinary significance because it will build, it will create, it will bring new things into being. For this you must have the right kind of education, which is not the kind that merely prepares you to get a job or to climb the ladder of success, but the education that helps you to think and gives you space—space not in the form of a larger bedroom or a higher roof, but space for your mind to grow so that it is not bound by any belief, by any fear. (Krishnamurti, 1964, pp. 46-48)

Krishnamurti's idea of creativeness as an outgrowth of discontent can be blended with Steele's recommendations earlier in this chapter about ways of dealing with consulting dilemmas. In quite different ways, both of these distinguished writers were concerned about the willingness to take risks for personal and professional growth. Discontent with the way things are comes from carefully evaluating the ways things are against an ideal of how things might be. The willingness to take risks emerges from a commitment to move closer to the ideal. Creativeness emerges as one struggles to overcome the obstacles to realization of the ideal. This necessitates having in mind some ideal of evaluation practice, which takes us back to the evaluation standards described and discussed in the first chapter. The creative imperative of evaluation is rooted in the standards that call for situationally responsive evaluations that are useful, feasible, ethical, and accurate. Those are indeed high ideals, sufficient to render most of us somewhat discontented if we carefully examine much current evaluation practice, including, perhaps, particularly our own.

Realities of Evaluation Practice

The test of a vocation is the love of the drudgery it involves.

Logan Pearsall Smith

This chapter began with a quote from the wise evaluation sage, Halcolm, admonishing the evaluator to "study and judge thyself." With that admonition establishing an introduction to the purpose of this chapter, I invited the reader to begin a process of actively and critically assessing her or his capacity for, interest in, and commitment to creative evaluation. The emphasis throughout has been on the professional creativity of individual evaluators and the people with whom they work. The theme of this chapter was established with the opening line: *Creative evaluation requires creative evaluators.*

The tone, I trust, has been optimistic, even enthusiastic, and clearly hopeful. Before finally defining creativity—or at least dealing with the issue—I want to temper the emphasis on creativity and personal/professional development with a clear recognition that a great deal of the day-to-day activity of evaluation is hard work, sometimes bordering on drudgery. Attending to details, setting up meetings, endless phone calls, managing budgets, dealing with the pressure of time lines that are always too short, and trying to prevent any of a host of foul-ups (then spending time correcting them when they occur anyway). Lest I be accused of seeing evaluation only through rose-colored glasses as a noble and glamorous profession filled with creative people doing marvelously creative things, I want to give a nod to the less inspiring and less attractive sides of evaluation practice. In between moments of creative expression and satisfying insight there are hours of making it happen. Earlier, I quoted Clarence Day to the effect that "creation is work." Here I want to reproduce his full statement.

> The creative impulse seems not to wish to produce finished work. It certainly deserts us half-way after the idea is born; and if we go on, creating is work.
>
> Clarence Day

As an evaluator, I have met and worked with highly creative, intelligent, and caring people. As with any public occupation, however, I have also met and worked with a fair number of dullards, incompetents, wackos, lamos, robots, and even a few crooks. I have had the satisfaction of helping programs make significant improvements, programs that were doing good things, programs with which I was proud to be associated. I have also been stuck with some real losers, programs and people impervious to evaluation, yet solidly funded for years to come by some thoroughly entrenched board, programs guaranteed a lifetime of perpetrating nonsense and interfering in the lives of needy people without in any way relieving those needs, sometimes making them worse. I have been outraged, saddened, and dejected. I can't even add, "but never a dull moment," for there have been lots of those, too.

These "realities" are not the subject of this book, but they constitute the backdrop against which efforts at creative evaluation will be undertaken. It is therefore important for the professional evaluator, as part of the overall self-assessment advocated in this chapter, to be in touch with and grounded in the realities of evaluation practice—both the creative, stimulating, and attractive sides of what evaluators do and the dismal, disappointing, and dull aspects of the profession. Since much of the work of evaluation is aimed at depicting reality for others, it is all the more important that we be firmly grounded in the realities of our own practice of evaluation. Without such a grounding, efforts at creativity may just become an exercise in setting oneself up for failure. Such a disappointed evaluator could have penned this poem.

> remember reality?
> didn't we play there once

the breakaway props didn't
    break away as planned
the spot burned out during
    my big scene
the curtain man was drinking
    mad dog 20/20 to keep warm
    and missed the cue
my agent won't book that
    gig
again
he didn't even want
his ten percent

                                    Kathleen Kolhoff (1980)

FINALLY, WHAT IS CREATIVITY?

He who does not know how to create should not know.

                                    Antonio Porchia

For nearly two chapters now I have talked about creativity without
defining what it is. In the first chapter I implied that the creative
evaluator was one who is able to move beyond the limitations of
conditioned responses represented by heuristics and standard operating
procedures to be truly active-reactive-adaptive in designing evaluations
that are situationally appropriate and responsive. In this chapter I have
further suggested that the creative evaluator is a lifelong learner open to
new ideas, willing to be challenged by new situations, and secure enough
to take risks that lead to continual growth and development of both
capabilities and awareness. While these notions hint at the parameters
of what is meant by "creativity," a clear, operational definition is still
lacking.

Definitions are fundamental to social science activity. It is clear that
we have to have definitions so that we know what we're talking about
with each other. That's a basic tenet of science. Still, I have deliberately
chosen not to offer an operational definition of creativity in this book.

How, then, could I put together a book on "creative evaluation"?

I managed to write the subsequent chapters without an operational
definition of creativity because I viewed those chapters as case materials
from which readers could extract and discover their own definition(s) of
creativity. While each reader's definition will therefore be unique, those

unique definitions may be all the more meaningful— and creative—for having been arrived at inductively.

I did search the literature for definitions of creativity. I found those existing definitions more limiting than expanding. I don't want to constrain the notion of creative evaluation practice to some small operational box. Indeed, it seemed to me that the existing definitions were far from creative—and often quite boring. (In the land of definitions, of course, boredom reigns supreme.)

Not quite satisfied by the definitions in the literature, I did attempt to write an operational definition of creativity. My greatest success in this worthy endeavor was inspired when I happened to come across a masterpiece of definitional writing from the Occupational Safety and Health Standards of the United States government. First, then, their definition, an operational definition of the term *exit*, followed by my corresponding definition of creativity.

> Exit is the portion of a means of egress which is separated from all other spaces of the building or structured by construction or equipment as required in this subpart to provide a protected way to travel to the exit discharge. Exit discharge is that portion of means of egress between the termination of an exit and a public way. (Reported in *Engineering Education*, April, 1972, p. 779)

Now, then, the corresponding definition of creativity. *Creative potential is the portion of a means of egress from the brain which is separated from all other existing spaces of the brain or neurological structures through construction of a unique and new protected way to travel to the brain's exit discharge. Creativity is the exit discharge of creative potential in a public way.*

I urge the reader to withhold enthusiastic endorsement and adoption of this definition pending examination of the case materials in the remainder of the book. Quite seriously, one of the purposes of this book is to encourage and stimulate thought about what constitutes creative work. This chapter began with an invitation to become actively involved in the creative process and to take responsibility for what happens in the process. The materials in the rest of this book are meant as resources to use on your journey into creative evaluation practice. To illustrate the demands that are placed on you as part of this invitation to personal engagement, this chapter concludes with materials aimed at beginning the process of inductively defining creativity. You are invited to take the occasion of reading this book as an opportunity to decide what it means to be creative, and when it is appropriate to consciously work at a creative evaluation process. By what standards will you judge your own performances?

The Cutting Edge of Intellectual Enterprise

At the 1979 meetings of the Midwest Sociological Society a panel of eminent social scientists were asked to discuss what it means to be on the cutting edge of a discipline. Janowitz focused on "creativity as the cutting edge of intellectual enterprise." He began by making a distinction between rote imitations of others and "true" creativity. He noted that the imitation of Frank Lloyd Wright's creative architectural work rapidly became "standard solutions to aesthetic problems until the solutions became cliches." Frank Lloyd Wright had hoped for emulation but all he found was imitation and solutions to problems that had more to do with the appearances of "modern" architecture than with creative approaches to emergent problems.

Janowitz also criticized much of the standardized work in social and behavioral sciences. He pointedly remarked that routinely using standard statistical packages in data analysis or simply adding new variables to regression equations can hardly be considered practices that provide much of a cutting edge in social science. Nor is the path to creative breakthroughs the common dissertation practice, fostered by many psychology departments, of looking for yet another reinforcer in some standard learning experiment. Janowitz said that he wanted to avoid naming any particular methodological development or theoretical approach as the cutting edge of social science because such accolades might falsely lead students to "imitate the solution rather than the creative spirit behind it." It is that creative spirit which is the cutting edge, not doing "routine, acceptable work contributing to routine, acceptable advancement in a routine acceptable profession."

Janowitz concluded by noting that creativity defies routine definition, standard operating procedures, or routine teaching, but there are certain professional techniques, attitudes, and commitments that when take together constitute the creative spirit of scientific endeavor.

I do not profess to know how one teaches creativity. Surely, creative activity is aided, in part, by providing alternative cognitive structures so that any problems or data sets may be seen in different lights. Surely, creativity is also aided by recognizing the tradeoffs associated with emphasizing different goals and ideals of intellectual endeavor. It is useful to set aside the usual requirements of acceptable work, on occasion, in order to play the kinds of mental games needed for breaking out of the routine and seizing on unlikely clues and insights. Finally, creativity is aided by a broad enough knowledge of previous procedures and results that unanticipated parallels and contrasts can be spotted, assuming that one is looking for promising parallels and contrasts.

These aids to creativity are not readily taught, especially as part of a discipline that must also insist on maintaining standards of valid and reliable knowledge. . . .

The final line, though, is still this: *the cutting edge of intellectual enterprise is creative thought.* (Janowitz, 1979, pp. 602-603; emphasis added)

Creative or Not Creative

How can one tell whether or not something is creative? Consider a possible subtitle of this section: "Creative or not creative, that is the question?" It is clearly a takeoff on Shakespeare's "To be or not to be," but is it a creative takeoff? Hardly. It is certainly not an original approach. I would guess that those lines from Hamlet are amongst the most often adapted and imitated in the Western world. It is hard to escape them. I was walking down the street in Bridgetown, Barbados, in the West Indies and a shoeshine boy came up to me and said, "To shine or not to shine, man, that is the question." I had the strong suspicion that he hadn't just received a sudden inspiration to create a new approach to the craft of hustling shoes for shining. My guess is that his "to shine or nor to shine" soliloquy was a very deep rut in his brain dug constantly deeper by reinforcing tourists who were really taken with the kid's creativity. More power to him.

Let's analyze a different example. I have purposefully selected a nonevaluation problem to examine at this point since the whole rest of the book presents materials that you can use in arriving at your own definition of creativity in evaluation. This example concerns musical and poetic creativity.

On the road from Port of Spain to Maracas Beach in Trinidad there is a beautiful ocean overlook where every Sunday afternoon a calypso singer sits with his guitar and makes up songs for passersby. As I was admiring the view he approached me and asked me what I was doing in Trinidad. When I replied "program evaluation" his reaction suggested that he had graduated *summa cum enthusiastica* from a major evaluation training program. "Evaluation, you say! Man, have I got a song for you."

(Sung to a lively calypso beat)

Evaluation, you say,
Will help improve we day.
You find out which way we going,
And whether not we be slowin'.

Evaluation, you say,
Can show we a better way.
Even though you hair I see you losin'
That evaluation brain is never snoozin'

Evaluation, you say,
Will make you lots of pay.
So you come visit me in Trin'dad
Eval'ate my act to tell me if it bad.

Evaluation, you say,
Will certainly make we feel gay.
You smiling, I think maybe I funny.
Now how 'bout eval'ate I some money.

The lyrics lose something of their effect without the music and the ocean setting, but I was quite taken with what came across as a very polished, though spontaneous, creation. "That," I said to myself, having gone to the beach to avoid working on this chapter, "is creativity."

I recalled being similarly impressed with performers in various improvisational theaters like Dudley Rigg's Brave New Workshop in Minneapolis and Second City in Chicago. But, as I reflected on the improvisational creativity of these performing artists it occurred to me that behind their spontaneous stage creations were long hours of practice. They train rigorously and work arduously so that at the moment of truth, on stage, they can quickly take off on whatever material the audience gives them. I wondered: Are they operating on some kind of situational heuristic that provides them with cues about what to do—how to "create"? And if their creativity is heuristically based, if it is practiced, is it still creativity? Perhaps this was the artistic corollary of Pasteur's comment on the nature of scientific discovery: "In the field of observation, chance favors only the prepared mind." *In the*

process of adapting to new situations, does creativity come only to the
prepared mind?

I decided to study the problem further. I needed more data. I asked
two other people I knew in Trinidad to separately visit the Maracas
overlook and tape record the songs created for them. One was a physical
scientist, the other a tourist. Here are their songs.

CALYPSO SCIENCE

Science, science, hooray,
Will give we all a better day.
Science helps keep we goin;
We never worry 'bout slowing.

Science, science, hooray
Can show we all a better way.
Your science head you never 'fraid a losin'.
You thinkin' even though ya may be snoozin'.

Science, science, hooray,
Will surely bring ya lots a pay.
Be sure ta bring you science to Trin'dad
So we can all be happy, not be sad.

Science, science, hooray.
Da sun will make we feel gay.
Before dis song is no more funny
I goin' ta ask ya for a little money.

THE TOURIST VERSION

Ya be a tourist ya say.
Well I sure wish you a very good day.
I wonder where ya be goin'.
Just don't go fast, try now slowin'.

Ya be a tourist ya say.
Ya maybe find here a better way.
Ya might try a little speedboat racin'
Or maybe just a little ocean gazin'.

Ya be a tourist ya say.
I hope you bring to Trin'dad all ya pay.
So while you here in dis fair land
You have a good time an' hear a fine steel band.

Ya are a tourist ya say.
Da sun will make ya feel gay.

Ya smilin', I think I am funny.
I want be tourist too, please give me money.

A comparison of the three different songs reveals some striking similarities. Creative, or not creative, that is the question.

I decided that I still needed more data before making a judgment. I wanted to interview the creator himself and get his views on his work. I would show him the three transcribed songs and get his answer to the creativity question.

MQP: Hey, man, what's happening? How goes the music?

Little Sparrow: All fine here, man. Ya come back for 'nother song, hey?

MQP: [It had been three weeks and he appeared to remember me. "He probably has a heuristic for remembering faces," I thought to myself.] No, I came back to find out how you do it. [He took the money I offered.]

Little Sparrow: What you mean, "how I does it"?

MQP: How you come up with the songs you sing.

Little Sparrow: What's matter, man? 'valuation no good? You want become calypso singer? Ya goin' have to work awful hard on dat accent ya gat, man.

MQP: Maybe you could teach me? No? Well, actually, I'm writing a book about creativity and, if you're willing, I'd like to include a bit about how you create your songs.

Little Sparrow: Me Little Sparrow, man. Me just sing. Da Mighty Sparrow is de Father of Calypso, de King. He's de greatest. I just Little Sparrow, but me have good time, no?

MQP: You remember I taped your song.

Little Sparrow: Yeah. [He started singing.] Evaluation, ya say, will give me much better day . . .

MQP: ["An amazing memory heuristic," I thought.] That's it. That's it. Well, I've also got two songs you did for some friends I sent to see you. [I showed him the three transcripts.]

Little Sparrow: I remember dem. Americans. One a man, de tourist a woman. Very pretty, she. Her *your* good friend or *his* good friend? [He broke out in a big smile and started singing]

Love in Trinidad, hooray,
Will make ya a very happy day.
If ya havin' trouble finding girl
I may be able to help ya have a whirl.

MQP: [I thought, "I bet that one gets a lot of play."] What I want to ask you is why all the songs are so much alike.

Little Sparrow: [Without hesitating] Ya all Americans.

MQP: What's that have to do with it?

Little Sparrow: Americans like one kinda beat; Brits like different beat. French, Chinese, Indians, Bajans, everybody like different beat.

MQP: Anything else?

Little Sparrow: Like ya see dere on de paper, I sings four lines, one always de same each time, each verse. Dat firs line gets de song started an' is easy ta rhyme. Da easy firs line give time to tink, if I needs sah more time—which I used ta, but don't no more. Everybody dat come dis way goin' somewhere so I always sings 'bout going. We in Trin'dad, so I sings 'bout bein' in Trin'dad . . . , and Trin'dad rhymes with lots other words, very easy. Americans always laugh at 'snoozin, so snoozin' guaranteed laugh. *You* American, ya tells me why. I don't knows, but sure 'nough, with Americans, snoozin is guaranteed, 100% laugh. That answer 'nough. Is just knowin' what's happen', man. Oh yeah, I also sings 'bout money, but ya sure 'nough know why dat.

[A car pulled into the overlook and he broke into another big smile.] Here come some more Americans. See how dey drive? I got go sing now.

MQP: Thanks for the help and the time. You're really creative, man.

Little Sparrow: [He smiled and started singing] Creativity, ya say, will bring we all a very nice day . . . [Then he was off to do business, to "create" some verse.]

* * *

Creative, or not creative? That is still the question. I will let you decide. I will venture this much. *He was aware of his own heuristics—and he had a set of heuristics that allowed him to adapt to different people.* Some of the adaptations were categorical (for example, Americans), and some were individual (for example, evaluation), but he appeared to have a fairly comprehensive repertoire. I didn't stay around to find out how many errors resulted from his heuristics. I lack sufficient data to judge the limitations of his heuristics.

The calypso problem really raises more questions about how to define creativity than it answers. That was the purpose of reporting this experience—to raise the question about what it means to be creative. The materials in the remainder of this book are aimed at helping you come up with your own definition of creativity.

Parameters of Creative Evaluaton

While declining to provide a universal definition of creativity, I did establish the parameters of "creative evaluation" in the first chapter.

Those parameters provide a fairly clear indication of my own notions about what it means to be creative as an evaluator. Creative evaluation means working within a framework, or paradigm, of multiple possibilities where new situations are approached without preconceptions about which particular evaluation methods or approaches ought to be applied. Creative evaluation means being situationally responsive, methodologically flexible, consciously committed to matching evaluation approaches to the needs and interests of those with whom one is working, and genuinely sensitive to the unique constraints and possibilities of particular people and circumstances.

Creative evaluation takes seriously the criteria of utility, feasibility, propriety, and accuracy that are specified in the emergent standards of of evaluation as the criteria against which professional evaluation practice should be judged. Creative evaluation is thus a problem-solving approach that emphasizes adaptation to change and changing conditions as opposed to a technical approach, which attempts to mold and define conditions to fit preconceived models of how an evaluation should be designed and implemented.

Creative evaluators are active-reactive-adaptive in working with decision makers, information users, and stakeholders to focus the evaluation on meaningful, appropriate, and researchable questions, the answers to which will be useful for program improvement and decision making. Throughout the consultative process, creative evaluators work to maintain an awareness of how their own routine heuristics, academic training, and preconceived notions may be limiting their vision and narrowing possibilities prematurely. Thus creative evaluators are keen observers of their own actions and influences as part of the ongoing process of observing and studying the entire evaluation endeavor. Those observations are used to help keep creative evaluators situationally responsive, open to new possibilities, and capable of reaching into their large repertoire of techniques, methods, and approaches to find or adapt a technique, method, or approach that is appropriate to the situation at hand.

These parameters and characteristics of creative evaluation fall short of being a formal definition. I have resisted offering a formal, universal definition that would allow one to say, "These evaluations were creative, and these were not." The same thing done in two different places might be considered "creative" in one situation, and quite routine in the other. The situation, the people with whom one works, the resources available, the political context, the evaluator's background, the nature of the problem to be studied—all these and many more factors must be considered to render a holistic judgment about the relative creativeness of a particular evaluation process and/or product.

Despite the situational complexities encountered in rendering judgment about the relative creativeness of particular evaluations, the basic premise of this chapter holds that at the core of those evaluations ultimately deemed "creative," one is likely to find a creative evaluator. Creative evaluation requires creative evaluators. This chapter has begun an examination of that premise and its implications for the personal and professional development of evaluation practitioners. Examination of that premise will continue in the chapters that follow.

CHAPTER 3: *The Calling of Evaluation*

Once, not so long ago, I was approached by a cynical colleague just after I had delivered a keynote address at a conference for human service managers. In the speech I had advocated taking evaluation seriously as a useful management tool. This academic colleague approached me and asked, "Why do you bother advocating useful evaluations? Nobody really cares, you know. Everybody's just caught up in their own little world. You shouldn't take those ideas of utility and creativity in evaluation so seriously. You're just blowing in the wind. But sometimes, when I hear you speak as you did today, I almost get the impression that you think evaluation is some kind of noble calling," at which point we were interrupted and he went off shaking his head at the very absurdity of the idea that evaluation could be a calling, noble or otherwise. That night I wrote "The Calling of Evaluation."

THE CALLING OF EVALUATION

It is good for a professional to be reminded that his profession is only a husk, that the real person must remain an amateur, a lover of work.

May Sarton

When I was young, I remember people talking un-self-consciously about being "called" to one's life work. This sometimes referred to a religious calling where "many are called but few are chosen." More generally it referred to finding one's calling—finding a purpose, a fit with one's capabilities, a meaning in work. The lack of a calling was believed to be the chief contributor to the ever-so-popular identity crisis of youth (or middle age or old age or death-bed despair).

The idea of a calling has ancient roots. Every culture has some manifestation of the calling—some ways of explaining how and why we end up doing what we do, being who we are. Each tribe, each culture has devised some sermon or ritual to help their young hear their calling and find out if they are chosen. Our modern rituals are entrance exams and graduation exercises, and it has become less a matter of being chosen than of making a choice. What will you be when you grow up? If you grow up?

There is a calling to evaluation. Part of the responsibility of the elders in our profession is to help the young experience this calling. Those inclined to the call can then make their choice, decide if the calling is true. It is the function and responsibility of the profession to elucidate and articulate the nature of the calling.

To what, then, are evaluators called?

We are called to help make the social technology of our era work to the service of humankind. We are called to enter the fray where knowledge combats ignorance, purpose attacks sloth, to reverse the entropy of routine mindlessness with the energy generated by insight and explication. We are called to care; to be intolerant of ineffectiveness and inefficiency even as we are tolerant of and sensitive to the individual human beings who are struggling in their own ways with their own callings. We are called to study, to understand, to hear and be heard, to act against the malaise and to expose the falsehood of self-indulgent impotency expressed in the cry, "There's nothing we can do." We are called to help people figure out what they can do and then to engender a commitment to get on with the doing.

But we are not called to do it for them.

We are not implementors. We do not deliver the service. We do not write the laws. We do not carry out the programs. We do not make funding decisions.

We help clarify what should be, facilitating the translation of vague visions into more concrete statements of purpose. We describe what exists—the "what is." We clarify, elucidate, reveal, analyze, and interpret. We help people see what could be. We present options—others must decide among those options. We show them the paths open to them. At our best, we try to help them anticipate what they will find along the way of each path. We may even work to equip and prepare them for the path they choose. We may accompany them along the path, shedding light backwards on the places they have been, casting our beam forward to expose the obstacles ahead. But we cannot walk the path for them.

And by whom are we called?

We are called by those who control resources and want to use those resources to build a better world. We are called by the service providers, the program administrators, the managers of resources, and the line staff, all of whom are answering their own callings. (We are sometimes called on to help them find out if they have chosen the right calling or if they have the competence and commitment to carry out their calling.)

We are called by teachers, police officers, health professionals, social workers, bureaucrats (someone has to move the paper through the system—even they can be called), farmers, energy conservationists, public officials, philanthropists, and politicians (*"many are called but few are chosen"*).

Most of all we are called by those whose very lives may depend on the quality of the services they receive—the poor and the weak and the powerless who daily experience the ravages of ineffectiveness, inefficiency, and incompetence. We are called by the victims of waste, greed, bureaucracy, regulation, and politics. We are called by the welfare recipients, the hungry, the uneducated, the victims of rape, the mentally disturbed, the chemically dependent, the casualties of discrimination, the children, and the sick.

We are called by them to hear, to see, to expose, and to care. We are called to use our training, our knowledge, our skills, our intelligence, our advantageous social position, our credentials, and our access to places of power to help make *the system*—whatever it may be—deliver on its promises—whatever they may be. We are called on to be strong, honest, forthright, forceful, rigorous—and creative.

It is a noble calling, this profession of evaluation. Behind the contracts, the statistics, the tenure systems, the fallibility of our methods, the paradigms that limit our vision, behind the trappings of our professionalism there is a noble calling.

Most of all, then, we are called on not to lose sight of our calling—to work together to deliver on the promises of our profession. At stake is the quality of human programs that express and embody the highest ideals of humankind. At stake is the quality of the lives of our fellow human beings.

PART II: *Toward A Creative Evaluation Repertoire*

- Evaluating a program is like shooting at a moving target. It's hard as hell to hit, and requires precise anticipation. The rare bullseye brings uncommon satisfaction. Improving your aim means lots of practice—and careful study of the non-random movements of the target.
- Where there is no resistance, there is no friction. There also is no movement.
- How you got where you are going can make all the difference.
- Don't underestimate the importance of helping people recognize what they already know.
- When a program is unjustly done in by an evaluation, or when a policy is inappropriately changed, the victims care not whether it was by malice or incompetence.
- Few things evade our attention so consistently as those things we take for granted.
- Unconscious thinking is a contradiction in terms.
- *Says he to she*: "Evaluators make better lovers because they are constantly assessing their performance to improve it."
  Says she to he: "Being aware of a thing and being able to do something about it are two quite different things."

From Halcolm's Evaluation Primer

CHAPTER 4: The Focusing Power of Concepts

> *The secret of living is to find a pivot,*
> *the pivot of a concept on which you*
> *can make your stand.*

> Luigi Pirandello

The concepts we use to organize and order the world are central in determining how we perceive and respond to evaluation situations we encounter. Creative evaluators are situationally flexible and adaptable, making sure that methods and measures are appropriate to the information needs of stakeholders and evaluation clients. Responsiveness and creativity are limited by our conceptual blinders. Creative consultants to corporations stress the need for mental leaps, frame-breaking, conceptual blockbusting (Adams, 1976), and imagineering to overcome conceptual barriers. This chapter examines the nature of conceptual thinking in creative evaluation and provides alternative conceptualizations of two major evaluation issues to illustrate the attention-directing power of concepts.

Concepts: Out of Chaos, Order

Concepts channel thought. Concepts order the world, telling us what things go together and what things are distinct from each other. The language we use is not neutral. It embodies and reinforces the meanings and perceptions that direct thinking and make judgment—and action—possible.

We have concepts to call our attention to the things we believe to be

important. We give names to those things we think are important so that
we can talk to each other about them. We learn in introductory
sociology that the Eskimos have many names for snow and that the
Arabs have many names for camels. Evaluators have many names for
evaluation:

- formative evaluation
- summative evaluation
- cost-benefit analysis
- discrepancy evaluation
- meta-evaluation
- utilization focused evaluation
- needs assessment . . .

I once asked Michael Scriven, who has probably identified and
named more evaluation concepts than anyone else in the field, how he
came up with new ideas and concepts. He replied that he really didn't
like "muddying up the field" with a lot of jargon and new terms, so he
only created a term when he felt it was absolutely necessary. He said that
as he noticed confusion about some issue or became sharply aware of
some gap in the field, he would find it necessary to create some new
terminology or to offer a new concept to help sort out the confusion and
fill in the gap.

Experiments aimed at studying the phenomenal capabilities of chess
masters illustrate the power of conceptual ordering. De Groot (1966)
showed complex chess board displays from actual games to poor chess
players and to chess masters. After seeing the boards for only five
seconds both amateurs and masters were asked to reconstruct what they
saw. The masters were able to reproduce what they had seen almost
perfectly, only occasionally making a minor error; the amateurs could
scarcely place any of the pieces in the correct positions. In a second
experiment the same two groups were shown new chessboards with the
same number of chess pieces as before. This time, however, a new
wrinkle was added to the experiment. Rather than arranging the pieces
in positions taken from actual games, the pieces were arranged
randomly on the board. Again the amateurs could scarcely place any of
the pieces in the correct squares. *But neither could the masters.* The clear
superiority of the chess masters over the amateurs disappeared when the
masters were unable to conceptualize the patterns of a particular chess

display because of the random ordering (the chaos) of the pieces.

The problem for evaluators is to know when a new situation can be appropriately handled by prior conceptualizations and when it cannot. The creative challenge is to resist imposing order through familiar concepts before taking the time to look for patterns unique to the circumstances at hand, circumstances that may require some new way of thinking about and labeling the evaluation process.

Reframing and Frame-Breaking

"Frames" are the boundaries we place around things to set them off from and make them stand out against the background. Concepts are frames. Like a picture frame, a concept places boundaries around an idea and makes it clearly identifiable. Reframing involves changing the boundaries, thereby changing the view. This may mean adding more to the picture, or framing a smaller portion of the original picture. It may mean placing a new and different picture alongside the original. Reframing often requires breaking the old frame and building a new one to fit the new picture.

Creative evaluation practice includes being open to the possibility that the usual frames are inadequate in a particular situation. Achieving conceptual flexibility through frame-breaking includes the following elements:

(1) awareness of the major conceptual distinctions in the profession;
(2) awareness of one's personal conceptual predispositions, that is, the concepts upon which one most often relies;
(3) knowing how to broaden or adapt concepts in new situations;
(4) considering the possibility that an altogether new frame is needed to do justice to a special situation; and
(5) a label to capture the new view.

I have been told by a number of evaluators that they are not interested in reframing issues or conceptual discussions; they simply want to get on with the business of doing evaluations. *The central point of this chapter is that practice is inevitably undergirded by conceptual distinctions that are far from esoteric. Whether one is aware of it or not, practice is guided by—indeed, controlled by—the concepts that order that world upon which one is "practicing." To ignore the conceptual distinctions that direct the day-to-day decisions taken in the field is to be controlled and limited by those conceptual predispositions.* Technicians may find satisfaction in that kind of evaluation practice; creative evaluators will not.

The remainder of this chapter moves from this general discussion of conceptual thinking to concrete consideration of two major conceptual issues in evaluation. These two examples illustrate what political scientist William Connolly would consider to be conceptual disputes that reveal basic theoretical positions in a discipline.

> Conceptual disputes . . . , when they involve the central concepts of a field of inquiry, are surface manifestations of basic theoretical differences that reach to the core. The intensity of commitment to favored definitions reflects intensity of commitment to a general theoretical perspective; and revisions that follow conceptual debates involve a shift in the theory that has housed the concepts. (Connolly, 1974, p. 21)

My primary concern in staking out a position in the "conceptual disputes" that follow is to illustrate with concrete and specific examples how the concepts we take into the field can determine what we do in the field. The first conceptual distinction describes the idea of "assets analysis." The second "conceptual contest," to use Connolly's term, concerns how we differentiate among major evaluation approaches.

ASSETS ANALYSIS

The idea of "assets analysis" is here offered as a way of calling attention to a conceptual weakness in the usual way evaluators think about "needs assessment." The idea of assessing client needs is one of the most important in the profession. A number of evaluators, most notably Michael Scriven, have made needs assessment the first and most fundamental step in program development and evaluation. The funding of many programs is now contingent on conducting some kind of needs assessment. The concept of needs assessment calls attention to the idea that programs should serve client needs—not staff needs, political needs, organizational needs, funder needs. First and foremost, programs of all kinds should meet client needs.

Needs assessment is a powerful conceptual frame. My concern is that the focus on client needs has become so pervasive and dominant that program staff and evaluators have largely ignored client strengths and assets.

Assets analysis is not the opposite of needs assessment. Rather, it highlights a different aspect of the assessment process. Where needs assessment suggests deficiencies to be corrected, assets analysis calls attention to strengths that can be developed. Just as programs are often unaware of the needs of their clients, so too they are often unaware of the capabilities of their clients. Those strengths or assets, if known, can be used to help clients meet their own needs. Assets analysis is also aimed at keeping intact in a program those things that may already be working quite well; this is in keeping with the spirit of the saying, "If it ain't broken, don't fix it."

Assets analysis provides a counterbalance to needs assessment. A focus on client needs to the exclusion of client assets and strengths can lead to a deficiency approach to educational and social action programming. The deficiency perspective exists when the student or client is viewed largely in terms of deficits to be removed or corrected, as an empty vessel to be filled, or yet again as clay to be molded. Program staff can become so concerned about what is to be done to and for the client that they lose sight of what can be done *by* the client. Clients in such programs come to view themselves in the same way; they become highly aware of their weaknesses and scarcely conscious at all of their strengths (Dewar, 1977; McKnight, 1976).

The deficiency perspective has clearly been dominant in American education. In setting instructional objectives teachers tend to think of all the things the children cannot do, things they will subsequently be taught in the educational program. Even the rhetoric of individualization often focuses more on the individual needs of children than on their individual capabilities. Tests are aimed at diagnosing individual needs and deficiencies. Assets, if considered at all, get defined as those things that the child does not need.

In welfare programs, manpower programs, and the full range of human service activities a problem-oriented approach dominates. Intake procedures are aimed at identifying client problems. Seldom is a procedure established to identify client capabilities and strengths.

At the community level the same phenomenon can be observed. Needs assessment surveys are widely used in community planning. Community residents are asked to prioritize their needs. Seldom are residents asked what strengths exist in their community that can serve as a basis for further development.

The danger is that without knowledge about assets, staff attempts to meet needs may be ineffective and in many cases may actually diminish or reverse client strengths and assets. Consider, for example, a study of housing needs that asks residents about the conditions of their homes, their needs for assistance in conserving energy, and their home repair problems. A planner might use such data to determine that a certain amount of older housing should be replaced by new housing. However, what if the assets of the community include a strong sense of pride attached to living in older homes? People in this community have chosen to live where they do because they like the environment of this older neighborhood. Residents have established a fairly close-knit community with organizations and activities that bring people together. Without knowledge of and attention to these community strengths the planner might proceed to implement a program of replacing older houses with new ones instead of building on local community organization and pride to restore and retrofit older homes.

The same potential exists in dealing with individual clients. People cannot be helped to help themselves unless the helpers are aware of individual strengths and assets. Indeed, the first real need for many students and clients may be to be made aware of their own individual strengths and assets. A formal assets analysis procedure will contribute to this process.

Finally, the same balance can be applied to program evaluation. Evaluation reports, especially the recommendations section, tend to focus on program deficiencies, things that need to be changed or improved, and areas in which a program is weak. But programs also need to be told what they have going for them, strengths upon which they can build, and assets they can use for program improvement. A balanced evaluation report will point out program assets as well as program needs, things that should be changed but also things that should be maintained.

It is important to understand that statements of assets are not simply observations about non-needs. Deficiency thinking can become so predominant that even strengths are stated as the absence of needs. For example, I once saw an evaluation report that concluded: "The program needs no new staff because it doesn't have a turnover problem and staff morale is not low." Such a conclusion hardly points out to program staff and others the basic strengths of the program: "The program has a stable and highly enthusiastic staff." The same thing can happen at the individual level. Diagnostic reports on students often come no closer to a statement of assets than to point out areas in which there are no needs or problems. Such a report will read: "The student has no family problems that would interfere with schooling." Instead it should read: "The student has a stable family that can be used to support learning." *Assets are not simply the absence of needs. Assets analysis is a positive affirmation of strength.*

Both planning and evaluation need to strike a balance between needs assessment and assets identification. A Sufi story makes this point quite nicely.

> Nasrudin was constantly harping away at his son's faults. He would tell him that he needed to study more, to work harder, to display more discipline, to be more assertive, *et cetera, et cetera, et cetera.*
>
> Nasrudin's wife told him he was far too hard on the boy. She urged him to say something positive to the boy.
>
> "Positive? You may whisper accolades in his ear if you want. That is what mothers are for. But I must push him to greatness. He is clearly superior to other young men. It is my responsibility as his father to see that he gets the push and drive he needs to achieve greatness. His strengths are obvious to all. It is his weaknesses that I am called on as his father to correct.

Imagine, then, Nasrudin's shock when he awoke one morning to find the following message from his son:

> I finally realized that I am unworthy to be your son. I have left so that I no longer bring shame to this household.

An Assets Analysis Example

Teenage pregnancies are a major problem among the Chippewa Indians in Minnesota. The tribe initiated a program to help young mothers develop their parenting skills. The program was based on a needs assessment that documented the high rate of teenage pregnancies, the problems experienced by children of such pregnancies, and information from key informants about the kind of program that was needed.

The pilot program run by health professionals had very low attendance. Young mothers did not participate in the program because they looked to their own mothers and grandmothers for advice about parenting in the tradition of the Chippewa. This intergenerational cohesion is a major asset of Chippewa culture. The respect given to elders and the integration of generations are strengths to build on, not barriers to overcome. A formative evaluation of the program included an assets analysis. The assets analysis suggested that any effective program for young mothers should include, in a very active way, mothers and grandmothers of the targeted teenage mothers.

There was initial resistance to this suggestion because of funder concern about the accuracy and value of the information that was being passed on from elders to the young. The funders finally agreed to try out the change when program staff pointed out that involving the mothers and grandmothers in the program would provide an excellent opportunity to expose the older generations to some new ideas and to find areas of flexibility where old ideas could be merged with new. Not only did this hold out the only hope for developing an effective program but it also enlarged the function and purpose of the program. By building on, reinforcing, and respecting the intergenerational ties among the Chippewa, it was possible to design a program for young mothers that did not alienate or separate them from their traditional culture. Moreover, the program provided a formal mechanism for systematically recording the wisdom of Chippewa mothers and grandmothers.

The point of this example is to illustrate the linkage between how we think about a situation and what we do about it. Conceptual flexibility and creativity help evaluators to be situationally responsive in designing useful and appropriate evaluations. It is in that spirit that I have offered these thoughts on the concept "assets analysis." It is in that same spirit that the concept of "user-focused evaluation" is discussed in the next section.

USER-FOCUSED EVALUATION

In writing the book *Utilization-Focused Evaluation* (Patton, 1986) I wanted the title to communicate the idea that how information is to be used should be the driving force behind how the evaluation is designed and conducted. Evaluation use is not something to be concerned about only at the end of an evaluation; how the evaluation is to be used is a primary matter of concern from the very beginning of the evaluation and throughout every step of the evaluative process. (The chapter "Going With the Flow" presents a flow-chart summary of utilization-focused evaluation.)

Ernest House (1980) wrote an important book categorizing various approaches to evaluation. His typology called to my attention an important conceptual omission in the profession. This section discusses and labels that missing approach by reframing House's categorization of utilization-focused evaluation.

House included utilization-focused evaluation among the "decision-making models" he reviewed. The primary characteristic of a decision-making model is that "the evaluation is structured by the decisions to be made. The evaluator is to supply information on these particular decisions" (House, 1978, p. 4). While utilization-focused evaluation includes the option of focusing evaluation questions in such a way that results will provide useful information for decision making, the overall approach emphasizes generating useful information that can serve a variety of purposes depending on the needs of specific information users. An evaluation can certainly provide information relevant to making decisions. But evaluations can be quite useful even where decisions are not at issue. For example, the evaluation process can be important in directing and focusing how people *think about* the basic policies involved in a program: evaluations can help in fine-tuning program implementation; the process of designing an evaluation may lead to clearer, more specific, and more meaningful program goals; and evaluations can provide information on client needs and assets that will help inform general public discussions about public policy. These and other outcomes of evaluation are entirely compatible with utilization-focused evaluation but do not make a formal decision the driving force behind the evaluation.

Nor does utilization-focused evaluation really fit within any of House's other seven categories: (1) systems analysis, which quantitatively measures program inputs and outcomes to look at effectiveness and efficiency; (2) the behavioral objectives approach, which focuses entirely on clear, specific, and measurable goals; (3) goal-free evaluation, which examines the extent to which actual client needs are being met by the program; (4) the art criticism approach, which makes the evaluator's own expertise-derived standards of excellence a criterion against which programs are judged; (5) the accreditation model, where a team of external accreditors determines the extent to which a program meets professional standards for a given type of program; (6) the adversary approach, where two teams do battle over the summative question of whether a program should be continued; and (7) the transaction approach, which concentrates on program processes.

What is omitted from the House classification scheme is an approach to evaluation that focuses on and is driven by the information needs of specific people who will use the evaluation findings. These people may be thought of as decision makers, stakeholders, information users, evaluation clients, policymakers, or any other term(s) you prefer. The point is that the evaluation is *user focused.*

The user-focused model is a clear alternative to the other models identified by House. In each of the other models the content of the evaluation is determined by the *evaluator's* presuppositions about what constitutes an evaluation: a look at the relationship between inputs and outcomes; the measurement of goal attainment; advice about a specific programmatic decision; description of program processes; a decision about future or continued funding; or judgment according to some set of expert or professional standards. In contrast to these models, user-focused evaluation describes an evaluation process for making decisions about the content of an evaluation—but the content itself is not specified or implied in advance. Thus any of the eight House models or adaptations and combinations of those models might emerge as the guiding direction in user-focused evaluation, depending on the information needs of the people for whom the evaluation information was being collected.

Utilization-focused evaluation is essentially a *user-focused approach.* In *Utilization-Focused Evaluation* I identified the "personal factor"— who cares about the evaluation—as the critical factor determining how evaluation information is used.

> The personal factor is the presence of an identifiable individual or group of people who personally cared about the evaluation and the information it generated. Where such a person or group was present, evaluations were used; where the personal factor was absent, there was a correspondingly marked absence of evaluation impact. The personal factor represents the leadership, interest, enthusiam, determination, commitment, assertiveness, and caring of specific, individual people. These are the people who are actively seeking information to reduce decision uncertainties so as to increase their ability to predict the outcomes of programmatic activity and enhance their own discretion as decisionmakers. These are the primary users in evaluation. (Patton, 1986, p. 45)

Utilization-focused evaluation begins with identification and organization of primary, intended information users, not vague, passive audiences. These primary, intended users are the people who will use the information that the evaluation produces. The evaluator works with these persons (often an evaluation task force representing several constituencies, for example, program staff, clients, funders, administrators, board members, and community representatives) to *focus relevant evaluation questions.* From these questions flow the appropriate research methods and data analysis techniques. Utilization-focused evaluation plans for utilization before data are ever collected. The question that underlies the ongoing interactions between evaluators and decision makers is, "What difference would *that* information make?" The evaluator asks: "What would you do if you had an answer to *that* question?" In answering the evaluation questions of decision makers and information users, utilization-focused evaluation does not preclude the use of any of the full variety of methodological options open to evaluations.

This summary of utilization-focused evaluation emphasizes that the focus is on people, not decisions. Thus I conclude that House's classification scheme makes a major conceptual omission—the omission of a user-focused model of evaluation.

User-Focused Examples

Laurence Lynn, Jr., Professor of Public Policy at the Kennedy School of Government, Harvard University, has commented on the challenge of meeting the information needs of specific policymakers. His observations and reflections provide excellent evidence for the importance of a user-focused way of thinking in evaluation. Lynn was interviewed by Michael Kirst for *Educational Evaluation and Policy Analysis.* He was asked, "What would be a test of a 'good policy analysis'?"

> One of the conditions of a good policy analysis is that it is helpful to a decision-maker. A decision-maker looks at it and finds he or she understands the problem better, understands the choices better, or understands the implications of choice better. The decision-maker can say that this analysis helped me. (Lynn, 1980, p. 85)

Notice here that the emphasis is on informing the decision maker, not the decision. This is a subtle but critical distinction.

Lynn argues in his case book on policy analysis (Lynn, 1980a) that a major craft skill needed by policy and evaluation analysts is the ability to understand and make accommodations for a specific decision maker's cognitive style and other personal characteristics. His examples are exemplars of user-focused approach.

> **Lynn:** Let me take the example of Eliot Richardson, for whom I worked, or Robert MacNamara, for that matter. These two individuals were

perfectly capable of understanding the most complex issues and absorbing details—absorbing the complexity, fully considering it in their own minds. Their intellects were not limited in terms of what they could handle. . . . On the other hand, and I do not want to use names, you will probably find more typical the decisionmakers who do not really like to approach problems intellectually. They may be visceral, they may approach issues with a wide variety of preconceptions, they may not like to read, they may not like data, they may not like the appearance of rationality, they may like to see things couched in more political terms, or overt value terms. And an analyst has got to take that into account. That is no point in presenting some highly rational, comprehensive piece of work to a Secretary or an Assistant Secretary of State who simply cannot or will not think that way. But that does not mean the analyst has no role; that means the analyst has to figure out how he can usefully educate someone who's method of being educated is quite different. The analyst needs to see and understand things in a different style. . . .

We did a lengthy case on the Carter administration's handling of the welfare reform issue, and, in particular, the role that Joe Califano and his analysts performed in the general process. It became very clear from listening to the accounts of everyone involved in that process that Joe Califano was very different in the way he could be reached than an Eliot Richardson, or even Caspar Weinberger. Califano is a political animal and has a relatively short attention span—highly intelligent, but an action-oriented person. And one of the problems his analysts had is that they attempted to educate him in the classical, rational way without reference to any political priorities, or without attempting to couch issues and alternatives in terms that would appeal to a political, action-oriented individual. And so there was a terrible communication problem between the analysts and Califano. I think a large part of that had nothing to do with Califano's intellect or his interest in the issues; it had a great deal to do with the fact that his cognitive style and the analyst's approach just did not match.

EEPA: Another example of that is Governor Jerry Brown of California who is trained in the Jesuitical debating style. He wants everything in thesis, antithesis. He wants oral, hard-hitting debate, and he is not too interested in long-written analyses.

Lynn: Yes, a lot of analysts, in listening to these examples of people who are not rational and analytical in the sense that they understand, would say we have no business dealing with those kinds of people then. Policy analysis cannot help them. I think that is the wrong implication. *One has to discover those art forms by which one can present the result of one's intellectual effort in a way that Jerry Brown will absorb.*

EEPA: Your book stresses that the analyst needs to have a pretty good grasp of the decision maker's reality, the complex blend of factors that the decision maker will take into account. How can I possibly do this if I am a systems analyst-economist dealing with a politician like Califano or Jerry Brown?

Lynn: Actually in my judgment, it is not as hard as it sounds. I think it is not that difficult to discover how a Jerry Brown or a Joe Califano or a George Bush or a Ted Kennedy thinks, how he reacts. All you have got to do is talk to people who deal with them continuously, or read what they say and write. And you start to discover the kinds of things that preoccupy them, the kinds of ways they approach problems. And you use that information in your policy analyses. I think the hangup most analysts or many analysts have is they they want to be faithful to their discipline. They want to be faithful to economics or faithful to political science and are uncomfortable straying beyond what their discipline tells them they are competent at dealing with. The analyst is tempted to stay in that framework with which he or she feels most comfortable.

And so they have the hangup, they cannot get out of it. They are prone to say that my tools, my training do not prepare me to deal with things that are on Jerry Brown's mind, therefore, I cannot help him. That is wrong. They can help, but they have got to be willing to use the information they have about how these individuals think and then begin to craft their work, to take that into account. (Lynn, 1980, pp. 86-87)

Lynn is here documenting the importance of the personal factor at the highest levels of government. Alkin, Daillak, and White (1979) have documented the operation of the personal factor at state and local levels as well. The importance of a conceptualization like *user-focused evaluation* is that it directs attention to the personal factor, giving direction to practitioners in the field about what to look for and how to proceed.

I would suggest that it takes a good deal of creativity to adapt an evaluation to the needs and characteristics of specific decision makers and information users. The personal factor is not the only factor in the evaluation to which one must adapt, but situational flexibility certainly includes sensitivity to the people involved in the evaluation process. Lynn's conceptualization of the ideal policy analyst bears a striking similarity to my description of the creative evaluator in the first two chapters of this book.

Individuals really do have to be interdisciplinary; they have to be highly catholic in their taste for intellectual concepts and ideas and tools. I do not think we are talking so much about acquiring a specific kind of knowledge or a specialist's knowledge in order to deal with environmental issues or energy issues. One does not have to know what a petroleum engineer knows, or what an air quality engineer knows, or what a chemist knows. Rather, one simply has to be able to ask questions of many disciplines and many professions and know how to use the information. And what that says is, I think, one has to be intellectually quite versatile.

It is not enough to be an economist, it is not enough to be an operations research specialist, it is not enough to be a statistician. One has to be a little bit of all of those things. One has to have an intuitive grasp of an awful lot of different intellectual approaches, different intellectual disciplines or traditions so that one can range widely in doing one's job of crafting a good analysis, so that you are not stuck with just the tools you know. I think, then, the implication is versatility and an intuitive grasp of a fairly wide range of different kinds of skills and approaches. (Lynn, 1980, p. 88)

CONCEPTUAL POWER

This chapter has examined how the concepts we employ to organize and order the world are central in determining how we perceive and respond to evaluation situations—and people—we encounter. Concepts direct attention *to* certain things and *away* from other things. Therein lies the power of concepts: the power to direct awareness and focus attention. Creative evaluation practice includes conceptual awareness, conceptual adaptability, and conceptual flexibility.

This does not mean that I am recommending a proliferation of new concepts and terms. The two concepts introduced in this chapter—assets analysis and user-focused evaluation—were meant to illustrate the power of concepts to guide practice and raise consciousness. I certainly do not intend to imply that every evaluation should include creation of a new concept. The cartoon on page 80 nicely satirizes concept creation.

Whether one thinks in terms of offering simple ideas or more grandiose *concepts*, the challenge of creative evaluation is situational responsiveness and sensitivity. This means avoiding the heuristic tendency to make new situations fit snugly into the few old conceptual boxes we happen to have with us. As for generating completely new concepts, the evaluation sage Halcolm has a few words of wisdom to close this chapter.

THE NEW CONCEPT

One day a student near the end of his training came to Halcolm. "As part of my training, Master, I have participated in and observed a great many evaluations. I believe that I have discovered among these a type of evaluation that has not previously been identified in the literature. I want to give it a name and thereby leave my mark on the field."

"It is not for me to pass judgment on the virtue of new concepts," Halcolm explained to the young man. "You must move among your peers and colleagues explaining your new concept to them. It is they who determine which concepts will become part of the profession and which ones will pass away unnoticed."

Following Halcolm's advice the young man went to many seminars and held many discussions with peers and colleagues advancing his new concept. While his notions generated some interest here and there, for the most part those with whom he talked thought his ideas were subsumed under other concepts and already taken care of by existing models. After a while the young man gave up his attempt to push the new concept. He completed his training and went forth to conduct many highly successful evaluations.

A number of years later his work brought him back to the site of his training. He dropped in on a seminar and listened with amazement as he heard a young student advancing a new concept to his peers. The concept was the very one he had attempted to introduce a number of years earlier. This time, however, it become clear that the new concept was being greeted with great acclaim and had already been accepted by the new student's peers and colleagues. Seeing this, the alumnus jumped to his feet and called for the attention of the assembled group.

"My fellow evaluators, students and colleagues, I am greatly heartened to hear you use and apply this supposedly new concept. I feel compelled to remind you, however, that it is I who first thought of this idea many years ago. I mention this now only to keep the record straight for those who follow us."

This led to heated debate between the two men over who should actually get credit for the concept, for the young student also believed the new concept to be his own original contribution. After all, he had introduced the concept based on his own experiences. To settle the conflict the assembled delegation went to see Halcolm, sage evaluator and teacher. They explained the situation to Halcolm and awaited his judgment.

"The prophet tells us that 'there is nothing new under the sun' and 'this too shall pass away.' Yet both of you believe that you have discovered something new and you hope that it will endure forever. Let us, then, consider the nature of new concepts.

"There are many who pass through the world without seeing a certain thing. Then there are many who see that certain thing, but for one reason or another, never name or label it. Then there are those few who see this certain thing and name it, thus calling the attention of others to it. Then still there are those who see it, name it, and convince their fellows that the label is worth preserving and that the thing is worth seeing, thus giving special importance to the concept. Finally, there are the many who follow and use the newly labeled concept but fail to really see or understand the thing and its importance.

"Each person plays a role in the nature of things. Some are given to seeing, some to naming, some to converting others, and some to distorting what others have seen and named.

"Being present at this time and in this place it is not our role to pass judgment on which of these deserves the greater credit. Future generations can look back and sort out the record. It is left to them to evaluate your new concept. Be content to understand your own role in these things. Be content to examine what it has been given unto you to do and see if you have done it well. Let others give credit where they will. You must decide for yourself, each of you, if what you have thought was useful and what you have done was done well.

"And, as a matter of only minor interest and no particular importance at all, I might point out—just for the record—that it was *I* who originally introduced the concept you've been arguing about when I was a student many, many years ago, but I couldn't get anyone else to pay any attention to it at the time . . ."

CHAPTER 5: *Evaluation Metaphors*

> *Authors of all races, be they Greeks,*
> *Romans, Teutons, or Celts, can't seem*
> *just to say that anything is the thing it*
> *is; they have to go out of their way to*
> *say that it is like something else.*
>
> Ogden Nash

Evaluators are highly familiar with statistical comparisons, but metaphorical comparisons can be no less powerful. Metaphors, similes, and analogies help us make connections between seemingly unconnected things, thereby opening up new possibilities by unveiling what had been undetected. Bill Gephart, in his 1980 presidential address to evaluators, drew an analogy between his work as a watercolor artist and his work as an evaluator. Gephart compared the artist's efforts to "compel the eye" to the evaluator's efforts to "compel the mind." Both artist and evaluator attempt to focus the attention of an audience by highlighting some things and keeping other things in the background. He also examined the ways in which the values of an audience (of art critics or program decision makers) affect what they see in a finished piece of work.

Nick Smith directed a Research on Evaluation Program in which he and others thought about evaluators as poets, architects, photographers, philosophers, operations analysts, and artists (Smith, 1981). They consciously and creatively used metaphors and analogies to understand and elaborate the many functions of program evaluation.

The last chapter focused on the power of concepts. This chapter considers the focusing power of various kinds of figurative speech—metaphors, similes, and analogies. Use of these forms of figurative speech can help evaluators communicate with others about the nature and practice of evaluation. Rather than explain an approach or finding directly, it is sometimes more effective to explain it metaphorically.

Metaphors and similes don't just happen. They are created by the aware and searching mind. Effective communication between evaluators and stakeholders is crucial if evaluative information is to be useful to those stakeholders. This chapter explores how creative evaluation metaphors and other forms of figurative speech can help increase our understanding of programs and enhance our effectiveness in communicating about evaluation process. The role of metaphor in evaluation has been discussed by Kelly (1975), Ortony (1975), Worthen (1978), Guba (1978), and Smith (1978). For a general discussion of *Models and Metaphors* see Black (1962).

The Classic Failure to Communicate

There is a poignant scene in the movie *Cool Hand Luke* in which Luke—a freedom-loving chain gang prisoner who has attempted numerous escapes—has once again been brought back to stand before the sadistic and cruel warden. Fully aware that the other prisoners are listening, the warden pauses before pronouncing some new and more severe punishment in his ongoing attempt to break Luke's spirit. Looking down at Luke, severely beaten and forced to his knees by the guards, the warden says: "What we have here is a failure to communicate."

There is a standing joke among people who employ organizational consultants that you can always count on them to find a "communications problem" and to recommend a solution that involves "improved communications." Despite the almost certain and mundane nature of such recommendations, the same truism applies to program evaluation processes. Many of the problems encountered by evaluators, much of the resistance to evaluation, and many failures of utilization occur because of misunderstandings and communications problems. What we often have is a "failure to communicate."

Studies of communication processes have increased our understanding of the important role that metaphor plays in facilitating interpersonal communications and stimulating thinking. The work of Milton Erickson, perhaps the world's foremost medical hypnotist, has demonstrated the power of the metaphor as a tool for communicating with both the conscious and the unconscious mind. Erickson was masterful in using metaphors. For example, Erickson was once asked to work with a florist dying of cancer. The man was experiencing great pain and drugs were no longer of much help in controlling his agony. The man had lost faith in medicine and refused to have any further contact with medical personnel. Erickson had a lengthy conversation with the florist in which he discussed a tomato plant, how the plant grows and what it takes to maintain a healthy plant. Using the metaphor of the tomato plant, Erickson was able to suggest ways that the patient could again experience healthy cellular growth. Communicating through metaphor, Erickson changed the man's thinking about his pain and illness. Without ever directly discussing the patient's condition, and using only the metaphor of the tomato plant, the therapy was quite successful and the patient experienced relief from pain and considerable improvement in the quality of the final days of life (Bandler & Grinder, 1975).

Metaphors and analogies can be extremely useful in stimulating creative thinking about evaluation and in facilitating communication about evaluation concepts, meanings, and processes. Creative evaluation approaches are of little use if they cannot be communicated. William James noted that "the most immutable barrier in nature is between one man's thoughts and another's." Failure to communicate is a common plague on all evaluation houses.

One reason for such failures is that the language of research and evaluation—the jargon—is alien to many laypersons, decision makers, and stakeholders. From my point of view, the burden for clear communications rests on the evaluator. It is the evaluator who must find ways of bridging the communications gap between the people who use evaluation findings and those who generate those findings.

The next section describes an exercise aimed at enhancing understanding about the nature of evaluation by having participants in an evaluation process reflect on evaluation by constructing metaphors and similes about evaluation. The exercise helps participants in an evaluation process discover their own values concerning evaluation while also giving them a mechanism to communicate those values to others. The exercise could be used with a program staff, an evaluation task force, evaluation trainees, workshop participants, or any group for whom it might be helpful to clarify and share perceptions about evaluation.

Getting at Evaluation Preconceptions

One of the first things I like to do with people who will be involved in an evaluation process is find out their preconceptions, their fears, their expectations, and their beliefs about evaluation. It is often appropriate to simply ask people to freely associate in stream-of-consciousness fashion with the word "evaluation":

"When you hear the word 'evaluation' what comes to mind?" On other occasions, when I'm working with a group of people who seem relaxed with each other or who seem open to a highly participatory style, I use a metaphor exercise to help focus what they have to say. The exercise goes like this.

> What I'd like to do to get the evaluation process started is have us share some perceptions about evaluation. One of the things that we'll need to do during the process of working together is come to some basic under- standings about what evaluation is and can do. In my experience, evaluation can be a very creative and energizing experience. In particular, interpreting and using evaluation findings for program improvement requires creativity and openness to a variety of possibilities. To help us get started on this creative endeavor I am going to ask you to participate with me in a little exercise.

> In this box I have a bunch of toys, household articles, office supplies, tools, and other miscellaneous gadgets and thingamajigs that I've gathered from around my house. I'm going to dump these in the middle of the table and ask each of you to take one of them and use that item or thing to make a statement about evaluation. Evaluation is like ＿＿ because . . .

I tell participants that being creative is really just a matter of practice and being open to thinking about new possibilities. To illustrate what I want people to do I tell them that I'll go first, and I ask someone to pick out any object in the room that I might use for my metaphor. What follows are some examples from actual workshops:

> Someone points to a coffee cup: "This coffee cup is like an evaluation framework. The framework specifies the evaluation process but doesn't specify its contents. The framework provides a structure for the evaluation process. This cup is a structure that can be used to hold a variety of things. The actual contents of the cup will vary depending on who is using it and for what purpose they are using it. But the basic form of the cup doesn't change. The framework or structure for an evaluation is empty until the group of people working on the evaluation fill it with focus and content and substance. The potential of the cup cannot be realized until it holds some liquid. The potential of an evaluation framework cannot be realized until it is given the substance of a concrete evaluation problem and

situation. One of the things that I'll be doing as we work together is providing an evaluation framework. You will provide the substance."

Someone points to a chalkboard: "Evaluation is like a chalkboard because both are tools that can be used to express a variety of different things. The chalkboard itself is just an empty piece of slate until someone writes on it and provides information and meaning by filling in that space. The chalkboard can be filled up with meaningless figures, random marks, obscene words, mathematical formulas, or political graffiti—or the board can be filled with meaningful information, insights, helpful suggestions, and basic facts. The people who write on the chalkboard carry the responsibility for what it says. The people who fill in the blanks in the evaluation and determine its content and substance carry the responsibility for what the evaluation says. The evaluation process is just a tool to be used—and how it is used will depend on the people who control the process.

I'll typically take a break at this point and give people about ten minutes to select an item and think about what to say. If there are more than ten people in the group I will break the larger group into small groups of five or six for sharing analogies and metaphors. The sharing process can take quite a bit of time if the group is too large. After about ten minutes each person is given an opportunity to make an evaluation statement. Below are some examples from actual workshops.

The empty grocery bag is symbolic of my feelings about evaluation. When I think about our program being evaluated I want to find someplace to hide and I can put this empty bag over my head so that nobody can see me and I can't see anything else, and it gives me at least the feeling that I'm able to hide. [She puts the bag over her head.]

Evaluation can be like this toothbrush. When used properly it gets out the particles between the teeth and the stuff that's on the teeth so that the teeth don't decay. It helps to keep the teeth healthy. If it's not used properly, if it just lightly goes over the teeth or doesn't cover all the teeth, then some of the foreign substance will stay on and cause the teeth to dacay. Evaluation can help get rid of the things that are causing a program to decay and help make the program healthy.

Evaluation for me is like a rubber ball. You throw it down and it comes right back at you. Every time I say to my staff we ought to evaluate the program, they throw it right back at me and they say, "You do the evaluation."

Evaluation is like this camera. It lets you take a picture of what's going on, but only takes a picture of what you point the camera at. And it only gets a picture of what you point the camera at at that particular point in time. My concern about evaluation is it can only capture a little bit of what's going on at a particular point in time and it doesn't give you the whole picture. It's helpful to have the picture but there's an awful lot that's left out.

Evaluation for me is like this empty envelope. You can use an envelope to send a message to someone. I want to use evaluation to send a message to our funders about what we're doing in the program. They don't have any idea about what we actually do. I just hope they'll read the letter when they get it.

Evaluation for me is like this adjustable wrench. You can use this wrench to tighten nuts and bolts to help hold things together. If used properly and applied with the right amount of pressure it holds things together very well. If you tighten the bolt too hard, however, you can break the bolt and the whole thing will fall apart. I'm in favor of evaluation if it's done right. My concern is that you can overdo it and the program can't handle it.

The process of sharing is usually accompanied by laughter, spontaneous reactions to what people have said, and much animated involvement. It is a fun process that communicates that the evaluation process itself may not be quite as painful as people thought it would be if this is any indication of what can happen. In addition, people are often surprised to find that they have something to say and that they can say it through an analogy. They are typically quite pleased with themselves. Most important, the exercise serves to express very important thoughts and feelings that can be dealt with once they are made explicit.

People often have very deep feelings about evaluating and being evaluated. They are typically not even aware that they have these feelings. By providing a vehicle for discovering and expressing their concerns it is possible to bring to the surface major issues that may later affect the evaluation. Shared metaphors can help establish a common framework for the evaluation, capturing its purpose, its possibilities, and the safeguards that need to be built into the evaluation process. Robert Frost once observed, "All thought is a feat of association: Having what's in front of you brings up something in your mind that you almost didn't know you knew." This exercise helps participants bring to mind things about evaluation they almost didn't know they knew.

By the way, I have used this exercise with many different groups and in many different situations, including cross-cultural settings, and I have never yet encountered someone who couldn't find an object to use in saying something about evaluation. One way of guaranteeing this is to include in your box of items some things that have a pretty clear and simple message. For example, I'll always include a lock and key so that a very simple and fairly obvious analogy can be made: "Evaluation is like a lock and key, if you have the right key you can open up the lock and make it work. If you have the right information you can make the thing work." Or I'll include a light bulb so that someone can say, "Evaluation is like this light bulb, it's purpose is to shed light on the situation."

To help evaluation students learn how to communicate more effectively I like to use a variation of this exercise to have them practice explaining evaluation to stakeholders. I begin by having the trainees think of something about evaluation that they want to communicate to a group with whom they might be working. It can be something about the evaluation process, something about methods, something about use, or anything at all. Once they have picked something they want to communicate, I then tell them to find a metaphor or analogy for making that point. They can pick anything in view in the room or they can make up an object that they would like to use and pretend that they have it in their hand. Each student then writes out the point they want to make, works out the analogy or metaphor, and then makes a presentation to the other trainees. Fellow trainees are invited to give feedback, either verbally or in writing, depending on how much time is available and what the situation is.

The Cutting Edge of Metaphors

Metaphors can open up new understandings and enhance communications. They can also distort and offend. At the 1979 meeting of the Midwest Sociological Society, well-known sociologist Morris Janowitz was asked to participate in a panel on the question, What is the cutting edge of sociology? Janowitz, having written extensively on the sociology of the military, took offense at the "cutting edge" metaphor. He explained:

> Paul Russell, the humanist, has prepared a powerful and brilliant sociological study of the literary works of the great wars of the 20th century which he entitled *The Great War and Modern Memory*. It is a work which all sociologists should read. His conclusion is that World War I and World War II, Korea and Vietnam have militarized our language. I

agree and therefore do not like the question "Where is the cutting edge of sociology?" "Cutting edge" is a military term. I am put off by the very term cutting edge. Cutting edge, like the parallel term breakthrough, are slogans which intellectuals have inherited from the managers of violence. Even if they apply to the physical sciences, I do not believe that they apply to the social sciences, especially sociology, which grows by gradual accretion. (Janowitz, 1979, p. 601)

"Strategic planning" is a label with military origins and connotations, as is "rapid reconnaissance," a phrase increasingly used to describe certain exploratory evaluation efforts. Some stakeholder groups will object to such associations. Evaluators, therefore, must be particularly sensitive in their selection of metaphors to avoid offensive comparisons. Of particular importance, in this regard, is avoiding the use of metaphors with possible racist and sexist connotations, for instance, "It's black and white." At the Educational Evaluation and Public Policy Conference sponsored by the Far West Regional Laboratory for Educational Research and Development (1977), the women's caucus expressed concern about the analogies used in evaluation—and went on to suggest some alternatives.

To deal with diversity is to look for new metaphors. We need no new *weapons* of assessment—the violence has already been done! How about *brooms* to sweep away the attic-y cobwebs of our male/female stereotypes? The tests and assessment techniques we frequently use are full of them. How about *knives, forks,* and *spoons* to sample the feast of human diversity in all its richness and color. Where are the techniques that assess the delicious-ness of response variety, independence of thought, original-ity, uniqueness? (And lest you think those are female metaphors, let me do away with that myth—at our house everybody sweeps and everybody eats!) Our workgroup talked about another metaphor—the cafeteria line versus the smorgasbord banquet styles of teaching/learning/assessing. Many new metaphors are needed as we seek clarity in our search for better ways of evaluating. To deal with diversity is to look for new metaphors. (Hurty, 1976)

It is because the connotations associated with metaphors are so powerful that evaluators were being encouraged by Hurty and her colleagues to think carefully about those connotations, and to "look for new metaphors" in evaluation. One of my favorite examples, of the power—and the humor—of metaphors is Donald Mazia's description of the nucleus of a cell.

In common language, we describe the nucleus as the administrator of the cell. It shares two attributes with more familiar administrators: it tends to perpetuate its kind, and it defies so successfully all efforts (by outsiders) to learn what it is doing that only by trying to get along without it can we satisfy ourselves that it is working at all. (Mazia, 1962, p. 5)

Metaphors and analogies can be overused. If an analogy is too obtuse or if the point is stretched too far, it loses its power. When properly used, however, metaphors and analogies can help alleviate the problem of "the failure to communicate." They can also be powerful stimulants to creative thinking and powerful aids to understanding. As Thoreau said:

All perception of truth is the detection of an analogy.

CHAPTER 6: *Going with the Flow*

In my early days of doing program evaluation workshops I once had a young man come up to me to express his disappointment at the day's handouts:

> Not a single flowchart the entire day! I must say that I'm much surprised to attend a whole day's workshop on program evaluation and receive not a single flowchart.

Reflecting afterwards on this bit of feedback I realized that my training had been inadequate in this regard. Not once in 22 years of formal education had I been schooled in the construction of flowcharts. I immediately set out to fill this vacuum and have subsequently included at least one flowchart of some sort in my workshops so as to meet the expectations of those who identify evaluation as "going with the flow" and to better communicate with participants who are graphically or visually oriented.

As I began to do some formal modeling with flowcharts I was surprised by the rigorous and creative thinking required. To construct a flowchart is to identify, clarify, and make explicit critical action and decision junctures in a problem or system. The relationships among the junctures must then be both elaborated and simplified. Initially skeptical that complex systems or processes could be accurately or fairly reduced to some display of boxes, circles, triangles, and arrows, I found that not only could it be done, but I discovered things in the process—important things of which I had previously been unaware. For example, I was convinced that the process of utilization-focused evaluation (Patton, 1986) was far too complex to represent as a flowchart. What I discovered instead was that not only could it be reduced to a reasonably understandable graphic, but in so doing the adaptive, reiterative, and dynamic nature of the process could be captured. The utilization-focused evaluation flowchart is included in this chapter, as are flowcharts of two other evaluation processes.

Serial Information Processing

There is substantial experimental evidence demonstrating that for most problem solving and decision making "the human is a completely serial information processing system" (Newell & Simon, 1972, p. 797). What this means is that, because of limited memory and information-processing capabilities, we can only attend to one thing at a time. To the extent that this is true, any process of decision making can reasonably be depicted as a set of sequential steps similar in format to a computer program. Graphically, this means that any process of decision making can be reasonably represented by a flowchart.

Kleinmutz (1966, 1968) has collected and reviewed a substantial literature showing how human problem solving and judgment processes can be formally represented by equations and flowcharts. Such work basically derives from careful fieldwork, which involves listening to the discussion of some committee or group of decision makers and then transforming their rambling interactions into a sequence of decision rules that can be displayed graphically. The people involved are typically not aware of their own decision-rule sequences and heuristics (a central point of the first chapter of this book), but they can learn a great deal about how they operate by having laid bare before them the sequence of critical problem points they have reached and the decision rules employed to resolve those critical problems. This sharpened awareness can be the first step toward more creative problem solving and decision making.

Flowchart Fundamentals

The symbols used in flowcharts derive their meanings from standard conventions. A circle is used for beginnings and endings (start, stop, or end). A rectangle is used to give process instructions or to designate an event, action, or procedure. A diamond shape indicates a question, usually a question that can be answered "yes" or "no" (a convention derived from the use of flowcharts in binary computer programs). Arrows are used to indicate the direction of the flow. Flowcharts are generally read from left to right and from top to bottom. To keep the flow understandable the chart is usually set up so that only one arrow will actually enter any symbol. If several lines are going toward a symbol, they will join together at some point just before entering the symbol. Only one arrow should leave a rectangle (an action symbol). Two arrows should leave a diamond (decision symbol), one for the *yes* path and one for the *no* path.

UTILIZATION-FOCUSED EVALUATION
FLOWCHART

Chart 6.1 depicts the process of utilization-focused evaluation. This is a process for making decisions about the focus and content of an evaluation. The decision-making process depicted in the flowchart does not preclude a priori any particular approaches, outcomes, measures, methods, typical questions, assumptions, or audiences. Utilization-focused evaluation is a strategy for making decisions about all these things by actively involving primary intended users.

Utilization-focused evaluation begins with identification and organization of primary intended users (not vague, passive audiences) who will use the information that the evaluation produces. The importance of gearing an evaluation to the interests, needs, and capabilities of particular people was discussed in Chapter 4 as *user-focused evaluation*, an alternative way of labeling the process depicted in Chart 6.1. The evaluator works with the primary intended users to *focus* relevant evaluation questions. From these questions flow the appropriate research methods and data analysis techniques.

Utilization-focused evaluation plans for utilization *before* data are ever collected. The question that underlies and drives the ongoing interactions between evaluators and decision makers is, What difference would *that* information make? The evaluator asks, What would you do if you had an answer to *that* question? Decision makers and evaluation task force members are expected to identify how answers to evaluation questions will be used before data are collected. Once questions are focused on useful issues, methods decisions are made with special attention to questions of methods appropriateness, believeability, feasibility, and data utility. Threats to utility are as important as threats to validity and reliability. Finally, the primary intended users are included in data analysis and interpretation.

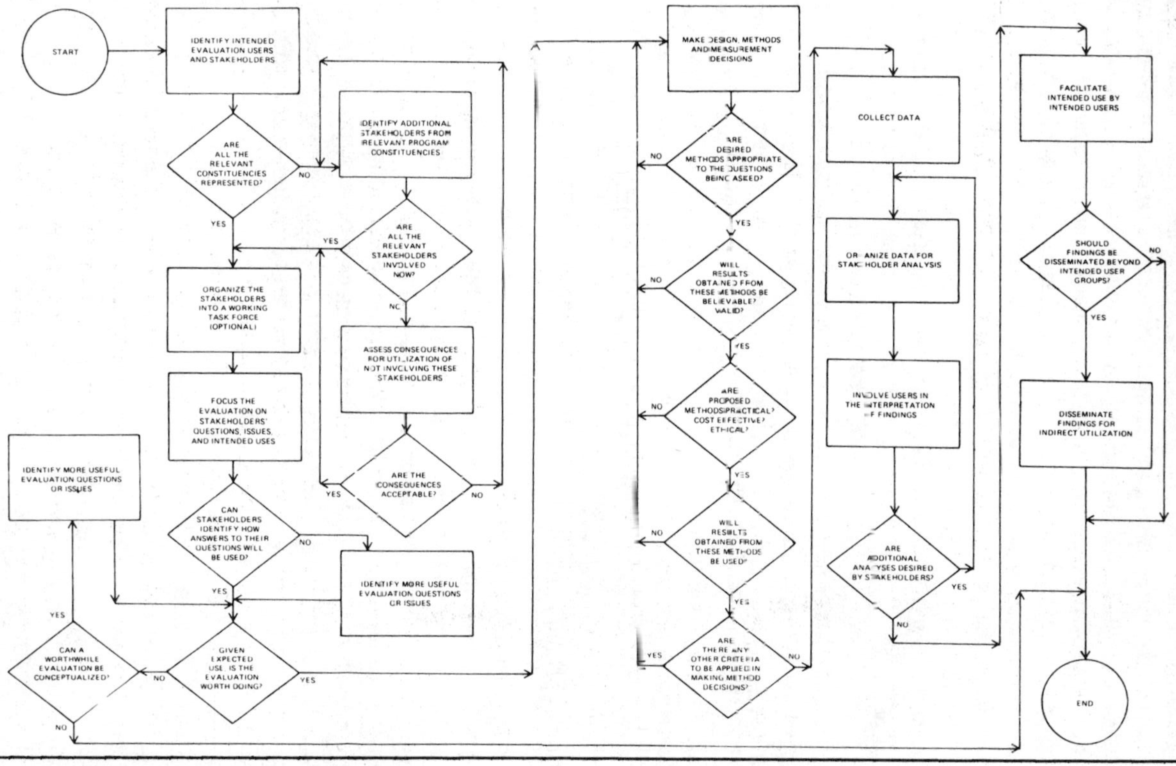
START
IDENTIFY INTENDED EVALUATION USERS AND STAKEHOLDERS
ARE ALL THE RELEVANT CONSTITUENCIES REPRESENTED?
NO
YES
IDENTIFY ADDITIONAL STAKEHOLDERS FROM RELEVANT PROGRAM CONSTITUENCIES
ARE ALL THE RELEVANT STAKEHOLDERS INVOLVED NOW?
YES
NO
ASSESS CONSEQUENCES FOR UTILIZATION OF NOT INVOLVING THESE STAKEHOLDERS
ARE THE CONSEQUENCES ACCEPTABLE?
YES
NO
ORGANIZE THE STAKEHOLDERS INTO A WORKING TASK FORCE (OPTIONAL)
FOCUS THE EVALUATION ON STAKEHOLDERS' QUESTIONS, ISSUES, AND INTENDED USES
CAN STAKEHOLDERS IDENTIFY HOW ANSWERS TO THEIR QUESTIONS WILL BE USED?
NO
YES
IDENTIFY MORE USEFUL EVALUATION QUESTIONS OR ISSUES
GIVEN EXPECTED USE, IS THE EVALUATION WORTH DOING?
NO
YES
CAN A WORTHWHILE EVALUATION BE CONCEPTUALIZED?
YES
NO
IDENTIFY MORE USEFUL EVALUATION QUESTIONS OR ISSUES
MAKE DESIGN, METHODS AND MEASUREMENT DECISIONS
ARE DESIRED METHODS APPROPRIATE TO THE QUESTIONS BEING ASKED?
NO
YES
WILL RESULTS OBTAINED FROM THESE METHODS BE BELIEVABLE? VALID?
NO
YES
ARE PROPOSED METHODS PRACTICAL? COST EFFECTIVE? ETHICAL?
NO
YES
WILL RESULTS OBTAINED FROM THESE METHODS BE USED?
NO
YES
ARE THERE ANY OTHER CRITERIA TO BE APPLIED IN MAKING METHOD DECISIONS?
YES
NO
COLLECT DATA
ORGANIZE DATA FOR STAKEHOLDER ANALYSIS
INVOLVE USERS IN THE INTERPRETATION OF FINDINGS
ARE ADDITIONAL ANALYSES DESIRED BY STAKEHOLDERS?
YES
NO
FACILITATE INTENDED USE BY INTENDED USERS
SHOULD FINDINGS BE DISSEMINATED BEYOND INTENDED USER GROUPS?
NO
YES
DISSEMINATE FINDINGS FOR INDIRECT UTILIZATION
END

Chart 6.1: Utilization-Focused Evaluation Flowchart

A potential weakness of any logical, narrative presentation of utilization-focused evaluation is that the process can seem quite linear in nature: (1) identify information users; (2) focus evaluation questions; (3) gather data; (4) analyze data; and (5) feedback findings. The flowchart depicting utilization-focused evaluation (Chart 6.1) at least has the virtue of showing that any one of these steps can keep you going in circles for a while.

Nevertheless, there are strategic decision points where one part of the process is brought to closure (at least *relative* closure) and the next part of the process is begun. For example, at some point you bring to an end the identification of primary intended users and the organization of an evaluation task force so that the process of focusing evaluation questions can begin. This does not mean that additional people may not join the group along the way. It just means that the evaluator has some responsibility to facilitate the process and keep it moving.

Fully absorbing the information in a flowchart requires some study. Let me pause here, then, to make a pedagogical point: Flowcharts are an excellent way of stimulating thought and discussion, but to do so, time must be allowed for absorption, reaction, and clarification. The full potential of the information in a flowchart is scarcely realized otherwise. I have attended too many workshops, conferences, and board meetings where chart after chart was handed out (or flashed on the screen) followed by a couple of quick highlights (while I was still figuring out what was before me)—then on to the next chart. Charts take time to digest. If it is worth putting all that information together in a carefully constructed flowchart, it is worth allocating sufficient time to discuss it. I remember attending a two-hour session on cost-benefit analysis at an evaluation conference where the presenter boasted afterwards that he got through all 45 of his charts. I didn't bother to tell him that I stopped trying to keep up with him and decipher his charts after the third one—and I lasted longer than most of the audience.

I therefore urge you to take the time to look carefully at Chart 6.1 on utilization-focused evaluation. Think about what is contained in the chart and what is left out. Think about the sequence of steps, the serial information processing depicted, and the reiterative loops. Do these make sense? Can you follow the flow? What are the gaps?

To help answer these questions the reader may find it useful to compare the process in Chart 6.1 with the evaluation process described in the next flowchart, Chart 6.2, which depicts "Evaluation à la Machiavelli."

EVALUATION À LA MACHIAVELLI

The creative and altogether too accurate view of much evaluation depicted in the flowchart by Krenkle and Saretsky (1973) is a sobering reminder of the highly political nature of program evaluation and the precarious nature of the utilization process. A major reason for conducting utilization-focused evaluations, which includes having decision makers develop a commitment to methods *before* data collection and analysis, is to avoid the kinds of subterfuge and sabotage represented so powerfully in the flowchart summarizing "Evaluation à la Machiavelli," Chart 6.2.

I use this flowchart in workshops to emphasize the importance of involving primary stakeholders in methods, design, measurement, and analysis decisions *before* data collection. I also use this flowchart as a centerpiece in that portion of workshops for program staff aimed at empowering the potential victims of poorly done and non-utilization-focused evaluations by teaching them how to protect themselves against unscrupulous evaluators. As Halcolm has observed:

> When a program is unjustly hurt by an evaluation, the victims care not whether it was by malice or by incompetence.

The next section, the "Martial Arts of Evaluation" (or how to defend yourself against unscrupulous evaluators), describes one of the ways the Evaluation à la Machiavelli flowchart has been particularly useful to me. It helps people about to enter into an evaluation process understand some of the options available to them and provides a stark contrast to the process of utilization-focused evaluation.

THE MARTIAL ARTS OF EVALUATION

What began as a joke turned out to be quite a serious matter. We offered a workshop entitled "The Martial Arts of Evaluation: How to Defend Yourself Against Unscrupulous Evaluators." The title was an advertising gimmick to get program people to come to a standard evaluation training workshop. As it turned out, the people who showed up were program staff and administrators who were genuinely interested in sabotaging what they considered to be burdensome and destructive evaluations that were sapping energy and resources from their programs. They came with stories of endless paperwork imposed by insensitive and

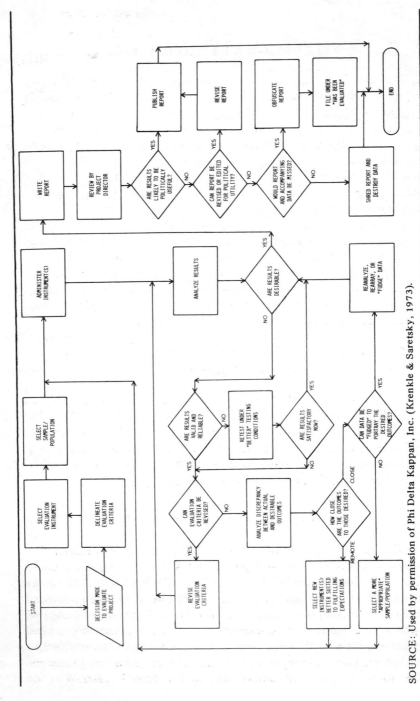

SOURCE: Used by permission of Phi Delta Kappan, Inc. (Krenkle & Saretsky, 1973).

Chart 6.2: Evaluation à la Machiavelli

incompetent researchers who seemed to have nothing better to do than create new forms to inflict on program clients, taking away as much data as possible without ever giving anything back in the way of understandable and useful information.

It was out of this first of what became many "Martial Arts of Evaluation" workshops that the section "The Goals Clarification Game" in *Utilization-Focused Evaluation* (Patton, 1986) emerged. The idea of keeping evaluators off balance by regularly changing program goals, endlessly reshuffling priorities, and purposely writing vague, unclear, and unmeasurable goals was a popular topic among participants who enthusiastically devoted themselves to thinking up ways to make the lives of evaluators difficult. They had an almost intuitive sense that if evaluators were deprived of statements of clear, specific, and measurable goals, they would be unable to do their work. Indeed, some of the participants described the evaluators' need as a kind of dependency. If deprived of their "goals fix" many evaluators exhibited symptoms of withdrawal and became unable to function.

Another popular topic of discussion was how to screw up data collection. Losing forms, wrongly filling out questionnaires, circling more than one number on a scale when the directions clearly stated that only one number should be circled for each item, leaving certain items blank, changing the code number on pre-post instruments, and otherwise subverting the data collection process revealed that the participants were both experienced and creative saboteurs.

While most of the participants claimed fundamental ignorance about research methods and design, they showed themselves to be quite sophisticated about how to undermine the credibility of evaluation reports if they didn't like either the reports or the evaluators who wrote the reports. They revealed considerable skill and experience in attacking sampling procedures, ridiculing sample size, casting aspersions at the comparability of comparison groups, doubting the validity and reliability of measuring instruments, pointing out all the important topics of study that the evaluation overlooked, and building powerful arguments proving the inappropriateness of the evaluation topics that were studied. Their ploys revealed a not altogether hidden killer instinct when it came to going after evaluators and evaluation reports. While they lacked the basic research jargon that would have allowed them to make their points with more circumlocution and pedanticism, their natural skill at locating actual flaws and potential flaws in evaluation designs would have done any graduate seminar proud.

Listening to these workshop participants get in the spirit of evaluation sabotage, it became quite clear that evaluations are very fragile and delicate. Far from being difficult to undermine and sabotage, evaluations are such easy targets that they hardly present a challenge to those who would attack them. There are so many points where almost any evaluation is vulnerable, so few places where an attack in force can be turned back, that the battle is usually over before it is really begun. Evaluators are outnumbered, outgunned, and usually less fanatic in their devotion to the cause than those who oppose them. The script reads more like a slaughter than a battle, for the odds against highly useful and credible evaluations are almost overwhelming when the process is conceptualized as one of conflict between the good guys and the bad guys—never mind which side is which.

The message from these workshops to program staff is that they have very little reason to fear evaluations as long as they pay attention to what is going on and intervene before any real damage is done. The message from these workshops to evaluators is that evaluators are almost sure to lose if they go into evaluation as if they are going into battle. The message to *both* program staff and evaluators is that, as in any war, a lot of resources are wasted and many people may be hurt for very little gain. Is it not better, then, to find ways to direct that energy into working together toward mutual interests?

I like to teach program staffs how to sabotage evaluations so as to make it clear to them that I recognize their power and then solicit their assistance in building a strong, defensible, and useful evaluation. By recognizing their power—indeed by using the evaluation process to empower them still further—the forces of evaluation and program delivery can be joined together for the common good.

In the active-reactive-adaptive process of working with decision makers, information users, and stakeholders to undertake useful evaluations the trick is not to attempt to build an evaluation structure that is invincible to attack. I am convinced that no such invincible evaluation exists. Rather, the trick is to so develop a sense of cooperation and commitment among the people with whom one is working that they feel no need and have no desire to attack. When the evaluation is perceived as being in their own interest and for their good, there is no need for a martial arts of evaluation. To attack the evaluation would then be to attack themselves and their own interests.

As Halcolm put it:

Belief in the value of evaluation is a shaky basis for undertaking a project. Such sincerity of purpose is like young love, easily given, equally easily withdrawn. Far more trustworthy is self-interest. If those involved know that they'll get something useful out of it, they'll stay with it.

From Halcolm's *Evaluation Politics*

A UNIFYING FRAMEWORK FOR
COMPARATIVE EVALUATION[1]

The flowcharts on utilization-focused evaluation (Chart 6.1) and Evaluation a la Machiavelli (Chart 6.2) depict contrasting evaluation processes. The third and fourth charts in this chapter present yet another model of a general process that can be applied to any kind of evaluation effort. Chart 6.3 presents a "Unifying Framework for Evaluation" (Comtois, 1981) as a flowchart. Chart 6.4 presents an enlargement of selected boxes from the flowchart put together as a work sheet for use in a training session.

The "Unifying Framework" is particularly powerful in its simplicity. It is meant to depict the fundamental comparative logic of evaluation, thus the "unifying" nature of the framework. It begins by emphasizing the importance of identifying the decision-making environment for the evaluation. The flowchart then depicts any evaluation function as a comparison of *what should be* to *what is* in order to arrive at a realistic assessment of *what can be* in program implementation and outcomes.

The flowchart shows that evaluators work with decision makers to determine the fundamental purpose of program evaluation and the basic goals of the program, both of which constitute "what should be" kinds of specifications. Evaluators examine the program (the "what is") separately from determining "what should be" because by carrying out their responsibilities for program operations, the staff and management at the program level determine what is actually happening in the program.

The focus of the analysis in evaluation is depicted in the flowchart as a fundamental comparison between what the decision makers believe should be happening and what is actually happening in day-to-day program operations. Any discrepancy between what is and what should be provides the data for determining what can be. As the assessment of "what can be" is applied to improve the program the utilization process

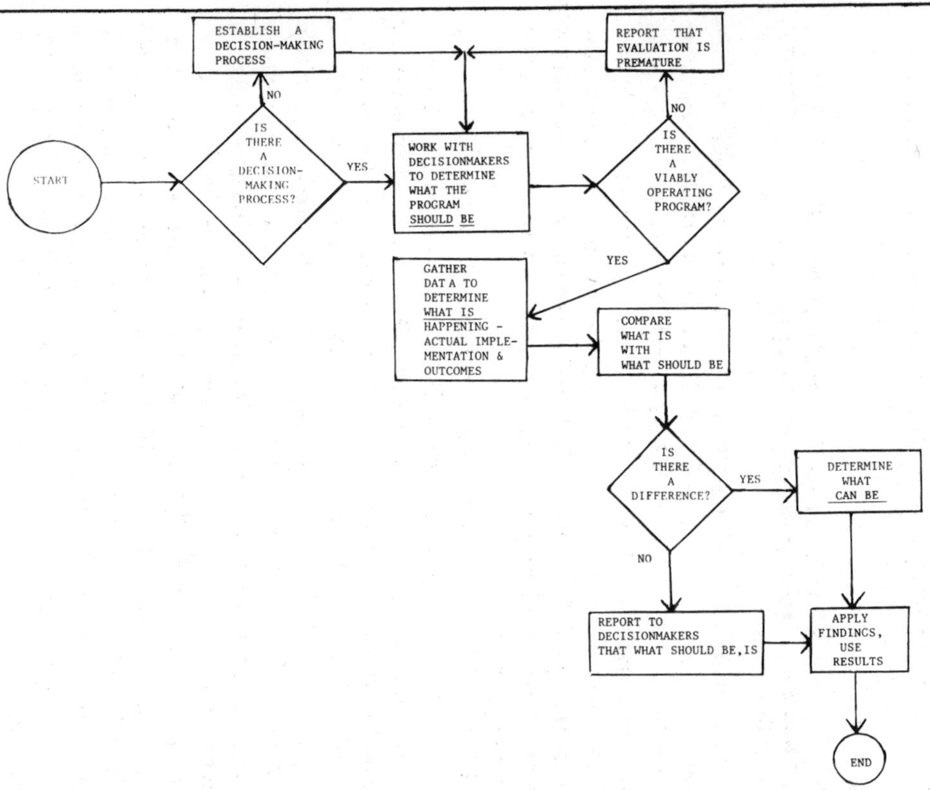

Chart 6.3: The Unifying Framework of Evaluation

The flowchart contains the following elements:

START →

IS THERE A DECISION-MAKING PROCESS?
- NO → ESTABLISH A DECISION-MAKING PROCESS
- YES → WORK WITH DECISIONMAKERS TO DETERMINE WHAT THE PROGRAM SHOULD BE

IS THERE A VIABLY OPERATING PROGRAM?
- NO → REPORT THAT EVALUATION IS PREMATURE
- YES → GATHER DATA TO DETERMINE WHAT IS HAPPENING - ACTUAL IMPLEMENTATION & OUTCOMES

COMPARE WHAT IS WITH WHAT SHOULD BE →

IS THERE A DIFFERENCE?
- YES → DETERMINE WHAT CAN BE
- NO → REPORT TO DECISIONMAKERS THAT WHAT SHOULD BE, IS

APPLY FINDINGS, USE RESULTS → END

102

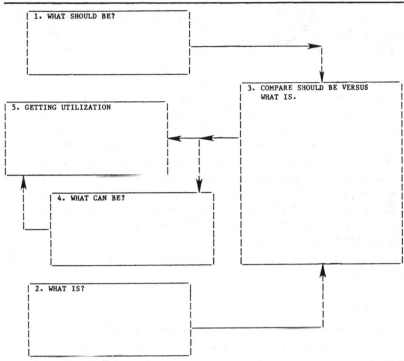

NOTE: This assumes identification of the decision-making context has already taken place.

Chart 6.4: Worksheet for Unifying Framework of Evaluation

occurs. The specifications of "what can be" become the new "what should be" for the next round of the evaluation.

This unifying framework also represents a concise conceptualization of needs assessment. One way of defining *need* is the difference between "what should be" and "what is." In conducting a needs assessment, then, it is necessary to gather data about both "what is" and "what should be." The comparison permits an assessment of "what can be" in the development of an actual program to meet the needs uncovered in the comparative analysis.

The power of the unifying framework lies in its simplicity, scope, and focus. In actuality the specification of "what should be" may require a complex goals-clarification process involving decision makers, information users, and stakeholders at multiple levels and with varying interests.

Determining "what is" involves a host of data collection, design, and methods decisions aimed at attempting to capture and describe what is happening in the program. The comparison between "what is" and "what should be" can become quite complex when various decision makers have differing views of "what should be" and the data about "what is" provide multiple and sometimes conflicting perspectives on actual program operations. The specification and determination of "what can be" takes us again into the arena where values merge with empirical data to create policies and programs. Moving toward "what can be" in a program involves all the complex processes of funding, program design, staff orientation, and client reaction. As these processes are reiterated and developed over time the full scope of program development and evaluation unfolds. Pieces of information that were initially missing can be filled in and added to the overall picture of both "what should be" and "what is." In this way evaluation provides a memory for the overall, ongoing planning process of a program (Comtois, 1981).

Chart Options

While this chapter has focused on flowcharts, there are clearly other diagrammatic ways of presenting information that do not involve all the circles, triangles, boxes, and arrows of a flowchart. Chart 6.4 shows one way of extracting major pieces of information from a flowchart and simplifying the presentation for quick and easy use in a workshop or planning session. Chart 6.3 is the full flowchart depicting each step in the "Unifying Framework." Chart 6.4 is a work sheet handout used to help evaluation participants identify the types of information to be generated in an evaluation based on the "Unifying Framework." Chart 6.4 is technically not a flowchart, at least not a complete one. Chart 6.3 is the technically complete flowchart elaborating all of the decision junctures that are only implicit in Chart 6.4, the work sheet extraction. The simpler work sheet has less information for participants to absorb and apply so it is particularly effective when time is short.

Clearly, *different charts and visual representations serve different purposes.* I have included both the original work sheet handout and the more complex flowchart of the overall process to illustrate this point. Which charts would be used in any given instance would depend on the sophistication of the group with which one was working, the time available, and the purpose of the working session. I have done workshops where I have used every chart presented in this chapter. I have also done workshops where I have used only the work sheet, Chart 6.4, the simplest of the four charts presented in this chapter.

Each of the three evaluation flowcharts highlights different aspects of program evaluation. Evaluation needs to be simplified and modeled for the same reasons that organizational decision-making processes in general need to be modeled and charted.

> Due to existential requirements and to the characteristics of man's limited information processing capability, the (quasi) totality of human and organizational problem solving and decisionmaking is per force heuristic; also, cognitive maps of the environment and of cause-and-effect relationships are at best truncated, and at worst a misleading imagery. Moreover, reliability, validity, and above all self-insight into the nature and quality of one's information processing (e.g., predictability of decisions, confidence in their accuracy, value of interviews, etc.,) are clearly limited. Together these considerations suggest that objectivizing in an articulated whole whatever formalized chain or process of complex organizational decision making can be effectively modeled is in itself an important contribution. . . . In short, for any given problem man needs help to unfold, follow, and check his own thought process. (Inbar, 1979, pp. 136-137)

The next section discusses modeling a program rather than evaluation.

Charting a Program's Theory of Action

In *Utilization-Focused Evaluation* (Patton, 1986) I suggested that one way of working with decision makers and staff in a program was to assist them in delineating their programmatic "theory of action" thereby making explicit their assumptions about the activities and linkages necessary for accomplishment of ultimate goals. A program's theory of action can also be displayed as a flowchart. Such a graphic display of the program's means-ends hierarchical and sequential chain of objectives serves two primary purposes. First, it helps those involved to identify and fill conceptual gaps in their programmatic theory of action, thereby making them aware of their major assumptions about program decision and action flows, and helping them decipher their organizational heuristics. Second, it serves as a mechanism for identifying where evaluative information is most needed in the overall flow of program action and implementation. This brings focus to the evaluation and enhances the potential for utilization by identifying where the evaluation would make the greatest contribution to increased program effectiveness. In effect, then, the implementation processes and activities of a human service program (or any organization) can be represented as a series of problem and decision junctures displayed as a flowchart.

Chart 6.5 is a flowchart depicting the theory of action for an agricultural development program. The initial agricultural system is unmanaged grazing of goats and sheep in West Africa. The animals are taken care of by children. They graze on whatever they can find to eat. Breeding involves no selection or timing. The goal of the program is to develop a managed system where animals are bred with superior stock, grazed on improved pastures, and cared for by adults for commercial purposes. The flowchart shows the research, interventions, and assumptions that will be necessary to move the system from its existing underdeveloped state to one of intensified, commercial production. Each linkage is critical to the theory of action. The flowchart essentially represents a long-term development plan for this agricultural program.

There is a fundamental difference between this kind of action/decision flowchart and the usual organizational chart that depicts lines of authority and responsibility. The organizational chart shows the sequence of persons through whom a decision or action should flow. In contrast, *the flowchart of a program's theory of action displays the critical assumptions, rules, linkages, conditions, and functions that constitute a program.* The traditional organizational chart displays the skeleton of a human service program. A theory of program action flowchart depicts the brain functions of the program. Used together, a great deal of information can be represented and communicated to make those involved more aware of what they believe they are doing, more realistic about what they are actually doing, and more open to the possibility that both their beliefs and actions ought to be altered.

Unlocking Creativity Through Flowcharts

In the first and second chapters I suggested that greater awareness of our heuristics, decision rules; standard operating procedures, and paradigms is of primary importance if we are to move beyond the constraints and limitations of conditioned reflexes and socialized unconsciousness. Charting programmatic action, decision, and information processes is one way of raising consciousness and sharpening

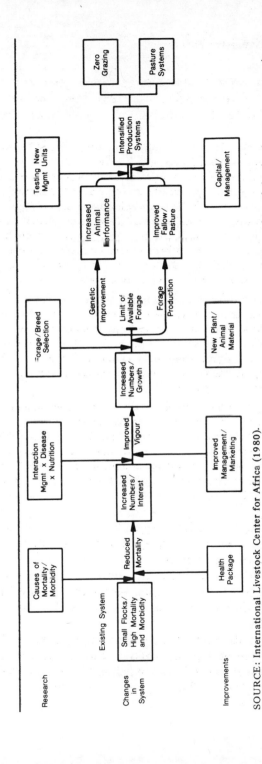

SOURCE: International Livestock Center for Africa (1980).

NOTE: Shows expected system changes for small ruminant production in the forest zone of West Africa if the development program is successful.

Chart 6.5: Theory of Action Flowchart for an Agricultural Development Program

awareness about these fundamental program processes. Decision theorist Michael Inbar has had considerable experience in modeling organizational systems in this way. I therefore quote him at some length.

> The flowchart mode of representation has the advantage of lending itself to use as an important conceptual aid. The reason is that it provides a basis for putting the particular organization of a process of decision-making into perspective. Specifically, by being able to disregard temporarily the actual constraints, role boundaries, and modes of organization within which an existing clerical bureaucracy operates, alternative modes of organization become immediately apparent. In the case of applications to clerical bureaucracies, *the stage of systems analysis which determines the decisionmaking logic of a system is therefore useful for breaking thinking habits.* (Inbar, 1979, p. 189; emphasis added)
>
> This proposition that decision charting is useful rests on the consideration that in a bureaucracy the overwhelming majority of the decisions are made by routine application of standard operating procedures, whether these are written, normative, or simply habitual (e.g., "discretionary" decisions). Accordingly, the day-to-day operations embody, in effect, the assumption that the standard operating procedures are valid solutions to the problems which evoke them.
>
> By objectivizing the referent process, such a model [a decision flowchart] provides a strategic meeting ground for administrators to probe their belief system, or for interested parties to whom they are responsible (e.g., the political system) to do so. . . . Models of this kind therefore constitute a natural means to validate both the decisionmaking procedures themselves and the rationale or rationalization which leads to their repetitive use. (Inbar, 1979, pp. 220-221)

The point of this chapter is to suggest that the ability to sequentially conceptualize and graphically display decision processes is one important technique that can increase awareness of routine behavior and autonomic heuristics thereby allowing conscious control and creative thinking to supersede those heuristics. This opens the way for creative problem solving, situational evaluation, and flexible/responsive decision making.

Flowcharts are also useful for communicating with the visually or graphically oriented person, and charting can be incisively helpful in simplifying and clarifying one's own thinking. *The ability to "go with the flow" in order to chart the flow may make it possible to exercise more control over the flow.*

Going with the Flow Sensitively and Creatively

It is important to keep in mind that the use of flowcharts is just one among the many creative options available to evaluators in working with decision makers, information users, and stakeholders. Many people are intimidated by flowcharts, put off by the arrows, the symbols, and the graphics. Far from simplifying and focusing, these people find flowcharts confusing and distorting. Even within the same task force some members may find a flowchart useful, while others are disdainful of exercises involving graphics. Thus evaluators are advised to use such tools with sensitivity and caution, keeping in mind that—as with all the other techniques in this book—flowcharts are simply a tool, one more among the many options available to evaluators in facilitating the evaluation decision-making process.

The trick in working with either individual clients or participants in an evaluation task force is to come to understand how *they* think about program evaluations. As one seeks this understanding it is well to keep in mind Halcolm's caution:

> Not to understand another person's way of thinking does not make that person confused.

NOTE

1. The Unifying Framework for Evaluation was developed by staff of the Program Analysis Division of the U.S. General Accounting Office (GAO). It was used by Joe Comtois, Lee Edwards, Robert Kershaw, Pat Patterson, John Scanlon, and me as part of a GAO training program in evaluation in 1980. The framework is discussed in greater detail in an article by Comtois (1981).

CHAPTER 7: *The Evaluation Version of Foursquare: Matrix and Quadrant Thinking*

> *The ability to simplify means to eliminate the unnecessary so that the necessary may speak.*
>
> *Hans Hoffman*

In the game of foursquare, a ball is bounced among four children each of whom plays in one of four squares.

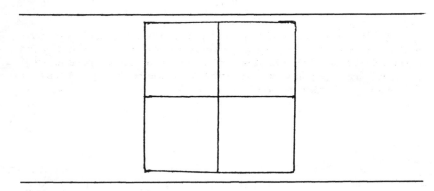

When a ball enters a child's square, he or she attempts to tap the ball to another square before it bounces more than once. If a tapped ball falls outside the boundaries, the errant child loses a point, or is eliminated from that round. Foursquare is a simple but lively game. There are few rules, all of which are relatively easy to understand. Minimal equipment is needed—some chalk to draw four squares, a hard and level surface, and a reasonably bouncy ball. It is a great game for developing eye-hand coordination in young children.

The evaluation version of foursquare is matrix or quadrant thinking. The object of foursquare evaluation-style is to construct models that illustrate the theoretical relationships between two (or more) dimensions or variables. The rule for playing evaluation foursquare is simple: The two dimensions must be conceptually distinct. To play, you simply cross the two dimensions, creating either a matrix or a graph. You then name and explain the relevance of the cells or quadrants created by having crossed the two dimensions.

Matrix and graph construction are similar in terms of basic logic. A matrix is constructed by dividing two separate dimensions into two or more mutually exclusive categories. The crossing of the two dimensions (each consisting of at least two categories) creates a table made up of separate cells, each cell being the product of the intersection of one category from each dimension. Each cell contains information about the relationship between the two dimensions.

| | | Second Dimension | |
		Category X	Category Y
First Dimension	Category A	Cell AX	Cell AY
	Category B	Cell BX	Cell BY

Model of a Simple Two-by-Two Matrix

In contrast to a matrix, a graph is created by crossing two continuous variables each with a conceptual midpoint that divides the variables into two halves—high and low. The variables are crossed at the midpoints creating four quadrants as shown below. Compared to the four-cell matrix, the graph gives a greater sense of dimensionality and variability. On the graph, the subjects or cases being plotted are placed in spatial relationship to each other, while in a matrix all cases are in one of four (or more) mutually exclusive cells without any distinctions made among cases in a particular cell. The graph allows an interval-based spread of cases throughout the quadrant space.

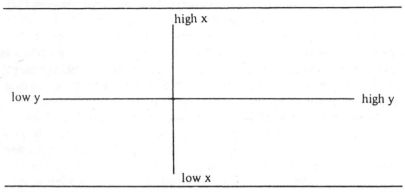

Model of a Two-Dimensional Graph

The creative challenge of both versions of the evaluation foursquare game is to come up with a meaningful label and accompanying statement of relevance for each cell or quadrant. It is a great game for developing mental agility as you hop back and forth between cells or quadrants trying to make sense out of each one while relating each one to the others. It can also be good for "mind building," that is, developing great "strength" of thought (as bodybuilding develops great strength of muscle) from forcing enormous amounts of material into a few small spaces, then carrying back out all the excess garbage you brought in. The purpose of evaluation foursquare manipulations and constructs is to simplify and focus complex evaluation realities.

Simplicity and Focus

A common theme of previous chapters has been the importance of simplicity and focus in making manageable the complex realities we encounter, and in facilitating communications about those complex realities. Metaphorical communications, conceptual thinking, and flowchart construction are all tools for simplifying and focusing evaluation problems and processes. Much of the creative imperative of the profession is a search for ways to simplify the enormous complexities of real-world programs and bring focus to what often appear to be diffuse, all-encompassing, haphazard, and/or multifaceted processes, many of which seem specially designed to keep evaluators (and decision makers) confused and off balance.

One of the most frequent complaints I hear from workshop participants and students is that they are overwhelmed by the complexity of program evaluation in the situations in which they find themselves. They cannot seem even to begin to identify and organize the options available to them. In working with them on their conceptual problems I often find that some variation of matrix or quadrant thinking is helpful to simplify and focus alternatives.

In the pages that follow I present two quite different but relatively simple examples of the foursquare approach to creative evaluation thinking—matrix and graph construction. In each case the matrix or graph is meant to simplify, elucidate, and focus complex issues, thereby facilitating the making of choices among a variety of options. At the end of each section you will be invited to reflect on and analyze your own thinking patterns in relation to the type of matrix thinking illustrated by the examples in this chapter.

AN EVALUATION
PROBLEM-SOLVING MATRIX

The next several pages discuss an evaluation problem-solving matrix. This matrix and the accompanying discussion permit me to elaborate some of my thoughts on creative evaluation from the first chapter, while at the same time providing an example of matrix thinking.

A basic premise of this book is that different situations require different evaluation approaches. The first chapter considered a number of different situational dimensions that could influence an evaluation. To simplify thinking about variations in evaluation this section presents a modest four-cell matrix of evaluation problem solving. The matrix (Chart 7.1) is built on two dimensions: (1) a dimension describing evaluation conceptual problems as ranging from routine to nonroutine and (2) a dimension describing evaluation analysis as ranging from routine to nonroutine. These dimensions are taken from the sociological literature on complex organizations. In that literature there is considerable discussion of how organizational structure is affected by the nature of the task performed by the organization. Tasks can be conceptualized in many ways: simple/complex; standardized/idiosyncratic; easy/hard;

unitary/differentiated; general/specialized; and a host of other descriptive dimensions. Charles Perrow (1970) has suggested that underlying these various ways of describing tasks is a fundamental distinction that encompasses all the others and captures the main factor affecting organizational structure. That fundamental distinction concerns the routineness of a task. Routine tasks are those where a production problem consists of a limited number of known factors and where there is a standardized search procedure or problem-solving process applied to that production problem. A factory assembly line consists of a series of routine tasks. Nonroutine tasks are those where each problem is unique and new search procedures or problem-solving processes must be developed to handle the problem. Building a high-performance race car is a nonroutine task. Part of what is interesting about Perrow's distinction is that the routine/nonroutine distinction is partly a matter of perception. Many tasks can be viewed as either routine or nonroutine. Which way the task is viewed and approached has profound implications for organizational structure (Perrow, 1970).

Routine production tasks are subject to standardized technical solutions. Nonroutine production tasks require creative solutions. Routine production tasks are handled by properly identifying the nature of the problem and then retrieving the predetermined solution to apply in solving the problem. Creative solutions to unique problems require innovation and invention. The routine production-system imagery is one of condition recognition, information retrieval, and solution matching. The nonroutine creative problem-solving system is geared to search, diagnosis, innovation, and adaptation processes. Production systems organize repetitive tasks. Creative systems organize search and analysis procedures for solving unique problems. Routine production tasks can be easily modeled and programmed. "This need not be the case for creative thinking and unique decisions. These processes are not sufficiently understood to be currently moldable to any significant extent . . . (in contrast to) what constitutes conceptually and experimentally *repetitive* and *routinized* decisionmaking" (Inbar, 1979, p. 105).

The Evaluation Problem-Solving Matrix (Chart 7.1) applies the routine/nonroutine distinction to problems of evaluation conceptualization and analysis. A relatively routine conceptual problem in evaluation is the process of specifying clear, specific, and measurable goals. An evaluator enters a new situation and the conceptual task is defined (by evaluator, decision maker, or both) as one of goals clarification: Does this program have clear, specific, and measurable goals? If the answer is "yes," the evaluator moves on to instrument design, data collection, and analysis. If the answer is "no," the evaluator writes a set of clear, specific, and measurable goals. The conceptual problem is routine: Write clear, specific, and measurable goals.

Nonroutine conceptual problems arise in evaluation when programs do not need, do not have, do not want, and/or cannot specify their goals. Program staff, administrators, or others sometimes resist "limiting" the program to some set of clear, specific, and measurable goals. Other nonroutine conceptual problems include situations where evaluating outcomes is not the focus of the evaluation. Programs may want help in reducing costs, determining *real* client needs, assets analysis, enlarging program functions, adapting to changed conditions—or any of a host of requests that involve the evaluation processes of information collection, analysis, and utilization, but are not routine outcomes evaluations (goal based).

The second dimension concerns the routineness of data analysis. *Routine analysis problems involve presenting statistical data to decision makers who understand statistical data.* The epitome of routine analysis is represented by *A Guide for Selecting Statistical Techniques for Analyzing Social Science Data* (Andrews, Davidson, Klein, O'Marley, & Rodgers, 1974). This excellent statistical guide from the staff of the Survey Research Center at the Institute for Social Research, University of Michigan, models all analytical decisions as a series of flowcharts. The evaluator analyst simply answers "yes" or "no" to a set of questions, follows the arrows, and selects the appropriate analytical technique. If the evaluation clients are able to understand statistical reasoning, the analysis is quite routine. Analyses of standardized tests and surveys typically fall into the routine analysis cell.

Nonroutine analysis problems may include any of the following: (1) integrating qualitative and quantitative data from a variety of sources, particularly where findings conflict; (2) working through an analysis with decision makers who have no analytical training but whose understanding of the evaluation data is critical; and (3) conducting analyses that depend heavily on the observations, insights, and perceptions of the evaluator, usually derived from site visits and informal consulting.

Purely Technical Evaluations

The four cells of the evaluation problem-solving matrix (Chart 7.1) are the product of crossing the conceptualization and analysis dimen-

	ANALYSIS DIMENSION	
	Routine Analysis Problems	Nonroutine Analysis Problems
Routine Conceptual Problems	Purely <u>technical</u> problem-solving (goals-based, statistical)	Space exploration problem-solving approach (standard goals-based conceptualization, unique/situational analysis)
Nonroutine Conceptual Problems	<u>Architectural</u> approach (Unique conceptual adaptation, standard analysis)	<u>Creative</u> <u>Consultation</u> (Situational conceptualization, situational analysis)

CONCEPTUALIZATION DIMENSION appears to the left between the two conceptual-problem rows.

Chart 7.1: Evaluation Problem-Solving Matrix

sions. The combination of routine conceptualization and routine analysis is a purely technical (production system) evaluation: measure the program's clear and specific goals; select the appropriate analysis technique from, for example, Andrews et al. (1974); and report the data. The evaluator is a technician who applies standard operating procedures throughout the process.

Space Exploration

Some evaluations involve a routine conceptualization but the analysis is nonroutine, often because the measurement of identified goals leads to collection of data that require special handling. I have labeled this cell in the matrix the *space exploration approach* because the (oversimplified) problem in space travel is always the same—getting from here to there (routine goal-oriented conceptualization)—but the data analyses required must be derived from and adapted to the particular space exploration conditions that emerge along the way. Unexpected problems in data reliability and validity can rapidly become unique analytical problems requiring highly creative solutions. For example, in one space flight the third of three monitors malfunctioned and the space flight engineers had to extrapolate and interpolate data from the two functioning monitors to supply the data missing from the third monitor, something they had never done before. Similar problems in data handling often arise unexpectedly in evaluation when data one planned to use in routinely measuring goals turn out to be unavailable or impossible to collect, and ways of estimating the needed indicators must be found by creatively analyzing those data that are available or possible to collect.

Another problem in the space exploration cell of the matrix is encountered when those to whom one is reporting (the viewing public in space flights, program staff in evaluation) lack analytical training. Creative ways of simplifying and presenting complex analyses may be required. I recall an evaluation of a displaced homemakers program that was quite routine in conceptualization (traditional goals-based evaluation) but presented a number of difficulties in the analysis/presentation/ utilization stages because the staff was intimidated by numbers, resistant to negative findings, and quite inexperienced in thinking analytically. We had to develop analytical approaches unique to this group and those data to solve the problem.

The Architect at Work

In still other cases the conceptualization is nonroutine, but once an adequate conceptualization is created, the analysis becomes routine. I have called this the architectural approach because an architect usually labors to create the overall concept of a building then turns the creative design over to builders to implement. The architect must know the requirements of technical analysis and provide sufficient guidance in the conceptualization to enable the builders to do their more routine work.

Similar situations arise in evaluation. I worked for 18 months with staff throughout Minnesota in conceptualizing an evaluation of early childhood/family education programs. Varying perceptions of the program, the evaluation, and the politics of the situation—plus the large number of people involved throughout the state—make the conceptual problems quite unique and difficult. Once conceptualized, however, the resulting data collection and analysis could be handled by a first-year graduate research assistant.

Creative Consultant

Finally, there are those evaluations where both conceptualization and analysis are nonroutine. Unique problems lead to collection of data that require unique analytical approaches. I have called this the "creative consultation approach" to evaluation because the evaluator must be adapting and responding to unique circumstances and situational constraints throughout the evaluation. This is what Barkdoll (1980) calls Type III evaluations (the "consultative model") as opposed to Type II ("technical" applications of state-of-the-art technology) or Type I (investigative auditing) evaluations.

Essentially, the creative consultation approach means being active-reactive-adaptive in responding to unique situational developments throughout the evaluation.

The thrust of this book, particularly the first two chapters, is that the profession of evaluation has been moving along the diagonal of the matrix from a point where most situations were defined as routine on both dimensions—purely technical evaluations—to a point where creative approaches are needed to handle the combination of unique conceptual and analytical problems. The mandate to conduct utility-focused, feasibility-conscious, propriety-oriented, and accuracy-based evaluations gives rise to a host of nonroutine conceptual and nonroutine analytical problems requiring creative evaluation solutions.

Matrix Reflection

To understand some of the strengths and weaknesses of matrix representations it may be helpful to pause for a moment and study Chart 7.1 more carefully, not to grasp the content of the matrix better but to examine more thoroughly *the kind of thinking* represented by the matrix. What is gained by reducing the enormous complexities of situational evaluation to a four-cell matrix? What is lost in such a presentation? Are the labels in each cell true to the relationships depicted and created by the matrix? In what ways and to what extent is the matrix misleading? Would the nature of the problem be better represented by a nine-cell matrix created by conceptualizing each dimension as a trichotomy instead of a dichotomy?

What's your personal reaction to the matrix approach? Are you stimulated by the sharp focus of the matrix? Annoyed by the oversimplification? Can you separate the content of the matrix (evaluation tasks) from the thinking process represented in the matrix (creating theoretical products or relationships by crossing two separate theoretical constructs)? To what extent and for what problems (or types of problems) do *you* use matrix thinking in your own work? Ask yourself the questions in this and the previous paragraph about a matrix that you have used, liked, or created. In what ways does matrix thinking work for you? In what ways might it hinder your understanding or your presentations to others?

Take the time to analyze your own style, your own heuristic, and your own thought patterns. Perhaps you can create a matrix to depict your own thought processes.

The problem-solving matrix is, of course, highly oversimplified. The purpose of such simplification is to focus and elucidate a few important issues. Some additional complexity can be introduced into the matrix conceptualization by presenting each dimension as a continuum rather than a dichotomy, that is, routine/nonroutine tasks are viewed as polar points along a continuum rather than as two mutually exclusive categories. The discussion of needs assessment and assets analysis in the next section illustrates the continuum approach to matrix thinking. Maybe your matrix style is more "graphic" than tabular. The next section presents a more "graphic" example of matrix thinking.

ASSETS-NEEDS PLANNING MATRIX

Chapter 4's discussion of conceptual thinking discussed the idea of assets analysis in contrast to traditional needs assessment approaches. What happens if we combine the needs dimension with an assets dimension to create a matrix? Chart 7.2 shows such a matrix, this time presented as the crossed dimensions of a graph to form four quadrants instead of the four-cell tables presented in the previous two sections. Both kinds of matrices achieve the same result. They are simply alternative graphic representations, although the graph gives a greater sense of dimensionality and variability. On the graph a community or group is not simply in one of four mutually exclusive cells but can be nearer or farther from the zero point at the center of the matrix, and higher or lower on either dimension, thus achieving an interval-based spread of cases throughout the matrix space.

The needs-assets matrix might be used to think about the kinds of programs that should be planned for different communities or target populations. Quadrant I is a community or group with high needs and high assets. I would suggest that self-help programs are particularly appropriate here so that the people in this situation learn to use their assets to meet their own needs.

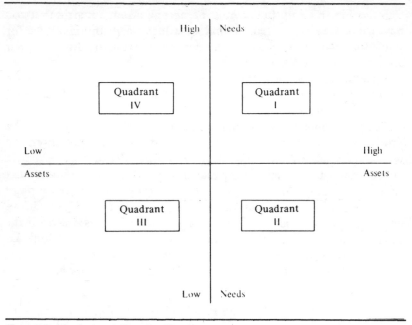

Chart 7.2: Needs-Assets Planning Matrix

Quadrant II is the case of high assets and low needs. Under conditions of limited resources (for example, from government) no program can be justified here until the other quadrants have been serviced.

Quadrant III is the situation where there are few needs and few assets. Given the limited assets of this group, a program of asset development might be initiated so that as needs arise these people can take care of themselves. This group should also be carefully monitored in case they drift toward Quadrant IV.

Quadrant IV is the primary target for human services. These people have high needs and few assets with which to meet their needs. This situation justifies an immediate influx of resources to meet the need for services while simultaneously undertaking an asset development program aimed at greater self-sufficiency over time.

Programs based on ability to pay have an implicit ideology derived from the kind of analysis represented by the needs-assets matrix. The problem is that such programs usually fail to deal with Quadrant I, the people with high assets *and high needs*. From a marginal utility perspective, self-help programs for these people may yield considerable benefit at relatively low cost.

Planners all too often ignore the situations in Quadrants II and III, the low needs quadrants, until these situations have deteriorated into Quadrant IV, where the most resources are required and the danger of long-term dependency is greatest.

Graphic Reflection

At the end of the section describing the problem-solving matrix of evaluation approaches, I suggested that some people are more comfortable with graphic representations of matrix constructs than with tabular representations of those constructs. Also, some problems are more appropriately depicted as graphs (yielding quadrants) and others are better represented as tables (yielding cells). To crystallize more fully the differences in the two approaches to the game of evaluation foursquare, reconstruct the matrix of evaluation tasks and approaches (Chart 7.1) as a graph, and reconstruct the needs/assets graph (Chart 7.2) as a four-cell table. How do the optional matrix representations affect the power and accuracy of the theoretical relationships being discussed? How is the content of each matrix affected by the format used to explicate the content?

Which approach do you prefer in each case? Why? What do your answers to these questions tell you about your own thinking style, your own heuristics, and your conceptual patterns, including both the strengths and weaknesses of those patterns, that is, the ways in which your patterns help you understand and respond to new evaluation situations, and the ways in which your thinking patterns constrain your situational understanding and creative responses?

SIMPLE MATRIX ADDITION

Matrix thinking is quite common in social science generally and evaluation specifically. It is sometimes called the "contingency" approach because what appears in a particular cell (or quadrant) is *contingent* on the dimensions or variables used to create the matrix (see Bryson & Delbecq, 1979). Nick Smith (1980) used a matrix approach to draw important distinctions among different kinds of utilization by asking if "techniques of effective evaluation utilization differ with regard to audience or entity studied." His matrix construct crossed a programs/policies dimension (what can be studied) with a program managers/policymakers distinction (who is to be aided) to show different kinds of utilization in each case. Paul Berman (1979) created a three-dimensional matrix to illustrate his thinking about how situational factors can affect program implementation and evaluation. He crossed three phases of program implementation (mobilization, implementation, and institutionalization) with two levels of analysis (micro and macro), and two approaches to human service programming (programmed and adaptive) to create a 12-cell matrix of evaluation situations and options.

Jeanne Campbell's (1981) "Conceptual Guide for Utilization of Planning, Evaluation, and Reporting" is a 500-cell matrix (Figure 7.3) that begins (but just begins) to reach the outer limits of what one can do in three-dimensional space. Campbell used this matrix to guide data collection and analysis in studying how the mandated, statewide educational planning, evaluation, and reporting system in Minnesota was used. She examined 5 levels of use (high school . . . , community, district), 10 components of the statewide project (planning, goal setting . . . , student involvement), and 10 factors affecting utilization (personal factor, political factors . . .). Chart 7.3 illustrates matrix thinking for methodological (data organization) purposes rather than theoretical/conceptual purposes.

The evaluation game of foursquare—matrix thinking—can be as simple as putting two plus two together, or as complex as putting x plus y plus z together. You can even try four-dimensional space (or x-dimensional space) if your audience is used to reading the output of multidimensional scaling computer programs. Personally, I find that three-dimensional space taxes my ability to comprehend.

Matrix thinking is as simple or as complex as you care to make it. Yet the purpose of a matrix is still to focus and organize. Part of the creativity of matrix thinking lies in the potential for turning empty cells in the matrix—cells created by crossing two dimensions—into new ideas, concepts, and options. For an excellent discussion of how to use matrix thinking to generate new concepts and social science theories see Hage (1972).

The *power* of matrix thinking resides in the *simplicity* of the tables created. As Hans Hoffman explained:

> The ability to simplify means to eliminate the unnecessary so that the necessary may speak.

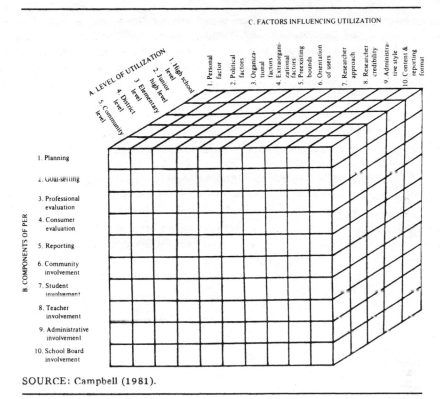

SOURCE: Campbell (1981).

Figure 7.3: Conceptual Guide for Data Collection and Analysis: Utilization of PER

Of course, evaluators and decision makers must keep in mind that simplification and focus capture only part of the picture—sometimes the wrong part. Henry Adams warned that "simplicity is the most deceitful mistress that ever betrayed man."

Creative evaluation includes the fun of trying to balance, sometimes even resolve, the many contradictions, paradoxes, and dilemmas that emerge in seeking to blend the appropriate amounts of complexity and simplicity in our attempts to understand and communicate about the world. Halcolm offers the following observations and advice:

> In the beginning you think.
> In the end you act.
> In-between you negotiate the possibilities.

Some people move from complexity
to simplicity
and on into catastrophe.
Others move from simplicity
to complexity
and onward into full-scale confusion.

Simplification makes action possible
in the face of overwhelming complexity;
it also increases the odds of being wrong.

The trick is to let
a sense of simplicity inform our thinking,
a sense of complexity inform our actions, and
a sense of humility inform our judgments. . . .

From Holcolm's *Sermon*
Under the Mount

CHAPTER 8: *Evaluation Simulations, Games, and Experiential Exercises*

We do not know when man begins to play. Play may start before birth, with the kicks and turns of the fetus; it certainly is present in the infant; and it continues throughout our lives.

When play is suppressed both the individual and society suffer. When play is encouraged, both benefit. The reasons for this are not clear, but somehow play is essential for man and many other social animals.

Editorial *in* Natural History, *the journal of the American Museum of Natural History, December 1971*

People learn in different ways. Different kinds of messages and different mediums for delivering messages affect people in different ways. One of the purposes of this book is to suggest some different ways of thinking about evaluation and some of the different ways of communicating to others about evaluation so that they can think about it for themselves. Workshops and task force sessions typically involve formal lecture presentations, discussions, practice exercises, and the use of a variety of communications techniques such as those discussed in preceding pages, including metaphors, flowcharts, and storythinking. This chapter describes some ways of providing learning experiences of a nonverbal nature.

A basic premise of this book is that creative, situationally responsive, and active-reactive-adaptive evaluators are called on to play a number of roles beyond those of researcher and scientist. One such role is that of trainer. Most program evaluations provide opportunities for evaluators to take on the role of trainer or teacher. Training is not something to be restricted to traditional classroom settings. When working with a group of nonscientists in an evaluation task force the situation *can be* defined as partly a training exercise aimed at empowering participants to exercise greater control over program implementation and outcomes through their increased knowledge about and understanding of both program and evaluation processes. When a program evaluation is defined as a learning opportunity for participants—learning about program evaluation as well as learning about the program being evaluated—the evaluator is helping build an increasingly sophisticated group of evaluation consumers better able to use information for program improvement.

This chapter presents training games, simulations, role-plays, and experiential exercises that can be used in working with a variety of groups to help them understand various aspects of program evaluation. These training materials are not designed solely for use in formal courses aimed at training professional evaluators. My premise is that all effective evaluators are trainers, and as trainers, all evaluators can enhance their professional practice by including a range of teaching approaches in their repertoire of communications and instructional techniques.

You Are Not Who You Thought You Were

The role-playing exercise that follows illustrates the power and effectiveness of actively and creatively involving workshop participants in their own training. Christine Crofton and Michael Hendricks developed this exercise for use in a training session for energy office evaluators in Nebraska in 1986. Michael Hendricks described what happened when he opened his training session with a surprise.

"As soon as the first session convened, we had introductions, but with a twist. Instead of the *participants* telling *me* their names, *I* told *them* their names—their new names. I did this by having them draw a name (only the last name, for reasons that will become clear) from a hat—Mr. Dieper, Ms. Keane, etc. There were a total of seven different names (about three times each) in the hat, one for each of the 21 participants.

"After folks drew a name, I had them move so that all persons with the same name (all three Mr. Diepers, all three Ms. Keanes, etc.) were sitting at the same table. (I had arranged the room into seven tables of three seats each.) Then I told them who they were going to be for the next two days. They were:

- *Mr. Dieper*—Rising young reporter for the *Lincoln Star*; hungriest of the hungry, sleaziest of the sleazy; great-nephew of Rupert Murdoch, knows that the road to *Newsweek* is paved with scandals; etc. Naturally, his full name is Doug Dieper.
- *Ms. Keane*—The world's most defensive program administrator; favorite dessert is sugar and syrup; sees the silver lining in a tornado; programmed her computer to reject the word "problem"; etc. For her flaming red name, known as "Peachie" Keane.
- *Mr. Snort*—Crusty state legislator; helped draft the state constitution; favorite song is "Roll Out the Barrel"; etc. Usually referred to as Senator Snort.
- *Mr. Prophets*—Chief stockholder in main utility company; his idea of "shared savings" is a secret bank account for his mistress; plays poker and golf weekly with Senator Snort; etc. Full name is Hyman, or just Hy Prophets.
- *Ms. Maynott*—Local elected official; says that the only good state offices are empty state offices; doesn't even like strings on her balloons; her idea of reporting requirements is a change of address card; etc. She's Mayor Maynott.
- *Ms. Peoples*—Citizen watchdog; had attended every legislative session ever held; checks the addition on budget requests; etc. Changed her name to Wetha—Wetha Peoples.
- *Ms. Ovark*—Energy Office evaluator; so humble, she's forgotten how to spell her own name; only human on Earth with no preconceptions toward anything; seeking "just the truth, and nothing but the truth"; etc. Friends call her Joanie, but she's really Joan Ovark.

"When folks knew who they were, I asked them, 'Now tell me what evaluation means to you (your character). What would you want an evaluation to do?' After they conferred a bit, I wrote each character's answers onto a flip chart as they gave them aloud. Much to my relief, it worked beautifully—folks got into their roles, they gave widely varying expectations and hopes for evaluation, and they argued back and forth among tables.

"Best of all, they saw that (a) it's impossible to talk about one, single definition of evaluation, since every stakeholder has a different perspective, and that (b) evaluation is at least as much a *political* activity as a *research* activity. For the next two days, they went back into these roles whenever an important issue cropped up in the training (Who should be contacted when planning an evaluation? What data should be gathered? How should findings be reported? Should recommendations be included?)."

This exercise illustrates the creative possibilities for actively involving participants in an evaluation learning experience. Before giving additional examples, the next section discusses the roots of the experiential alternative.

The Experiential Alternative

The ideas and exercises presented in this chapter are derived from three bodies of knowledge. First there are the theories, research, and literature on "experiential education"—the idea that people learn best and most when they are actively involved in doing and personally experiencing that about which they are learning. There is a vast literature in this area (see Bruner, 1960, 1967; Geertsen, 1979; Hoopes, Pederson, & Renwick, 1978; Hoopes & Ventura, 1979; Patton, 1973; Rogers, 1977; Wright & Nammons, 1970), and a network of professionals from a full range of disciplines interested in further developing these techniques; thus their membership in the Association of Experiential Education, which publishes the *Journal of Experiential Education.*

The second tradition represented by and applied in this chapter is the field of simulation gaming. Simulation games are a specifically structured and formal approach to experiential education. Again, there is a vast literature for evaluators to draw on in developing simulations for virtually any training purpose (see Duke & Greenblat, 1979; Horn & Cleaves, 1980; Stadsklev, 1974, 1975; Tansly & Unwin, 1969; Taylor & Walford, 1979). There is also the journal *Simulation & Games.* In a simulation what happens is:

1. Participants take on roles which are representations of roles in the real world, and then make decisions in response to their assessment of the setting in which they find themselves.

2. They experience simulated consequences which relate to their decisions and performances.

3. They monitor the results of their actions and reflect on the relationship between their own decisions and the resultant consequences.

Whether the simulation has obvious *structure* or not, inter-relationships between a large number of factors can be displayed, visibly manipulated and adjusted. (Taylor & Walford, 1978, p. 7)

Simulation games in particular and experiential educational in general are ways of creating microcosms of real-world situations in classrooms, workshops, and staff training sessions. The action is compressed, accelerated, and debriefed to provide an intensive and engaging learning experience for participants. One of the major figures in evaluation research, Clark Abt, is also a major figure and pioneer in simulation gaming (Abt, 1966, 1974). Work on simulation games played an important part in the early development of Abt Associates, now one of the leading contractors in the conduct of program evaluation.

Three major attributes of simulation games make them particularly attractive for use by evaluators who have assumed the role of teacher/trainer in working with participants in an evaluation process.

1. It is a technique oriented towards activity in the (teaching/learning situation), and in such activity both teachers and pupils participate. It represents an informal and corporate approach to the understanding of a situation.

2. It is usually problem-based and therefore helpful in the development of inter-disciplinary approaches to learning. It also frequently involves the use of social skills which are directly relevant to the world outside the (immediate learning situation).

3. It is a technique which is fundamentally dynamic. It deals with situations that change, and which demand flexibility in thinking and responsive adaptation to circumstances as they alter. (Taylor & Walford, 1978, p. 27)

This last point is particularly relevant to creative evaluation, with its emphasis on situational flexibility and adaptability derived from increased awareness of one's typical heuristic responses and exposure to new situations that permit one to move beyond the limitations of those conditioned heuristic responses.

The third body of knowledge on which this chapter is based is the study of play and its role in learning and creativity. Social scientist M. Brewster Smith observed in 1974 that "a renaissance of scientific interest in play" was taking place (Smith, 1974, p. 5). Mary Reilly has written with great insight and feeling on the power of play to channel and unlock human creative impulses. I quote her here at length.

Play is a behavior whose central mode of operations is to puzzle, to tease, to doubt at reality. The "as-if" of the metaphor, the contradiction of the paradox, and the specificity of rule are the realities of its substance. For in play man puts himself totally and freely in a position of decoding the complexities of reality. . . . In the action of play reality is explored via curiosity and conflict for the rules of how things, events, ideas and people operate. As meaning is generated, the searching process produces learning. The symbolization system becomes enriched as playing man constructs the rules of space, time, and purpose. In play inquisitive man seeks out first the sensorimotor rules, then the rules of objects and of people, and finally even the rules of thinking. The capacity to know the rules enables man's intellect to know, and particularly to know-how. . . .

The curiosity of man differs from that of animals in that man's response to the environment is to ask questions, hence the stimuli to his exploratory activities are novelty, surprise, conflict, or uncertainty. Play is the behavior in which the exploratory drive receives its purest form of expression. When the drive is directed toward specific targets, it results in latent learning and, in a more complex form, it becomes problem solving. While play is self-rewarding, in problem solving the search as well as the solution act as incentives to move on to another problem. In this way means and ends become chained to keep the learning going as the nervous system processes information continuously. (Reilly, 1974, pp. 141-142)

Reilly (1974) presents both theory and research to show that play is an important vehicle for both children and adults to develop new ways of responding to situations, thereby breaking out of old, self-limiting heuristics. There is a growing body of literature on the nature and functions of play (Bruner, 1972; Fluegelman, 1976; McLellan, 1970; Millar, 1968; Sutton-Smith, 1971) suggesting that creative evaluators might be able to incorporate play usefully and effectively in their work. This chapter is dedicated to that end.

The exercises and games described here can be used with a program staff about to be involved in an evaluation, with workshop participants, with students, and/or with professional groups interested in evaluation. Each of the exercises aims to involve participants in an active way in the learning process so that they directly experience something that can stimulate reflection, new ways of thinking, and new understandings. The first experiential exercise presented here is quite simple and short, illustrating a minimum level of experiential activity. Other exercises, games, and role-plays are longer and more involving, some requiring an entire day.

Focusing the Evaluation Question

In an introductory session on evaluation I will typically spend a fair amount of time discussing the importance of focusing evaluation questions and issues in the context of anticipated decisions and expected utilization of the findings. I will talk about different ways of focusing evaluation questions, different types of focus, and the importance of focus to the overall success of the evaluation (see Patton, 1978, Chap. 5).

The idea of focus is to make sure that the evaluation concentrates on those issues that will produce the most useful information, yield the greatest insights, and/or provide the most solid basis for action. The notion here is to focus on those "vital few" facts among the "trivial many" that are really high in payoff and information load (MacKenzie, 1972). The "20-80 rule" expresses the importance of focusing on the right information. "The '20-80 rule' states, as a rule of thumb, that 20% of the facts account for 80% of what is going on" (Anderson, 1980, p. 26). To help people understand the idea of focus and its importance I use a short exercise. It goes like this:

"We've been talking a lot about focus and its importance. Let's try doing it for a moment.

"Let me ask you to put your right hand out in front of you with your arm fully extended and the palm of your hand turned toward you. Now focus on the center of the palm of your hand. Really look at your hand in a way that you haven't looked at it in a long time. Get to know your hand. Look at the lines—some of them long, some of them short; some of them deep, some of them shallow; some of them relatively straight, some of them nicely curved, and some of them quite jagged and crooked. Look at the colors in your hand—reds, yellows, browns, greens, blues, different shades and hues, and notice the textures, hills and valleys, rougher places and smooth places. Become aware of the feelings in your hand, feelings of warmth or cold, perhaps tingling sensations. (Those of you who, at this point, are having trouble maintaining your attention on the center of your palm may notice you have a problem with focus . . .)

"Now, keeping your right hand in front of you, I'd like to ask you to extend your left arm and look at your left palm in the same way, not comparatively, but just focus on the center of your left palm in its own terms, looking at it, focusing on it, seeing it, feeling it. Really allow your attention to become concentrated on the center of your left palm, getting to know your left hand in a new way . . .

"Now with both arms still outstretched I want you to *focus*, with the same intensity that you've been using on each hand, I want you to focus on the center of *both* palms at the same time. [Give participants a little time to try this.] Unless there is something unusual about your eyes you're not able to do that. There are some animals who are able to move their two eyes independently of each other, but human beings do not have that capability. We are only able to look at one thing with intensity at a time. You can go back and forth between the two hands, you can use peripheral vision and get a general look at both hands at the same time, but you can't focus with intensity at the center of both palms at the same time.

"Focusing involves a choice. The decision to look at something is also a decision not to look at something. A decision to see something means that something else will not be seen, at least not with the same acuity. Looking at your left hand or looking at your right hand or looking more generally at both hands provides you with different information and different experiences.

"The same thing is true in the evaluation process. Because of limited time and limited resources it is never possible to look at everything. It is particularly never possible to look at everything in great depth. Decisions have to be made about what is worth looking at. Choosing to look at one area in depth is also a decision not to look at something else in depth. Utilization-focused evaluation suggests that the criteria for making those choices of focus be the usefulness of the resulting information. That information that would be of greatest use for program improvement and programmatic decision making becomes the focus of the evaluation."

Before going on to the next section and having simply read this description of the exercise, I suggest that you take a couple of minutes and experience the exercise for yourself. Focus on your own right hand in the way suggested above, and then your left hand, and then both. Experience the exercise and make your own judgment about the kind of nonverbal understanding that can emerge from the exercise.

Unraveling the Tangle

This next exercise involves considerably more action and takes a good deal more time. I have done this exercise with all kinds of people in many different settings and for a number of different purposes. It is an exercise adapted from the noncompetitive games movement. It can be used to illustrate a number of different things about research and evaluation.

A group of 8 to 12 participants are asked to come together and form a circle. Initially standing shoulder to shoulder in a tight circle, all the participants are asked to do a left-face so that they are looking at the back of the person in front of them. They are then asked to move in still closer and make the circle a bit tighter. Indeed, the circle must be tight enough for participants to reach across with their right hands and grasp the hand of one other person. If there are an even number of people everyone will have grasped the right hand of one, and only one, other person; if there are an odd number of people, one person will be left holding air. Participants are then asked to reach into the circle with their left hands and grab the hand of another person, not the same person whose hand they are already holding. With an odd number of people, the person whose right hand was left hanging will take the hand of the person whose left hand was the odd hand out.

Instruction: "Without letting go of each other's hands and without talking you are now to unravel the tangle so that you are standing in a continuous circle, side by side, unknotted. You may make noises and whatever sounds you want to, but you are not to talk to each other."

Depending on how people have gotten themselves tangled up it may or may not be possible to get completely unknotted. With a smaller number the solution is sometimes quite easy and can be found in a few minutes. With a larger number of people a considerable amount of gymnastics may be necessary, and it may still not be possible to become completely untangled. Sometimes it turns out that there are two circles, one within the other or one looped through the other. If the group is having considerable difficulty after having struggled for at least five minutes with the exercise, the facilitator may, at his or her discretion, select one coupling of hands to break so that there are now two ends in the tangle. The object of the exercise is now to get in a straight line rather than a continuous circle.

The change in instructions can be introduced as follows: "As your formative evaluator I have shrewdly observed that you're having certain difficulties completely implementing the program as designed. Therefore I'm going to make a couple of suggestions for change. The first recommendation is that we change the goal and instead of trying to get into a circle, that you get into a straight line. To facilitate the implementation of activities that will bring about that desired goal I'm going to uncouple one pair of hands. Now you can continue." After this

Figure 8.1: Unraveling the Tangle

modification, if it is needed, there should be no difficulty untangling the knot.

I sometimes use this exercise simply as an ice-breaker and make the following observation: "I like this exercise as a way of beginning a workshop (or time of working together) because solving the problem of the tangle is a lot like understanding an evaluation process. At the beginning of an evaluation everything usually is all tangled up. It's very difficult to sort out the different elements or even to tell exactly what the connections are and what is supposed to happen. By the end of the process, sometimes after some modifications along the way, the evaluation begins to take shape and finally emerges with clear, smooth, and manageable lines. An evaluation process involves sorting a lot of things out, getting things unknotted, and getting the pieces of information arranged in some manageable order."

The exercise also works well just before or just after a break, to make the same simple point. Most recently I have tended to use this exercise in the early afternoon as a way to combat the drowziness that can set in after lunch when it gets very difficult to keep the attention of the participants.

Modes of Inquiry

The tangle or knot exercise can also be an excellent mechanism for illustrating the differences between participant observation and external-spectator observation. As an experience in participant observation one simply asks the participants, as they engage in the exercise, also to observe what goes on, both in the group and in their own experience of the exercise. They are told that they will be asked to write down their observations when the exercise is over. Immediately upon completing the exercise, then, participants are asked to write their observations. After about 20 minutes of writing, participants share observations and discuss their experiences in trying to observe the exercise while participating in it. They are also asked to discuss their experiences in trying to write about their observations.

If there are enough people it is possible to have those participants who are not actively involved in the exercise take on the role of external, spectator observers. Their assignment is to move around the outside of the group and take notes on what they observe.

Both groups, the participant observers and the spectator observers, are asked to write down their observations. In sharing their observations the group is asked further to observe differences between the observations of those who participated in the exercise and those who observed it from outside. They are also asked to discuss what each observational experience was like.

Yet another variation is to use the exercise to let people experience the difference between inductive and deductive approaches to research. This requires a considerably larger group because it consists of an experiment. In one case I was working with 60 people. I divided the group in half and told one group that they would undertake a deductive research exercise while the other group did an inductive bit of research. The inductive half was sent out for a break while I worked with the deductive half to identify a set of dimensions and scales that would be used to rate two groups, different groups, both attempting to unravel a tangle. The participants were given a choice about how to construct the two groups, for example, a male group versus a female group, a group of older participants versus a group of younger participants, random assignment to the two groups, or any other dimensions of interest that permit composing two separate groups and observing the differences in how the two groups go about the exercise.

Ten dimensions for standardized rating of the two groups are then generated usually using a rating scale of 1 to 10. Examples of dimensions on which groups can be rated are noisy/quiet, enthusiastic/reserved, cooperative/competitive, and so on. The deductive group is then given a break while the inductive group returns to be given about 15 minutes of quick instruction on how to be participant observers.

The inductive group is the source for the two groups that will actually unravel the tangle. They are *not* told what the other group will be looking for or the basis for composing the two different groups, although in many cases that basis will be quite obvious, for example, males versus females. Any members of the inductive group who cannot participate in the tangle are given the role of spectator observers, but they too are not told what to look for. They are simply told to experience, observe, and record what they experience. The deductive group then returns to the room and the experiment proceeds. The deductive group is involved in measuring what goes on along predetermined, standardized scales, and are testing some hypotheses about differences between the groups, that is, hypotheses about how the two groups will differ on the dimensions being rated. The inductive group is simply remaining open to whatever the experience provides and whatever data may emerge from their observations.

Following the exercise all the participants are given time to carry out their analysis. The deductive group must tabulate the ratings of all the observers, compute the appropriate percentages and means, and compare the results for the two groups thus testing their hypotheses. The inductive group begins by writing their individual analyses of their experience and then sharing their individual experiences to identify common patterns and emergent themes in the observations.

Having conducted their separate analyses, representatives of the two groups report to the entire assembly about their findings. The entire group then discusses the nature of the two different kinds of processes. One of the glaring contrasts that has emerged every time I have done this exercise is that the inductive group reports a great deal of information about the dynamics of the exercise and how participation in the exercise changes from its beginning to a point where a solution is completed. This fluid and dynamic description contrasts sharply with the cross-sectional analysis of the deductive group because their measuring procedures were established in such a way that they have to summarize the entire group experience on each dimension with a single number.

The point is not to make the two approaches examples of how one would conduct either deductive or inductive research. The point, rather, is to give the participants a direct experience with the conduct of the two types of research so that they can begin to identify the differences for themselves and understand what it is like to generate measurement dimensions and hypotheses before doing field work, compared to going into an experience without prior determination of the focus of study. The entire exercise takes about three hours. In my experience it has been a very powerful and memorable learning experience for participants.

Exploring the Environment

This next exercise also has multiple possibilities to illustrate different things. It is a nice exercise for getting participants to think about what is needed to conduct an evaluation. It can also be an exercise in participant observation, and for data analysis workshops it is an excellent exercise to get the participants thinking about the differences between empirical observations, interpretations, judgments, and recommendations. *The basic exercise is the same in all cases. What varies is what one does with the participants and the instructions given following the exercise. It is possible to take the postexercise discussion in a number of directions depending on the purpose of the session in which the exercise is used.*

A Setting

It is shortly after 8 a.m. on a damp summer morning at Snow Mountain Ranch near Rocky Mountain National Park. Some 40 human service and education people from all over the country have gathered in a small, dome-shaped chapel to participate in an evaluation workshop. The session begins like this:

> Okay, let's get started. Instead of beginning by my haranguing you about what you should do in program evaluation, we're going to begin with a short evaluation exercise to immerse us immediately in the process. That is, we're going to take an experiential or simulation approach to learning about the stages of program evaluation.
>
> So what I'm going to do is ask you to engage in an exercise as both participants and evaluators (since that's the situation most of you find yourselves in anyway in your own agencies and programs—where you have both program and evaluation responsibilities). We're going to share an experience through this exercise to loosen things up a bit . . . perhaps warm you up, wake you up, and allow you to get more comfortable. The exercise will also allow us to test your participant observation skills and

provide us with a common experience as evaluators. We'll generate some personal data about the process of evaluation that we can use for discussion later.

So what I want you to do for about the next five minutes is to move around this space, to get up and move around in any way you want to, to explore this environment. You can explore the environment in any ways you want to—touch things, move things, experience different parts of this setting. And while you're observing the physical environments, watch what others do. Then after about five minutes I'll ask you to find a place where you feel comfortable to write down your observations about the exercise, what you observed, and also to evaluate the exercise. Experience, explore, observe, and evaluate. That's the exercise.

Oh yes, there are two rules. First, I'd prefer that you not talk to anyone, second, I'd prefer that no one leave the room. The exercise works best if people hang around for it! But otherwise, you're free to explore, and remember, while you are participating in this experience, this exercise, you're also evaluating it.

At the end of the exercise the participants were asked to write an evaluation report based on their own observations of what had occurred. Several people were then asked, on a voluntary basis, to share with the group what they had written.

First observer: People slowly got up. Everybody looked kind of nervous 'cause they weren't sure what to do. People moved out toward the walls, which are made of rough wood. The lighting is kind of dim. People sort of moved counterclockwise. Every so often there would be a nervous smile exchanged between people. The chairs are fastened down in rows so that it's hard for people to move in the center of the room. A few people went to the stage area, but most stayed toward the back and outer part. The chairs aren't too comfortable but it's a quiet, mellow room. The exercise showed that people are nervous when they don't know what to do.

Second observer: The room is hexagonally shaped with a dome-shaped ceiling. Fastened-down chairs are arranged in a semicircle with a stage in front that is about a foot high. A podium is at the left of the small stage. Green drapes hang at the side. Windows are small and triangular. The floor is wood. There's a coffee table in back. Most people went to get coffee. A couple people broke the talking rule for a minute. Everyone returned to about the same place they had before after walking around. It's not a great room for a workshop, but it's okay.

Third observer: People were really nervous about what to do because the goals of the exercise weren't clear. You can't evaluate without clear goals so people just wandered around. The exercise shows you can't evaluate without clear goals.

Fourth observer: I said to myself at the start, this is a human relations thing to get us started. I was kind of mad about doing this because we've been here a half hour already and we haven't done anything that has to do with evaluation. I came to learn about evaluation not to do T-group stuff, or nonverbal communications stuff. So I just went to get coffee and I talked to someone because I didn't like the rule about not talking, but the other person was really nervous about breaking the rule. I didn't like wasting so much time on this.

Fifth observer: I felt uneasy, too, but I think it's natural to feel uneasy when you can't talk and aren't sure what to do. But I liked walking around looking at the chapel and feeling the space. I think some people got into it, but we were stiff and uneasy. People avoided looking at each other, but by kind of moving in a circle most people went the same direction and avoided looking at each other. I think I learned something about myself and how I react to a strange, nervous situation.

The five observers had five different perspectives on the same experience. The exercise and reports were followed by a discussion of what it would take to produce a more focused set of observations and evaluations. Suggestions included establishing clear goals, making up criteria for what is being evaluated, figuring out what is supposed to be observed in advance so everyone can observe it, giving clearer directions of what to do, stating the purpose of the evaluation, and training the evaluators so that they all know how to observe the same thing.

This exercise can also be used to provide practice in participant observation and/or as a stimulus for discussing the extent to which participants were able to separate their observations from interpretations and judgments in their written report on the exercise.

Variability of Evaluation Criteria

This next exercise takes only a few minutes and is easily used with most any group in virtually any setting. Lee Edwards of the U.S. General Accounting Office told me about this exercise after he used it in an evaluation training program at GAO.

"Let me start the morning off this way: Let us assume that each of you is a very busy person. Your old car is on the verge of collapse but you just don't have time to shop around for a new one. So you ask me to do it for you, but you aren't at all sure what make and model of car you want.

Take a sheet of paper now, if you will, and put your name on top of it. Then take just two minutes and list the factors you want me to consider in shopping for your car."

Later in the morning: "During the break, I looked at some of the factors each of you said you wanted me to take into account in purchasing your car.

"There were some common elements such as [list some] but there were also a lot of differences.

"The point is that if I were buying a car for you, it would make a difference which of you I were doing the evaluation for. Well, the same is true of programs." This is a nice exercise for quickly introducing the importance of "user-focused evaluation" (Chapter 4), and the personal factor in evaluation utilization (Patton, 1986).

The Evaluation Priorities Simulation Game

As noted in the introduction to this chapter, there is an already vast and still rapidly growing literature on simulation games that offers evaluators myriad alternative exercises that can be adapted and applied to evaluation training. In this section I will describe only one such game in detail by way of illustrating the potential of formal simulation games.

The "prisoner's dilemma" game (Johnson, 1972, pp. 49-52) is representative of a common type of simulation game in which the rules are structured to force choices that have clear and immediate conse-quences of either a positive or negative nature. Only in playing the game do participants become aware of the full consequences of their choices. In subsequent discussion they can reflect on what they learned about themselves—the rule following and interpersonal interaction heuristics that guided their responses to the game.

The original "prisoner's dilemma" game revolves around choices between competition and cooperation. In adapting the game to evaluation I changed the number of teams from two to four and changed the choices to these:

(1) We insist that this issue be studied in the evaluation.
(2) We insist that this issue be omitted from the evaluation.
(3) We don't care one way or the other about this issue.

As adapted, the game simulates the problem of whose issues will be included in an evaluation when there are multiple decision makers and information users with evaluation concerns. Whose perspectives will be taken into account? What are the consequences of trying to include all perspectives and concerns? What are the consequences of ignoring some concerns?

The rules and procedures for playing the Evaluation Priorities Game are in the Appendix to this chapter.

Other Simulation Games

By way of illustrating the possibilities let me just mention a few other simulation games that I have found to be relevant in working with evaluation groups. The experiments of Alex Bavelas (1960) on patterns of communication in groups permit comparisons of efficiency, leadership, and morale in two or more five-person groups with different systems for communicating with each other. One group is arranged in a circle, the other in a line. Each person in both groups is given a list of different symbols. Using only written messages the participants are to determine which symbol is on everyone's list. Any given message can contain information about only one symbol and the words "yes" or "no." When both groups have agreed that they have identified the common symbol, the time to complete the task for each group is recorded *and* the total number of messages needed is recorded for each group. After the experiment has been repeated a few times, evaluation sheets are given to each group member. On these sheets they are asked to circle their position in the group (A-E) and answer the questions dealing with perceived leadership and enjoyment of the work.

> Except where participants violate the rules and set up their own communication channels, the results will show greater efficiency and agreement on leadership in the line pattern of communication. However, greater overall enjoyment will be found in the circle pattern. The persons on the ends in the line pattern will show the lowest enjoyment or morale. ·
> (Geertsen, 1979, p. 49)

This exercise is an interesting and enjoyable way to introduce the problem of trade-offs in programs. Most programs have multiple goals (such as efficiency, leadership, high staff morale) that may conflict to some extent. How can evaluators take these trade-offs into account in determining overall program effectiveness? Does it make sense to combine levels of attainment on separate dimensions into an overall effectiveness score? Would it be fair to compare the two groups in the experiment on only one criterion (for example, efficiency) and ignore morale? These and other questions are highly relevant in many real-world evaluation situations.

A more complex and sophisticated game simulates the problems of (1) multiple goals; (2) conflicting goals; (3) priorities development; (4) trade-offs; (5) analyzing separate issues to arrive at an overall evaluation of a program; and (6) bringing values to bear in making evaluation judgments. The game was developed for planning simulations, but it is easily adapted to evaluation scenarios. The game is called "At Issue" (Duke & Greenblat, 1979). It uses a set of wheels on which are displayed (1) factors that have an impact on the situation, (2) values that are to be brought to bear, and (3) outcome variables that are to be monitored. Game participants are asked to estimate the positive or negative impact of each factor on various issues. They must also prioritize values and estimate outcomes of various scenarios. The game takes about two hours, requires preparation of materials in advance, and is best used for specific situations, that is, to look at the options in a specific program evaluation situation. The full directions and materials for the game are in Duke and Greenblat (1979).

Before moving from simulation games to role-playing exercises, let me add one final example that was used at a 1976 evaluation conference on Educational Evaluation and Public Policy, organized by the Far West Laboratory for Educational Research and Development. The following description is from the proceedings of that conference.

Immediately after registration on Friday afternoon, the 150 conference participants gathered to view a frightening slide-tape presentation [copyright 1975, John R. Rader], concerning the year 2000. In sepulchral tones, the narrator described a United States on the brink of total disintegration. The only hope, the viewers learned, lay in rigorous selection of the cream of the nation's youth for special schooling and advancement to leadership positions.

The lights came on. As we sat pondering the point of the disturbing presentation we had just seen, each of us was given a packet consisting of information about 10 hypothetical youthful candidates for special educational treatment in the year 2000. We were informed that just two of the 10 candidates could be admitted to the special program and that our selection would determine not just the educational future of the individual candidate but also the general well being of the nation and the allocation of considerable funding. But how to decide? The descriptive data we received included demographic information, physical descriptions, intelligence quotients, social quotients, health evaluations and information about goals, interests, skills, and political beliefs.

By one set of standards, the decision seemed simple. Two of the candidates stood far above the rest in terms of intellectual performance. Indeed, most of the remaining eight were clearly inferior in intelligence and had serious behavior problems to boot. In small groups, we discussed the data and choice we had to make. Some wanted to discount the criterion of intelligence in favor of ethnic balance or gender balance or income balance, but on the whole, the two "superior" choices were voted in. Then the slide show recommenced and we discovered that all of the applications had pseudonymously described gifted individuals and that we had excluded Albert Einstein (IQ of 82, very poor school adjustment, etc.), Isadora Duncan (low social quotient, behavior problem), Eleanor Roosevelt (erratic, withdrawn, seeks attention, fails often) and four others of the most illustrious individuals of our times.

A somber mood prevailed after the Rader presentation. Probably no one among the participants had arrived at the conference believing evaluation problems to be simple of solution, but the slide show drove the point home with a vengeance: evaluation, at least as currently interpreted, means sifting, separating good students and programs from bad; wheat from chaff. But where human beings are concerned what is wheat and what is chaff? Who is to say what is good or bad? As the complexity of the issue registered, it became apparent that there were no quick answers, that we were all, in a sense, equally expert and equally ignorant. (Far West Laboratory, 1976, pp. 17-18).

Evaluation Role-Playing

Role-playing is a powerful and proven technique for helping people (1) *understand* perspectives and situations other than their own, (2) *empathize* with those who have different perspectives and find themselves in different situations, and (3) *practice* new behaviors, skills, and approaches (see Patton, 1970).

This section presents just a few of the many possibilities for using role-playing in a variety of evaluation training sessions.

Consider the following situation. Human service directors from counties throughout the state are brought together for a one-day session on evaluation. These human service directors are responsible for providing evaluative data to their county boards and state legislators who fund their programs. They must also encourage (force?) and assist local programs to conduct evaluations. They are busy people, full-time managers of underfunded and understaffed human services (at least they believe their programs are underfunded and understaffed). They are required to include program evaluation among their responsibilities, though they have no formal training in evaluation. Their antipathy toward the idea of devoting scarce time and resources to evaluation is only thinly veiled.

The opening session has three purposes: (1) make them open to learning about evaluation based partly on a recognition that there are things one should know and be able to do in order to instigate, supervise, and be accountable for the results of evaluation processes; (2) help them better understand the respective functions, roles, and responsibilities of human service directors, elected public officials, and evaluators; and (3) bring before the group in an interesting and stimulating way the evaluation issues that will be of concern throughout the day.

Faced with precisely this situation I opted to open the session with a role-play. I began with something like the "invitation" in Chapter 2, inviting participants to take responsibility for the quality of their own learning experience during the day. I then asked for a volunteer who had a specific program in mind on which he or she was about to instigate an evaluation. When the volunteer joined me in front of the group I asked him to assume the role of the key elected county or state official who would be interested in the results of the evaluation. I then asked for a second volunteer willing to work and consult with this elected official to determine what kind of evaluation should take place. The first volunteer played the role of the elected official to whom he is ultimately responsible and the second volunteer played the role of evaluation consultant. I then asked them to introduce themselves to each other and the group using real or fictitious names *other than their own* (to help them move into being a new person and playing an assumed role).

What happened in this case (and what usually happens) is that the elected official was (hyperbolically) vague about what kind of information was needed and the evaluation consultant was quite frustrated in trying to figure out what questions to ask to move the evaluation consultation forward. The elected official wanted to know "if the program is worth the taxpayer's money," and the evaluator wanted to know what criteria to use to answer that question. In the 10-minute role-play (they were pretty well stuck after 10 minutes) the importance of resolving the following evaluation questions was demonstrated:

(1) Who is the evaluation for?
(2) What should be the focus of the evaluation?
(3) What measures of program activity and outcome are possible to collect and worth collecting?
(4) How would evaluation data be used to make judgments and decisions about the program?

These questions could easily be abstracted from the role-play though they were not explicitly dealt with by either the elected official or the evaluation consultant. The role-play proved to be a frame of reference for discussions and demonstrations throughout the day. At the end of the day all participants were paired in these two roles (for a different situation and program in each case). Using what they had learned and discussed throughout the day, the second role-play was a chance to practice and reinforce their new knowledge and skills.

Many opportunities to use role-playing are missed because we rely so heavily on the standard operating procedure (heuristic) of having people make monologic presentations when an interactive demonstration would bring to the surface basically the same information in more interesting fashion and allow the accomplishment of secondary objectives like practice in consulting, learning to ask and answer questions under pressure, and taking another person into consideration in an interaction. For example, many evaluation meetings or training sessions include the opportunity for one or more persons to describe their program, or evaluation, or whatever. Instead of calling on these volunteers for a monologue or speech to those assembled, a role-play can be created in which another volunteer solicits the desired information through a consulting interaction.

The same process, though admittedly somewhat more time-consuming than a monologic presentation, can be used in evaluation practica or seminars. For several years I have offered a field experience seminar for graduate students actually doing evaluations. All progress reports are rendered through role-plays, and work on problems students are experiencing is often undertaken by role-playing the situation. Students become eager for the chance to refine their consulting skills under the critical but basically supportive scrutiny of the group. One of the rules I impose on the seminar role-plays is that the consultant's question must always build in some way, or at least recognize, the "client's" last answer or comment, and the client is to answer *only* the question asked. Thus if the consultant asks a question in a form that structurally implies a dichotomous answer—"Can you tell me what criteria are used to admit people into your program?"—the "client" answers either and only "yes" or "no." Consultants must also ask only one question at a time. These artificial rules force attentive listening on all sides, including those observing the role-play, for they are instructed to interrupt when either rule is broken. Under these constraints and pressures the quality of student/consultant open-ended interviewing rapidly improves (see Patton, 1980, pp. 195-266, on interviewing).

Demonstrations

There is one hazard in using role-playing in workshops, task force meetings, and seminars about which I feel obliged to warn my colleagues. The attentive reader will have noticed that I am always on the sidelines of the role-plays I set up, kibitzing at will, but not on center stage where I would have to demonstrate the correct way of avoiding all the mistakes those under my scrutiny have made—mistakes I have usually pointed out to the group. Participants in these sessions with whom one works over time, particularly students, will put up with this double standard, where only they are in jeopardy, for so long. The pressure gradually builds for a demonstration by the "master," a label that emerges with sarcastic endearment as the pressure builds to move center stage. While it is true that some of the best coaches were poor players, this argument has never been much help to me in reducing the demand for a demonstration of "how it should really be done."

While for a long time I adamantly resisted these pressures, once I yielded I found that I was hooked. The most fruitful and important experiences I have had in learning about my own consulting style and heuristics have come from these sessions where I have attempted to demonstrate evaluation consulting processes and skills before a group of colleagues, students, and/or program people. In all evaluation classes I teach I now eagerly look for opportunities to do a live, unrehearsed classroom demonstration by offering a free hour of consulting to someone who has called me for help on an evaluation. The rules for the demonstration are that we meet for the first time in front of the class, that I be given no prior information about the program or evaluation problem, and that the class be allowed to comment afterwards on what they have heard. I have had no difficulty finding program people to work with under these conditions, and I have learned a tremendous amount from observer feedback. Students typically consider these demonstrations and the ensuing discussions to be the highlight of the course because of the intensity of the demonstration and the amount of action compressed in a very short time. I also find that demonstrations have much more impact, and make a deeper impression on observers, if those observers (students) have first found themselves center stage in either a role-play, simulation, or real consulting field experience.

Discussion-Generating Materials

Experiential exercises, simulation games, and role-playing performances are techniques for generating discussion and helping participants develop insight, empathy, and understanding into real-world processes. The "debrief" or postexperience discussion is a critical part of these techniques if they are to be allowed to have their full impact. The exercises are not ends in themselves. Too little time left at the end for discussion and reflection can defeat the whole purpose of using these techniques. I prefer to cut the exercise short to guarantee discussion time rather than let the exercise run overtime and lose the discussion.

In this section I want to refer briefly to some other materials I have found useful to generate discussion on important issues where there wasn't time for an appropriate simulation. Again, these examples are offered by way of stimulating thinking about discussion-generating possibilities.

Racism, sexism, classism, and ethnocentrism are problems that impinge on evaluation no less than other areas of society. The proceedings of the Conference on Educational Evaluation and Public Policy (Far West Laboratory, 1976) include some excellent materials that can be used to generate discussion on these issues. Consider, for example, the following excerpts from the women's caucus at that conference.

As a woman, I would like to raise the issue of dealing with diversity honestly. In these comments I am dealing specifically with sexism, though in my view racism and sexism are intrinsically intertwined.

To deal with diversity is to look at *every* tool of assessment from the standpoint of inclusiveness—does the tool reflect diversity in terms of sex? *Visually:* are pictures, graphics, balanced in number (frequency) and in terms of diversity of experience in nonstereotypical roles? *Linguistically:* is there balance in terminology? Generic terms such as "man, men" need not be used to describe both the male of the species and all people! Have biased linguistic assumptions been challenged? (Men by the thousands headed west. Not true! We know they didn't go alone! Why not "men, women and children by the thousands . . .") *Observationally:* is observation used in a way that shows reflective and sensitive awareness of both boys and girls? There are not boys' and girls' ways of learning—there are diverse *human* ways of learning and we needn't describe them in male modes. . . .

I want to be sure, as a woman evaluatee/evaluator, that

1. women be included in the dialogue at every level of decision-making about educational evaluation and public policy—on panels, boards, local, statewide and national committees, legislative groupings, editorial groups, etc. . . .

2. women be included in the *language* of our dialogue—as has been succinctly pointed out: not to substitute women's language for men's language, but to be sure that men's language is not paraded as the whole.

3. women be freed from the stereotypical roles, the "boxed-in-ness" that our educational and evaluational systems perpetuate (or at the least, allow). I want to be, for example, included in the books of our classrooms, even if it means taking liquid paper and marking pens and editing in balance, because I want my reading growth as a girl-child to be assessed from a common baseline of human experience.

4. women be able to fully share in the common commitment to humanness and concern in educational evaluation-humanness defined in its most diverse and colorful richness! (Report by Women's Caucus, statement written by Kathleen Hurty, Far West Laboratory, 1976)

The proceedings also include a dialogue written by James A. Johnson, Jr., in which an evaluator and program director discuss (from different points of view, pro and con) whether a white, middle-class evaluator can fairly evaluate a program run by and for low-income, black people (Far West Laboratory, 1976, pp. 102-105). There is also an excellent piece by Michael Scriven written as a role-play in which he argues (as an evaluator) with a program administrator who is presenting reasons (excuses?) why his program should not be evaluated (Far West Laboratory, 1976, pp. 75-77). Both of these dialogues are excellent materials for generating discussion on important evaluation issues. Where more time is available in a session these role-plays can be simulated in a group by assigning the respective roles to different participants (pro and con on these issues). To facilitate the role-play, participants representing each point of view would be given materials supporting only their role-play perspective. Participants could then translate these arguments into their own language and enrich them with their own experiences.

Another excellent way to stimulate discussion and provide participants with an active, involving learning experience is to use case materials and have students analyze, critique, and dissect illustrative cases (illustrative of whatever one wants to demonstrate). Lawrence Lynn has developed the case study approach to a fine art in teaching policy analysis (Lynn, 1980a). Ann Lieberman (1979, pp. 72-82) has written two case studies that are useful for examining the role of evaluation in planned change. Five evaluation case studies put together by Alkin et al. (1979) are excellent case materials for discussion and analysis of evaluation processes. While any evaluation report can serve the purpose of being a case study, reports often tell only part of the story and are too lengthy with too much irrelevant material to serve well under severe time constraints. Case materials are most effective when carefully prepared to illustrate a particular point and to generate discussion on specific issues.

LEARNING THROUGH EXPERIENCE

The best substitute for experience is being sixteen.

Raymond Duncan

This chapter has presented examples of various approaches to *experiential* learning: group exercises, games, simulations, role-plays, and critical case analysis. The premise underlying the use of these materials is that evaluators are *trainers* whenever and wherever they take on the task of working with a group of people who want to learn about either a specific program or evaluation more generally. As trainers, creative evaluators need a large repertoire of training techniques to deal effectively with different learners and different situations.

As noted at the beginning of this chapter, these materials draw on three areas of research and study: experiential learning, simulation games, and the function of play in human experience. The exercises and games in this chapter are by no means an exhaustive set of evaluation exercises. Part of the fun of conducting workshops is thinking up new ways to engage participants actively in the learning process or adapting old approaches to new situations. *The first step is to figure out exactly what you want participants to understand and experience, then an exercise can be designed or adapted to provide them with that experience and the desired understandings.* Experiences of these kinds can be a powerful stimulus to helping people think creatively about evaluation.

The exercises in this chapter are purposefully *playful.* They assume that learning—and evaluation—can be enjoyable, engaging activities. They also assume a potential linkage between playfulness and creativity. Franz Alexander (quoted in Reilly, 1974, p. 17) commented on that linkage as follows:

> It is paradoxical that when man through scientific knowledge has become too efficient in securing with little effort his basic necessities of life, he becomes deadly serious and looks nostalgically at the creative centuries of the past when he still had time and detachment for play and creativity. In this paradox lies the secret of understanding the crisis of Western civilization.

Of course, there are limitations to how much experience one can absorb in a simulation, a game, or a role-play. Experiential exercises are merely one strategy for helping people prepare for the "games" played in real life and in real program evaluation situations. A story about a ritual exercise used by evaluation sage Halcolm from his *Evaluation Parables* makes this point to close this chapter.

YCKE!

All day long the passersby outside the courtyard where Halcolm taught his students could hear a chorus of voices saying rhythmically over and over again:

YCKE! YCKE! YCKE! . . .! YCKE! . . .

The people of the village paid no particular attention because several times a year they had grown used to hearing this chorus of shouts. A stranger, however, was much perplexed by the unusual shouting. He entered into the courtyard and spotted Halcolm at the side, looking over the students. He went up to him and asked what the students were shouting.

"Many years ago I began a ritual wherein the students would come into the courtyard as part of their evaluation training and repeat over and over again the phrase 'YOU CAN'T KNOW EVERYTHING!' Over the years the students shortened the phrase to the acronym 'YCKE!' "

The passerby, it turned out, was himself a teacher and was much fascinated by the ritual. After watching a bit more he turned to Halcolm and asked, "And what is the effect of this ritual on your students? Have they absorbed and understood that 'you can't know everything'?"

Halcolm smiled at the newcomer. "Your question is well put. Many understand but many more have to learn by experience. As a teacher I have discharged my responsibility by planting the germ of this idea in their head so that the real teacher, Experience, can water it and make it blossom."

APPENDIX: THE EVALUATION PRIORITIES SIMULATION GAME, RULES AND PROCEDURES

The game is played by four teams, with two or more players on each team. One team is designated to represent "program staff" concerns; a second team represents "funders"; a third team represents the concerns of program administrators; and the fourth team represents "client" concerns. There are 15 different evaluation issues presented to the participants. For each concern the respective teams decide among themselves whether or not they are personally (in the roles they represent) concerned about the issue before the group. They then decide whether to (1) insist that this concern be included in the evaluation, (2) insist that this concern be omitted from the evaluation, or (3) remain ambivalent or essentially uncaring about the issue at hand. No team can insist on including more than 10 issues. No team can insist on excluding more than 10 issues. No team can remain ambivalent about more than 5 issues. Each team must vote to include at least 3 issues, to exclude at least 3 issues, and to abstain on at least 1 issue.

Points are awarded to the teams as follows:

(a) If all four teams vote to either exclude or include an issue, all teams receive four points.

(b) If a majority of teams vote to exclude or include an issue (ambivalent votes are counted as abstentions and do not figure in computing the majority view), each of the teams in the majority win as many points as there are teams in the majority and the minority team loses the same number of points. Those voting "don't care one way or the other" neither win nor lose points.

(c) In the event of a tie vote all teams voting either to include or to exclude the issue lose two points; those abstaining, if any, win four points.

(d) If all four teams vote that they don't care one way or the other, all teams lose four points.

For each issue the teams are given a maximum time period to determine their vote. The time alloted can be as short as one minute for two-person teams or sophisticated players and can be much longer for larger teams and/or less experienced participants. In any case, a maximum time is set and any team not ready to report or unable to agree on a vote within the alloted time loses four points and is counted as an abstention in the voting.

After votes on the 15 issues have been recorded, the total group is permitted to discuss and negotiate briefly on the 5 issues about which there was least consensus (tie votes, then majorities of one, then four "don't care" votes). New votes are then taken on those five issues with no restrictions on how teams vote (that is, all five votes could be cast to include, exclude, or remain neutral—or any combination of these). Throughout the voting the facilitator keeps score on a board clearly visible to all participants, but no talking can go on between teams during the game. Only members of the same team can talk to each other. (A variation of the game would allow alliances and negotiations between teams before each vote, or once before the start of voting, but such variations, though more realistic in some ways, take longer to play out.)

At the end of the 20 votes the facilitator totals the score and reports the final outcomes for each team in rank order. Participants are then asked to discuss the experience with emphasis on (1) what they learned about their own strategy-making heuristics and (2) what similarities exist between the simulation and the real world of evaluation priorities decision making. Certain teams usually emerge as highly conciliatory, others as relatively ambivalent, and still others as aggressive or exploitative. At least 20 minutes should be allowed for a "debrief" of the exercise; the debrief or postexercise discussion is critical to the overall learning experience. The debrief begins with descriptive reporting ("Who did what?" "What were the patterns for each team?") and then moves to interpretation and judgment ("Why did that happen?" "What did you learn?" "What's the relevance to real-world evaluations?").

The 15 issues for voting can be specific to a particular program (the actual program to be evaluated by those in the exercise or a case example constructed for the exercise), or the issues can be more general and abstract. For example, a review of the types of evaluations listed in Chapter 11, Evaluation Alphabet Soup, would easily yield 15 alternative evaluation issues on which teams could vote. I find that using an actual program or case example to set the context for the game helps participants get into their roles and makes the choices more real.

CHAPTER 9: *Picturethinking*

> *When the artist is alive in any person,*
> *whatever his kind of work may be, he*
> *becomes an inventive, searching,*
> *daring, self-expressive creature. . . . He*
> *disturbs, upsets, enlightens, and opens*
> *ways for better understanding. Where*
> *those who are not artists are trying to*
> *close the book, he opens it and shows*
> *there are still more pages possible.*

> *Robert Henri (1923)*

The connecting thread of thought that runs throughout this book is the proposition established in the first chapter that our situational flexibility, adaptability, and creativity in evaluation practice are limited by conditioned reflexes, paradigmatic perception, unconscious rules of thumb, socialized definitions of the situation, and autonomic standard operating procedures. In short, we are constrained by our internal neurological computer programs—our heuristics. Creative potential has a greater chance of realization as we develop heuristic awareness, unveil and move into consciousness our paradigms, allow ourselves to try new ways of behaving, practice new skills, and *see things in new ways*. It is this last path to greater creativity that is the subject of this chapter.

This chapter has special meaning for me because it represents a personal commitment to move beyond the limitations of my past experience into a realm of perception and experience that has been largely closed to me. By self-definition and definition of others, especially school teachers, "I am not artistic." I don't remember when I was first told that I lacked artistic talent, though I'm sure it was quite early. I do remember that artistic inclinations were considered "sissyish" in the poor, working-class neighborhood where I spent my childhood, so I would have been highly motivated to repress any artistic flair if ever I had any. At different times along the way "I'm not an artist" became "I don't have an eye for art," "I don't really understand art," "I don't appreciate art," and "I'm not into art." I hasten to add that having thus defined away a whole realm of human experience I felt no vacuum, remorse, loss, guilt, or limitations. "Different strokes for different folks" being the order of the day, I graciously accepted the obvious fact that I was not among the artistic strokes folks.

Then in 1977 I was asked to do a three-day evaluation research workshop sponsored by Lesley College in Cambridge, Massachusetts. A number of the participants in that workshop were artists and poets interested in enlarging their horizons to come to terms with scientific research, including several learners in the graduate program of the Union for Experimenting Colleges and Universities, a nonresidential, advanced degree-granting institution. As I challenged them to be open to scientific ways of understanding and experiencing the world, they turned the tables on me and challenged me to be open to the experiences and understandings of artists.

Since that time I've come to think of my artistic self as underdeveloped rather than nonexistent. I've had the opportunity to work with artists on evaluations, and to bring picturethinking into my evaluation practice. This chapter is meant to enlarge the realm of picturethinking possibilities for others who, like myself, may have inadvertently omitted it from their evaluation repertoire. Without offering an equation about how many words a picture is worth, this chapter explores evaluation artistry.

SEEING

Work in psychology (Grinder & Bandler, 1976, 1979) suggests that different people have developed different *primary* "representational systems" for understanding and experiencing the world. Some people are primarily language oriented; some are touch oriented; some rely most heavily on auditory information; and many are primarily visually oriented. One of the reasons the different chapters in this book emphasize different approaches to creative evaluation thinking is that no single modality of communication and experience is effective with everyone.

Picturethinking is a general term for using visual stimuli to understand and communicate about the world. Drawings, paintings, pantomimes, videotapes, movies, photographs, and diagrams are all forms of picturethinking. Visualizations involve different neurological and perceptual processes than do words, sounds, scents, and kinesthetic stimuli (Grinder & Bandler, 1979). What is of special import for our purposes is the evidence from Grinder and Bandler that one can develop and learn to use representational systems that have been relatively dormant and of minor importance in one's usual experience. One need not go deaf to realize the extent to which the potential of the visual sense has been unrealized. Through practiced awareness and directed experience, Grinder and Bandler have helped people enlarge their sensorial and perceptual repertoire. They have learned to *see*.

A major research tradition that is relevant here is the work on brain hemispheres (Bogen, 1969; Ferguson, 1973; Jaynes, 1976; McGulgan & Schoonover, 1973). Simply stated, the "dominant" side of the brain (the left side in right-handed people) is the location of verbal, analytical, and linear reasoning and information processing, while the "other" side is the locus of nonverbal information processing: visualizing, imagining, and spatial, holistic understanding. Dr. Roger Sperry, a California Institute of Technology psychobiology professor, is one of the country's leading brain scientists. He has summarized the implications of hemispheric brain research as follows:

> The main theme to emerge . . . is that there appear to be two modes of thinking, verbal and non-verbal, represented rather separately in left and right hemispheres, respectively, and that our educational system, as well as science in general, tends to neglect the non-verbal form of intellect. What it comes down to is that modern society discriminates against the right hemisphere. (Sperry, 1973, p. 209)

Again, what is important for our purposes is that the usual domination of the verbal, analytical hemisphere need not be permanent. We can learn to use both sides of the brain (Buzan, 1976). Betty Edwards has developed "a course in enhancing creativity and artistic confidence" by *Drawing on the Right Side of the Brain* (1979). She works on the premise that you can develop "a new way of seeing by tapping the special functions of the right hemisphere of your brain" (p. vii). Her "cognitive-shift model of teaching" encourages mental shifts from verbal, logical thinking to "a more global, intuitive mode." The conclusion she reaches about the potential for artistic seeing in all people is based on her own studies of student artistic success rather than the validity of hemispheric brain theories and studies.

> Regardless of the degree to which future science may eventually confirm the strict cerebral lateralization or separation of brain functions into what I termed left-mode and right-mode, the two cognitive modes and the related principles presented in this book have empirically been proven to be successful with students at all levels and therefore hold up irrespective of how strictly lateralized the brain mechanisms may be. In its present form, the model has provided me with a method of teaching that solves the problem I started out with: how to enable *all* of the students in a class instead of just a few to learn the skill of drawing. (Edwards, 1979, p. vii)

There is yet another tradition that is relevant here, the Zen emphasis on understanding the world through the senses unencumbered by words, labels, categories, and analytical distinctions. In Frederick Franck's *The Zen of Seeing* (1973) and the companion volume, *The Awakened Eye* (1979), he illustrates what he calls "*seeing/drawing*" as a way of experiencing and understanding the world.

> When I SEE—suddenly I am all eyes, I forget this Me, am liberated from it and dive into the reality of what confronts me, become part of it, participate in it. I no longer label, no longer choose. . . .
>
> It is in order to really SEE, to SEE ever deeper, ever more intensely, hence to be fully aware and alive, that I draw what the Chinese call "The Thousand Things" around me. Drawing is the discipline by which I constantly rediscover the world.
>
> I have learned that what I have not drawn I have never really SEEN. (Franck, 1973, p. 6)
>
> And so I speak, again and again, about experiencing first-hand and about the gift of our eyes to really SEE. (Franck, 1973, p. 24)

The zen of seeing, the potential of "right brain" understanding, the variety of nonverbal experience, and the development of multiple representational systems all converge in an evaluative question: To what extent am I using my full human creative potential as an evaluator? There are two ways in which *seeing* and picturethinking constitute potentially underdeveloped creative processes in evaluation. The first concerns the potential for alternative ways of understanding programs through artistic perception. The second concerns the potential for more effectively communicating about evaluation, in particular facilitating communications between traditionally verbal, analytical evaluation researchers and nonverbal, intuitive evaluation consumers or clients. Nonverbal and experiential approaches to understanding and thinking about evaluation provide a mechanism for including "right brain" types in the evaluation process. Evaluation research is usually perceived as an entirely "left brain" activity—deductive, cognitive, linear, and analytical. Perhaps evaluation and evaluators can be enriched by being open to "right brain" influences—induction, affect, imagination, and nonverbal information processing. The remainder of this chapter is devoted to sharing a few modest endeavors to explore the possibilities of picture-thinking in evaluation.

In the Shadow of the Dominant Paradigm

The first selection, Plate 9.1, is a collage titled "In the Shadow of the Dominant Paradigm." Take a moment to do more than just *look* at the picture—*see* it. Let yourself move into the setting being depicted. Be there. Observe the expressions of the people and of the cat. Take in the background, the details. Focus without staring. *See* what the artist saw. Experience the picture first without analyzing it. Then let the *seeing* and the experiencing become *picturethinking*. What thoughts and feelings flow from what you *see*?

Before reading on, try one more thing. Put the book aside, close your eyes, and allow the picture to emerge on the movie screen in your mind. What stands out? What have you chosen to emphasize in your internal visualization? What do you retain from what you've *seen*? What images? What thoughts? What feelings?

The collage was created by New York poet/artist Sandy McIntosh after attending the evaluation workshop at Lesley College mentioned in the opening section of this chapter. Sandy was beginning an evaluation of New York's Poets in the Schools program. He was reacting to the discussion of methodological paradigms that took place at the work-shop. That discussion was based on my concerns about methodological prejudices and paradigmatic blinders in evaluation as described in *Utilization-Focused Evaluation*.

Evaluation research is dominated by the largely unquestioned, natural science paradigm of hypothetico-deductive methodology. This dominant

SOURCE: Sandy McIntosh.

Plate 9.1: In the Shadow of the Dominant Paradigm

paradigm assumes quantitative measurement, experimental design, and multivariate, parametric statistical analysis to be the epitome of "good" science. This basic model for conducting evaluation research comes from the tradition of experimentation in agriculture, which gave us many of the basic statistical and experimental techniques most widely used in evaluation research. . . .

By way of contrast, the alternative to the dominant hypothetico-deductive paradigm is derived from the tradition of anthropological field studies. Using the techniques of in-depth, openended interviewing and personal observation, the alternative paradigm relies on qualitative data, holistic analysis, and detailed description derived from close contact with the targets of study. The hypothetico-deductive, natural science paradigm aims at prediction of social phenomena; the holistic-inductive, anthropological paradigm aims at understanding of social phenomena. From a utilization-focused perspective on evaluation research, neither of these paradigms is intrinsically better than the other. They represent alternatives from which the active-reactive-adaptive evaluator can choose; both contain options for identified decisionmakers and information-users. . . . *The problem from a utilization-focused approach to evaluation is that the very dominance of the hypothetico-deductive paradigm with its quantitative, experimental emphasis appears to have cut off the great majority of its practitioners from serious consideration of any alternative evaluation research paradigm or methods.* The label "research" has come to mean the equivalent of employing the "scientific method," of working within the dominant paradigm. There is, however, an alternative. (Patton, 1978, pp. 203-204, 207)

What Sandy's collage did for me was tell me that I was drawing too stark a contrast between quantitative and qualitative methods in my writings and workshops. I discovered that in some cases I had been feeding and encouraging certain kinds of antimeasurement, antinumbers feelings. His visual representation of what I was communicating helped stimulate me to be more descriptive of concrete methodological alternatives, a task I undertook in the writing of *Qualitative Evaluation Methods* (Patton, 1980). In the second edition of *Utilization-Focused Evaluation* (Patton, 1986), I have provided a synthesis of qualitative and quantitative methods that moves beyond the original notions of dominant and alternative paradigms to a genuine paradigm of choices.

I have used Sandy's collage on a number of occasions to help program staff, evaluation task force members, and participants express their feelings about social science methods and/or evaluation. It is clear that many people can relate to Sandy's imagery, particularly people who feel his collage depicts not just a methodological paradigm but *evaluation* writ large. Many staff who see the collage immediately identify it as a representation of the monster, *evaluation*. Picturethinking about evaluation and research methods with the "In the Shadow . . ." collage has helped to open up both verbal and nonverbal communication channels in these instances.

One of the things I find most interesting about reactions to the collage is the variation in what people *see* in the cat's eyes. Some people see fear in the eyes. Some sense an amusement in the cat. Still others find an intense alertness or guardedness in the eyes. For me, part of the power of the feline expression is what I experience as a detached, unemotional, matter-of-fact, this-is-the-way-the-world-is stance, a chilling neutrality about what is going on since what is going on is simply in the nature of things.

It is important when using a picture or visual projection approach that participants be given sufficient time to get into the visualization. Picturethinking and picture*see*ing don't happen when, as I once experienced, a session facilitator handed out a drawing and said, "I think this drawing nicely shows what we've been talking about. Take a quick look at it and we'll move on. You can look at it more carefully when you get home."

If a picture is worth introducing to a group, it's worth taking the time—then and there—to let people experience, *see*, discuss, and think.

The Evaluation Horserace

The next selection consists of four pictures, Plates 9.2 through 9.5. These drawings were done by my son, Brandon, at age seven. The idea for the drawings came from Nick Rayder, who used horse drawings by his daughter, Tara, in a presentation on "Methodological and Ethical Problems of Research in Early Childhood Education" to illustrate "the absurdity of what is being done in the Follow Through Evaluation" (Rayder, 1977, p. 70). Rayder argued that Follow Through programs were as different as different kinds of horses (thoroughbreds, Clydesdales, leisure horses, work horses, circus horses, studs) but the evaluation design for Follow Through entered all programs into an academic achievement race regardless of whether the program was suited for that kind of race. He called the Head Start and Follow Through planned variation evaluation/experimental design the "Horse Race paradigm" of evaluation.

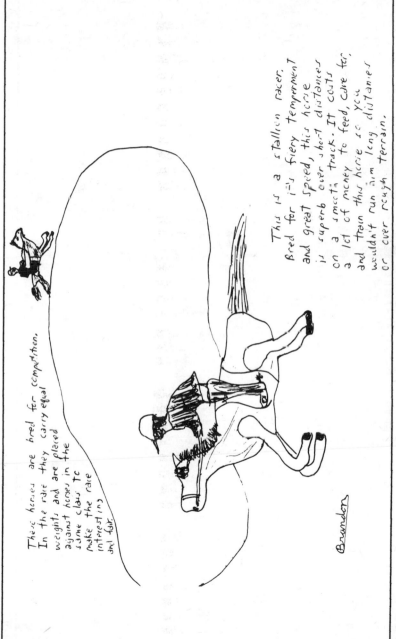

Plate 9.2

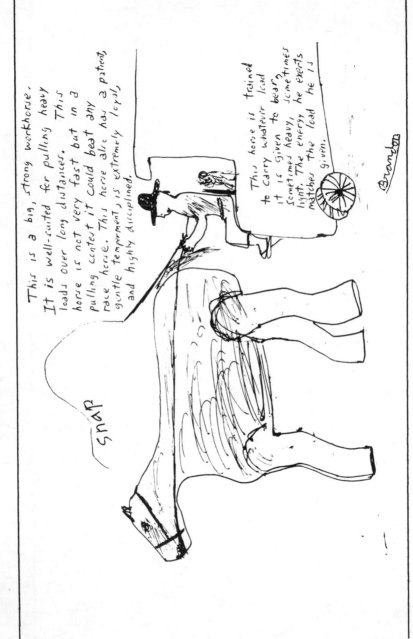

This is a big, strong workhorse. It is well-suited for pulling heavy loads over long distances. This horse is not very fast but in a pulling contest it could beat any race horse. This horse also has a patient gentle temperament, is extremely loyal, and highly disciplined.

This horse is trained to carry whatever load it is given to bear, sometimes heavy, sometimes light. The energy he exerts matches the load he is given.

snap

Branton

Plate 9.3

162

This is a mare with her newborn foal. The mother is completely absorbed in her task of nurturing this new life. Nurturing is her purpose, and all she wants to do at the moment. At other times she might be a race horse, a work horse, or even a circus performer.

Brendan

Plate 9.4

This is a high performance, finely tuned, custom built race car. It has 400 horses under the hood. It is enormously expensive, but it could outrun even the fastest racing thoroughbred... if it didn't wreck or break down.

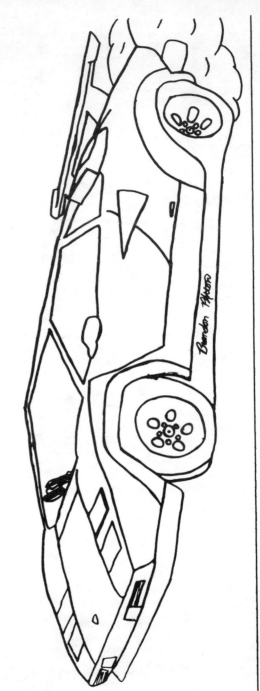

Brandon Hylton

Rayder's point can be extended to evaluation generally. The horse drawings presented here are meant to illustrate the basic premise of situational responsiveness in creative evaluation: that different types of programs demand different types of evaluation. This premise is the corollary of and takes seriously the emergent philosophy of the discipline that evaluations ought to be utility-focused, feasibilty-conscious, propriety-oriented, and accuracy-based (see the "Ten Commandments of Evaluation," this volume). The routine heuristic operational among many dominant paradigm adherents of automatically turning every evaluation into an experiment (horse race) comparing programs on standardized quantitative outcomes is incompatible with situational responsiveness, which recognizes and takes into account unique program characteristics and circumstances.

The horse race paradigm is appropriate where all the programs in an evaluation are geared to strive for high attainment of common goals. Even here, however, for the race to be fair and interesting the producer of the show (the evaluator) will want to consider handicap data and only enter horses of similar capability and desire into the same race. An experiment (or race) pitting the thoroughbred in Plate 9.2 against the horsepower in Plate 9.5 would be neither interesting nor fair. The horses in Plates 9.3 and 9.4 don't belong in a horse race at all, though they clearly have other attributes that are worthy of study and comparison.

One of the side benefits of requesting my son to provide these illustrations was an opportunity to discuss my evaluation work in a way that, for the first time, made some sense to him. It occurred to me then that part of the power of picturethinking may be its connection with the child in us. Children relate to pictures before they relate to words. When working with people for whom evaluation is a totally new (and often frightening) experience, the place to begin may be with certain childlike understandings. Sages throughout time have urged adults not to lose touch with childlike wisdom. Picturethinking may play an important role in stimulating, connecting with, and building on childlike perceptions of elemental, but crucial, evaluation principles, thereby returning to the evaluation process an important reservoir of childlike wisdom.

Brandon: But Dad, why would anybody try to race these horses together anyway. That's just dumb, especially against a car.
Dad: Maybe they want to be sure. Maybe they don't see the differences among the horses and they won't see them without a race.
Brandon: Anybody can see that a new mother horse can't beat a stallion racer.

Dad: No matter what: Can you think of any way the mother could win?

Brandon: Sure, like the turtle and hare, if the stallion just went to sleep or didn't try. Or if he was sick or hurt. Wait, I know. If you stole the baby horse and the mother was chasing you, I bet she could beat any horse alive.

Dad: Would that be a fair race?

Brandon: A chase is different from a race. A lot of things are faster in a chase than they could ever be in a race, but they still wouldn't be any good in an ordinary race. Plus, a chase is really dangerous, because you can run into things, or get hit, or step in a hole, or get hurt just from trying too hard, like hurting your muscles. The mother horse could beat the stallion trying to get her baby colt back, but she might be dead afterwards from running so hard. That wouldn't prove nothing except she loved her baby, but nothing about who was faster. [Pause] You don't do that kind of thing in evaluation stuff, do you—make mother horses run so hard to get their babies that they kill themselves, just so you can see how fast they are?

Dad: Well, um, not on purpose, but, well, you have to understand that. . . .

Brandon: I get it now. I get it. I get it. That's why you wanted me to draw the picture, so you could tell people in the book they shouldn't do that, even by accident. Right?

Dad: You got it, son. You got it.

Brandon: Then I think I better draw a better picture showing the mother horse kissing the baby so they know she really loves him, not like this just standing there together.

Dad: Thanks son, that will help a lot.

Matrix Vision

A very different kind of visual stimulus is shown in Plate 9.6. The exercise[1] is introduced as a "speed of analysis" exercise. Participants are shown an enlarged version of the square matrix in the upper left-hand corner of Plate 9.6. "As quick as you can, now, tell me how many squares there are." It is important that the participants provide spontaneous and rapid answers. Record the responses and ask individuals to explain how they came up with their answers. After several different answers have been generated participants are invited to discuss the reasons for their perceptual differences. They can then be shown the full variety of possible responses displayed in Plate 9.6. This provides an introduction to a discussion of perception, data interpretation, and judgment in evaluation. In studying the number of squares in the matrix no single answer shown in Plate 9.6 is wrong, but no single answer is entirely right either. If perceptions can differ this greatly in a simple

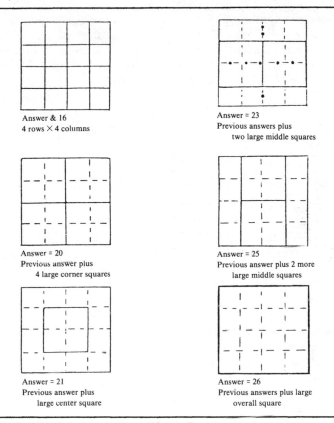

Answer & 16
4 rows × 4 columns

Answer = 23
Previous answers plus
two large middle squares

Answer = 20
Previous answer plus
4 large corner squares

Answer = 25
Previous answer plus 2 more
large middle squares

Answer = 21
Previous answer plus
large center square

Answer = 26
Previous answers plus large
overall square

Plate 9.6: Possible Solutions to Square Matrix Exercise

square-counting exercise, and if multiple answers are needed to completely answer this straightforward counting problem, how much more complex and prone to error (or partial truth) may be the task of perceiving, observing and counting things in human service programs.

Visual Impact

> Things seen are mightier
> than things heard.

Alfred Lord Tennyson

Pictures are not the only way of making visual contact and of having visual impact. Flowcharts (Chapter 6), matrices (Chapter 7), and illustrations (see Chart 10.1) all have a visual dimension, though each relies on words in ways that a picture or painting does not. This section contains two examples of how attention to the impact of nonverbal presentations can enhance communications and stimulate thinking.

The first selection is an excerpt from the Proceedings of the Far West Laboratory Conference on Educational Evaluation and Public Policy, which describes how a dance presentation was used to stimulate thinking about problems of ethnocentricity in evaluation research, given the discipline's roots in Western science.

> The second key large-group experience of the conference occurred Friday night. Settling back after dinner, we were electrified by the Wajumbe Dancers' presentation of black rhythms from across the centuries. But it was more than a dance show. As the dancers and drummers performed their final selection, narrator Blanche Brown melodically and rhythmically informed the audience, "Chinese are Chinese wherever they are; Japanese are Japanese wherever they are . . . and we are an *African* people . . . we are an *African* people . . ."
>
> Brown didn't need to say, since it was apparent to those who watched, that American educators and evaluators must recognize that the dominant culture's definition of valid learning experiences and styles is not all-encompassing or, indeed, sufficient. To say that the Wajumbe Dancers taught a lesson in pluralism is merely an inadequate verbal attempt to convey a highly charged, nonverbal and convincing experience. (Far West Laboratory, 1976, p. 18)

Another performance medium that contains lessons for evaluators is magic. Perhaps in nothing is the problem of confusing illusion with reality better demonstrated than in magic. A demonstration of magic opens up a multitude of analogous evaluation research questions, while providing rich material for stimulating thinking about particular issues. For example, I have had a great deal of fun with Houdini's Escape Ring trick, illustrated in Plate 9.7.

The Escape Ring trick involves removing a ring from an unbroken loop of thread placed around the two forefingers of a volunteer. The ring "escapes" from the loop of string without cutting it. The trick is quite simple to learn and perform, and the visual illusion is quite striking. While performing the trick I use the following "misdirection" dialogue:

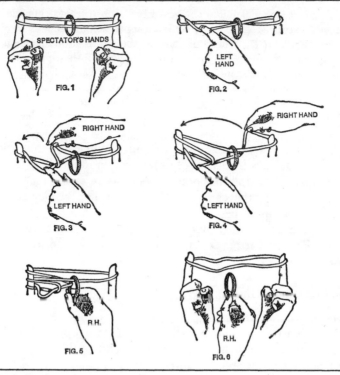

Plate 9.7: Escape Ring Trick

The two fingers represent two different participants in the evaluation process. One finger represents the evaluator, and the other finger represents the person or persons who will use the evaluation for decision making. The two lines of string formed by the loop represent the two-way flow of communication that is established between the evaluator and program decision makers during the evaluation process. The ring moves freely back and forth between the fingers along the lines of string [step 1], such that the ring represents the information that passes back and forth between evaluators and decision makers throughout the evaluation process.

The evaluator moves the ring back and forth a couple of times and then performs the trick while saying:

The utilization of evaluation findings depends on this smooth flow of information between evaluators and decision makers. Unfortunately, the lines of communication often get mixed, obstructed, entangled, or otherwise twisted. [The loops are overlapped at this point as shown in steps 2-4, Plate 9.7.] When this happens the information that should be going back and forth gets lost or diverted, sometimes slipping away so unobtrusively that there isn't even a trace afterwards that the lines of communication had been completely severed. The information is gone [and the ring is magically slipped from the string, step 5, leaving an empty loop and nothing to move back and forth between the two poles, step 6].

The trick takes only a couple of minutes, but I find that it leaves a powerful visual imprint of unused or lost evaluation findings, an imprint that can be recalled at any point by simply referring to "the ring of evaluation findings that can so easily slip away, like the magical ring that you saw slip away earlier."

For those of you interested in expanding your creative evaluation repertoire to include magic tricks, a good beginning primer is Wright (1976).

Visual Evaluation Data

The preceding sections have presented examples of how picture-thinking and visual communications can help people understand and relate to evaluation concepts, processes, and problems. This section briefly addresses the second contribution of picturethinking in evaluation: the collection of visual images of programs as part of the overall data collection in an evaluation. Photographs, videotapes, and films can be important sources of qualitative data on programs (Patton, 1980, p. 166). Patricia Templin (1979) has been working on the uses of photography in evaluation. She has also used photography to study evaluation. The April 1980 issue of the Northwest Regional Educational Laboratory newsletter *Research on Evaluation Program* presents the beginning of her study of the 1979 Evaluation Network national meeting through photographs. She worked under the assumption that "visual information available in settings chosen as sites of program evaluations can inform our appraisal of a situation" (Templin, 1980, p. 6).

Eminent sociologist and qualitative methodologist Howard Becker wrote in 1979 that "visual social science isn't something brand new . . . , but it might as well be."

It is only in the last eight or ten years that a sufficient number of people have had a joint interest in the two fields to create the critical mass of some real progress to be made. One advantage of a field which has just reached that state is that there has not been time for standard procedures and paradigms to get established. As a result, people come into the work with a variety of backgrounds, training, and experience, of necessity make a great variety of experiments (almost anything you do is an experiment at this stage), and the ratio of novel ideas, procedures, and results to the total volume of work produced is very high. The complementary disadvantage is that it is all very confusing, so that it is at present a field for people who can tolerate disorder. (Becker, 1979, p. 7)

The issues involved in visual evaluation data are the same issues of validity, reliability, accuracy, confidentiality, propriety, and utilization that are central to any kind of data. Experienced visual social scientist Jon Wagner (1979) offers a number of suggestions for "avoiding error" in photographic data that are applicable to evaluation studies:

- Use several photographers.
- Photograph from preplanned scripts to provide a basis for inclusion and selection.
- Assess photographs in light of other data.
- Make randomized exposures to supplement personal, subjective, and purposeful sampling.
- Use several analysts in the analysis of visual data.
- Edit analytically to "assess the contribution of each photograph to statements about the whole set" while also "trying to say different things with the same set of images" (Wagner, 1979, p. 153).
- Examine random samples of photographs.
- Code photographs and perform systematic content analysis of visual data.

Photographs can serve two major, but quite different, purposes as evaluation data. Visual data can be (1) systematically collected and analyzed to *learn about* program implementation and outcomes and/or (2) used to illustrate and communicate findings established through more conventional data collection and analysis techniques. The journals *Afterimage* and *Studies in the Anthropology of Visual Communications* are excellent resources for the evaluator who wants to pursue picture-thinking for either of these purposes.

The Evaluator As Artist

Elliot Eisner has developed an image of the evaluator as artistic connoisseur. An artistic approach to evaluation involves expert judgment based on qualitative inquiry that is openly and explicitly subjective. The result is an evaluation of a program that takes the form of art. It is art to the extent that it constitutes a "qualitative whole . . . that has the capacity to evoke in the intelligent perception a kind of experience that leads us to call the work art" (Eisner, 1979, p. 190).

The subjectivity of Eisner's evaluation has been the subject of considerable attack. But for Eisner, the evaluation issue is not one of objectivity but rather one of capturing essence. The criterion to be applied in such cases is not whether the artistic criticism of the evaluator is "true" but rather whether it is useful by contributing to understandings of and communications about a program. Thus Eisner holds forth a creative vision of the evaluator as artistic connoisseur. "What is needed is to see more precisely how artistic vision is integrated into the process of conceptual and empirical analysis as they function within the context of evaluation" (Alexander, 1986, p. 270).

Beyond Limited Vision

Unlike Chapter 5, this chapter is not metaphorical or allegorical. I have not been discussing how being an evaluator is *like* being an artist, or how the process of evaluating a program is *like* the process of painting a picture (Gephart, 1979, 1980; Seefeldt, 1980). This chapter is about evaluators as artists, performers, visual communicators, and image creators.

This chapter merely hints at the possibilities of expanding our vision—and visualizations—in evaluation. As a communications medium and as a source of data, the world of pictures, and all the many forms picturethinking can take, represents both an outlet and an inlet for creative evaluation. Picturethinking is a way of *see*ing the world and also of helping others *see* the world. The possibilities include new ways of gathering data and new ways of reporting data. On the reporting side, I understand that at least one evaluator has already delivered a report entirely in pantomime. Then there is the suggestion from Robert Brown, reported in the Spring 1979 Evaluation Network newsletter, that evaluation reports literally be paintings.

> In this way reports would surely get more notice than they do at present. They could be hung on the walls in the school cafeteria. We could, of course, still maintain our different schools of evaluation, with responsive evaluators painting impressionistically while systems people could paint by the numbers. (Evaluation News, 1979, p. 9).

NOTE

1. My thanks to Lee Edwards of the U.S. General Accounting Office for introducing me to this exercise.

CHAPTER 10: *Storythinking*

> *"Tut, tut, child," said the Duchess.*
> *"Everything's got a moral if only you*
> *can find it."*

> Lewis Carroll

Storythinking is the art of drawing morals from a good tale or case example. Storythinking is a time-honored tradition in all cultures, a technique used by teachers throughout the ages and around the world to get a point across to students. While the moral may not always be remembered, the good story will be, and upon recalling the story the teacher hopes the point of the story may also sneak back into consciousness.

In seminars I will sometimes ask students to think of some children's story and draw an evaluation point or moral from it. Initially skeptical, the students soon get into the exercise and surprise themselves at the associations they can make and the meanings hidden within those seemingly simple children's tales. But then, most traditional fairytales and classic children's literature were written for purposes of education, political satire, spiritual reflection, or all three.

One common example is the story of Little Red Riding Hood. What approach to evaluation is exemplified as Little Red Riding Hood makes observations about the wolf and gathers data to draw the conclusion that things are not what they should be with grandmother? Or what evaluation roles are represented by the characters in the story? I've heard interesting comparisons drawn between evaluators and the wolf ("trying to disguise being big, bad, ugly, and mean by appearing in grandmother's clothes"). The evaluator as Little Red Riding Hood is innocent, bewildered, and slow to recognize the obvious. The grandmother is the evaluator held captive or hostage by a powerful program administrator or funder, or the evaluator's role being usurped by same.

One can have similar fun with other stories: Alice in Wonderland as evaluators (or program staff) who don't know where they are or where they're going; the White Rabbit worried only about meeting deadlines, always in a hurry, popping in and out; the Queen as the authoritarian evaluator reaching a verdict before hearing any evidence. Dr. Seuss stories are particularly rich with allegory and potential for analogy (*Sneeches, Zaks,* and *Empty Pants* are my favorites). Then, of course, there is the rich tradition of Sufi stories and other folk tales that can be used to apply ancient wisdom to the new discipline of evaluation.

One of my favorite stories was often told by Gregory Bateson in his lectures. It's the story of attempts to create a computer that could think. Two scientists became particularly enthralled with this idea and devoted their lives to it. Each time, their efforts failed the critical tests and they had to go back to the drawing board trying again to make the breakthrough that would lead to thinking computers.

At last they thought they had it. They had made revisions based on all their prior failures and they felt certain that this time they would succeed. The moment for the critical test came and the two scientists asked the computer, "Can you think like a human being?"

The tapes on the computer rolled, the computer processed the question, and milliseconds later the computer printed an answer. The two scientists anxiously read what the computer had printed. It said:

THAT QUESTION REMINDS ME OF A STORY

They knew then they had succeeded (Bateson, 1977).

A good story or case example lends itself to multiple meanings, allows the teacher to make many different points depending on the occasion. The story that follows, "History's First Evaluation," was originally published in *Qualitative Evaluation Methods* (Patton, 1980) to make a point about the adaptability of research designs. In this chapter the same story will be used instead to illustrate the major points encompassed in the processes of conducting a utilization-focused evaluation, and then again to illustrate the philosophical issues that can emerge in asking the question, To evaluate or not to evaluate?

History's First Evaluation

The young people gathered around Halcolm. "Tell us again, Teacher of Many Things, about the first evaluation."

"The first evaluation was conducted a long, long time ago," he began. "It happened in Ancient Babylon when Nebuchadnezzar was King. Nebuchadnezzar had just conquered Jerusalem in the third year of the reign of Jehoiakim, King of Judah. Now, Nebuchadnezzar was a shrewd ruler. He decided to bring carefully selected children of Israel into the palace for special training so that they might be more easily integrated into Chaldean culture. This special program was the forerunner of the compensatory education programs that would become so popular in the twentieth century. The three-year program was royally funded with special allocations and scholarships provided by Nebuchadnezzar. The ancient text from the Great Book records that

> the King spake unto Asphenaz the master of his eunuchs that he should bring certain of the children of Israel, and of the King's seed, and of the princes;
>
> Children in whom was no blemish, but well-favored and skillful in all wisdom, and cunning in knowledge, and understanding science, and such as had ability in them to stand in the King's palace, and whom they might teach the learning and the tongue of the Chaldeans.
>
> And the King appointed them a daily provision of the King's meat, and of the wine which he drank: so nourishing them for three years, that at the end thereof they might stand before the King. (Daniel 1:3-5)

"Now this program had scarcely been established when the king found himself faced with a student rebellion led by a radical named Daniel who decided for religious reasons that he would not consume the king's meat and wine. This created a real problem for the program administrator who was responsible to the king. If Daniel and his co-conspirators did not eat their dormitory food they might fare poorly in the program and endanger not only future program funding but also the program director's head! The Great Book says:

> But Daniel purposed in his heart that he would not defile himself with the portion of the King's meat, nor with the wine which he drank; therefore he requested of the prince of the eunuchs that he might not defile himself.
>
> And the prince of the eunuchs said unto Daniel, I fear for my lord the King, who hath appointed your meat and your drink; for why should he see your faces worse liking than the children which are of your sort? Then shall ye make me endanger my head to the King. (Daniel 1: 8, 10)

"At this point, Daniel proposed history's first educational experiment and program evaluation. He and three friends would be placed on a strict vegetarian diet for ten days (nothing but pulse and water), while other students continued on the king's rich diet of meat and wine. At the end of ten days the program director would inspect the treatment group for any signs of physical deterioration and judge the productivity of Daniel's alternative diet plan. As Daniel described the experiment:

> Prove thy servants, I beseech thee, ten days; and let them give us pulse to eat, and water to drink.
>
> Then let our countenances be looked upon before thee, and the countenance of the children that eat of the portion of the king's meat: and as though seest, deal with thy servants.
>
> So he consented to them in this matter, and proved them ten days. (Daniel 1:12-14)

"During the ten days of waiting Aspenaz had a terrible time. He couldn't sleep; he had no appetite; and he had trouble working because he was preoccupied with worrying about how the evaluation would turn out. He had a lot at stake. Besides, in those days they hadn't quite worked out the proper division of labor so he had to play the roles of both program director and evaluator. You see . . ."

The young listeners interrupted Halcolm. They sensed that he was about to launch into a sermon on the origins of the division of labor when they still wanted to hear the end of the story about the origins of evaluation. "How did it turn out?" they asked. "Did Daniel end up looking better or worse from the new diet? Did Aspenaz lose his head?"

"Patience, patience," Halcolm pleaded. "Aspenaz had no reason to worry. The results were quite amazing. The Great Book says that

> at the end of ten days their countenances appeared fairer and fatter in flesh than all the children which did eat the portion of the King's meat.
>
> Thus Melzar took away the portion of their meat, and the wine that they should drink; and gave them pulse.
>
> As for these four children, God gave them knowledge and skill in all learning and wisdom; and Daniel had understanding in all visions and dreams.
>
> Now at the end of the days that the King had said he should bring them in, then the prince of the eunuchs brought them in before Nebuchadnezzar.

And in all matters of wisdom and understanding, that the King inquired of them, he found them ten times better than all the magicians and astrologers that were in all his realm. (Daniel 1: 15-18)

"And that, my children, is the story of the first evaluation. Those were the good ole days, when evaluations really got used. Made quite a difference to Aspenaz and Daniel. Now off with you—and see if you can do as well." (This story is from Halcolm's *Evaluation Histories*.)

THE POINT OF A GOOD STORY IS . . .

A good story will often have multiple layers of meaning and permit the making of more than one point. A story may have meanings for listeners that are unanticipated by the storyteller. In any case, it is important to make sure that your audience understands what *you* intend to communicate with a story. You can do this either before or after you've asked them for their interpretations of the point of the story. I prefer to get *their* interpretations and meanings before adding or elaborating my own point. A good story is worth some discussion time. It's important *not* to assume that listeners understand the reason you told the story. While the point of the story may be quite obvious to you, listeners may infer a quite different (and contrary) point from the story you've told.

In the pages that follow I shall elaborate three quite different lines of thought about evaluation that can be drawn from the story "History's First Evaluation." First, I shall use the story to illustrate the major principles or points of utilization-focused evaluation. Second, I shall focus on the design and measurement approaches illustrated in that historical first evaluation in ancient Babylon. Third, and last, I shall use the story to introduce a distinction between instrumental and intrinsic goals. These examples are meant to illustrate the power of storytelling and storythinking as part of the repertoire of creative evaluators.

Utilization-Focused Evaluation

In reading this story at workshops I ask the participants to identify the factors that appear to be related to the high degree of utilization that took place in history's first evaluation. After a bit of discussion something like the following points will emerge.

First, *the intended users of evaluative information are clearly identified and involved at every stage in making decisions about the evaluation.* After hearing me use this story in a workshop for the Government Accounting Office, Lee Edwards of GAO constructed Chart 10.1, which shows the potential stakeholders in this evaluation. Clearly, not all those stakeholders actually became involved in the evaluation. Given the particular situation that emerged in the story, the information was intended to be used only by Aspenaz and Daniel. They were the principal information users and they were the ones who conceptualized the evaluation, designed it, interpreted the data, and applied the findings.

Second, *the decision makers and information users negotiated the precise nature and content of the evaluation.* Daniel and Melzar discussed the primary decision to be made, the information needed for making that decision, and the design that would give them that information. It was a shared decision-making process. Reading between the lines a bit, I suspect that considerable negotiating was involved in arriving at the final design. I imagine Daniel proposing a six-month trial period with Melzar suggesting that they initially try the changed diet for only two days; Daniel counters with a request for three months and Melzar moves up to five days; Daniel pleads for at least a six-week trial and Melzar offers him ten days, "Take it or leave it." Daniel then proposes an independent panel of judges to inspect the countenances of the students and Melzar responds that it's his head (or other part of his anatomy) at stake so he'll gather the data himself. These negotiations, in a situation where power was not altogether balanced, led to the final design as it is recorded for history.

Third, *the evaluation was clearly focused.* There are a number of potential areas of study in this program. A longitudinal evaluation involves student achievement. There are also some implicit socialization and acculturation criteria. It would be possible to study student satisfaction, student cooperation, cognitive outcomes, affective outcomes, and so on. But the evaluation is very specifically focused on changes in the countenance of the students. It's information about countenance that Melzar and Daniel identify as the critical information needed for making a decision about the change in diet.

Fourth, *the evaluation question is clearly focused in terms of action, decision, and utilization.* Before any data are collected it is clear that Melzar and Daniel have agreed on what actions will be taken based upon the potential outcomes of the study. If there is a deterioration in the countenances in any of the four students, the students will remain on

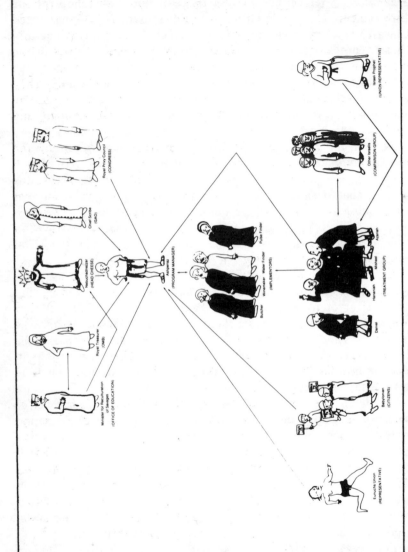

Plate 11.1: Stakeholder Environment for History's First Evaluation

a wine and meat diet. If there is no deterioration in countenance, or if the countenance is actually improved (a largely unexpected outcome) then the diet will be changed to allow the students to partake of pulse and water. *The decision framework is clearly cast before data collection.*

Fifth, *the methods and measures being used for the evaluation have credibility with and are understandable to the people who will use the information for decision making.* This credibility and understandability are direct consequences of their involvement in making the evaluation decisions. Melzar clearly trusted his own judgment in this matter, but Daniel also had to decide to trust Melzar's judgment or else the evaluation would not have had credibility with Daniel and his compan ions, and they would not have accepted the evaluation results.

Sixth, *the methods were appropriate to the evaluation question being asked.* This point takes us into the area of methodological quality and the meaning of methodological appropriateness, points that can be elaborated in their own right without attention to the utilization factors listed above. In the next section the example of "History's First Evaluation" is used to illustrate this methodological point.

Methodological Quality and Appropriateness

A meta-evaluation

A meta-evaluation is an evaluation of an evaluation. A great deal can be learned about evalution designs by conducting a meta-evaluation of history's first program evaluation. Let us imagine a panel of experts conducting a rigorous critique of this evaluation of Babylon's compensatory education program for Israeli students.

(1) Small sample size (N = 4).
(2) Selectivity bias since recruitment into the program was done by "creaming," that is, only the best prospects among the children of Israel were brought into the program to begin with.
(3) Selectivity bias because students were self-selected into the treatment group.
(4) Failure to specify and control the nature of the treatment clearly, thus allowing for the possibility of treatment contamination. We don't know what other things besides a change in diet either group was involved in that might explain the outcomes observed.
(5) Possibility of interaction effects between the diet and the students' belief system and/or relationship to God.

(6) Outcome criteria vague.

(7) Measures of outcomes poorly operationalized and nonstandardized.

(8) Single observer with deep personal involvement in the program introduces possibility of selective perception and bias in the observations.

(9) Validity and reliability data are not reported for the instruments used to measure the final, summative outcome ("he found them ten times better than all the magicians and astrologers . . . ").

(10) Possible reactive effects from the students' knowledge that they were being evaluated.

Despite all of these threats to internal validity, not to mention external validity, the information generated by the evaluation appears to have been used to make a major decision about the program. Indeed, it is difficult to find a more exemplary model for the utilization of research in making educational policy decisions than that first evaluation conducted under the auspices of Nebuchadnezzar so many years ago. Immediately following determination of the evaluation results a policy decision was made to allow Daniel and friends to maintain their diet of pulse and water. The longitudinal indicators collected over the three-year period suggest that the decision was appropriate; Daniel did place first in his class.

To my knowledge there is no better example of evaluation research having an immediate, decisive, and lasting impact on educational policy. Modern evaluation researchers, flailing away in seemingly futile efforts to affect contemporary government decision makers, can be forgiven a certain nostalgia for the "good old days" in Babylon when evaluation research really made a difference. *But should the results have been used?* Given the apparent weakness of the evaluation design, was it appropriate to make a major policy decision on the basis of data generated by such a weak research design?

I would argue that not only was utilization exemplary in this case, but that the research design was also exemplary. The evaluation design was exemplary because the study was set up in such a way as to provide precisely the information needed by the program director to make the decision he needed to make. Certainly, it is a poor research design to study the relationship between nutrition and educational achievement. It is even a poor design to decide if *all* students should be placed on a vegetarian diet. But those were not the issues. The question that the program director had to deal with was whether or not to place four specific students on a special diet at their request. The information he needed concerned the consequences of that specific change and only that specific change. He showed no interest in generalizing the results beyond those four students, and he showed no interest in convincing others that the measures he made were valid and reliable. He was the only person who had to trust the measures used, and so data collection was designed in such a way as to maximize his belief in the meaningfulness of the observations. If any bias existed in his observations, given what he had at stake, the bias would have operated against a demonstration of positive outcomes rather than in favor of such outcomes.

While there are hints of the whimsical in the suggestion that this first evaluation is exemplary, I do not mean to be facetious. I am absolutely serious in suggesting that the Babylonian example is an exemplar of utilization-focused evaluation. The decision maker who was to use information generated by the evaluation was clearly identified and deeply involved in every stage of the evaluation process. The evaluation question was carefully focused on needed information that could be used in the making of specific decisions. The evelution methods and design were appropriately matched to the evaluation question. The results were understandable, credible, and relevant. Feedback was immediate and utilization was decisive. Few modern evaluations can meet the high standards for evaluation set by Aspenaz and Daniel several thousand years ago.

The next section discusses yet another point about program evaluations that can be drawn from this story of history's first evaluation.

Means and ends

As noted in the previous section, evaluators can be forgiven a certain nostalgia for the "good ole days" in Babylon when evaluation research really made a difference. But, alas, a high-level commitment to making programmatic decisions on the basis of explicit and observable productivity criteria can be a mixed blessing.

What if Daniel's experiment had failed to produce the desired results? Suppose God had decided to test Daniel, as he tested Job, allowing the experiment to fail so that Daniel's commitment rather than his diet could be put to the empirical test? Would Daniel have capitulated in the face of statistically significant results showing that his diet of pulse and water was detrimental to his appearance? Indeed, did Daniel's very participation in the experiment obligate him as well as his masters to abide by the results? Or would Daniel have maintained that the issue was not the outcomes achieved by different diets, but rather the righteousness of the diet itself?

The modern equivalent of these questions can be found in virtually all contemporary education and human service programs. Is desegregation of schools to be evaluated on the basis of its effectiveness as a method for increasing minority achievement test scores or is desegregation of schools an end in itself desired because it is right regardless of its effects on student achievement? Is educational mainstreaming a means of improving the educational achievement of disabled children or is it promoted because of its intrinsic value? In the area of criminal justice, are community corrections programs for juvenile offenders to be evaluated according to their effectiveness in reducing recidivism—or have we as a society simply decided that it is wrong to incarcerate young people despite the potential deterrent value of prisons? Are community mental health programs to be evaluated in comparison to state institutions using cost-effectiveness criteria—or are community mental health programs to be judged on intrinsic value because it is inhumane to lock people away in institutions?

In effect, these questions suggest a critical distinction between two different kinds of program goals. Some program goals symbolize the very values and principles of a society. Such goals are ideals to strive for because they represent basic notions of what is good and right. These goals are ends in themselves. The second category of goals is more instrumental in nature. These represent a means of attaining more basic ideals. Instrumental goals represent the methods by which higher-level ideals are to be achieved.

In evaluation research and policy analysis this distinction between intrinsically valued goals and instrumental goals can be critical. Goals that express intrinsic values imply evaluations that focus on program implementation questions (see Patton, 1978, pp. 149-178)—and *only* implementation questions. If Daniel's diet of pulse and water had been intrinsically valued because it was "*right*," then the only evaluation question would have been whether he was getting the diet he wanted. The diet would not be required or expected to accomplish any specific objectives, that is, there would have been no effectiveness criteria like improved countenance by which to judge the diet because the diet would be perceived as an end in itself. Likewise, where humane or humanistic treatment of criminal offenders in prison is *right* in itself, the only legitimate evaluation question is the extent to which the program is humane or humanistic (an implementation question). Such a program cannot fairly be evaluated in terms of the extent to which it reduces recidivism. Treating criminal offenders humanely becomes an end in itself. Similarly, programs of racial integration require only implementation evaluation (Has integration been achieved?) when integration is intrinsically valued as good in itself. Student achievement scores are not an issue in such cases.

By way of contrast, instrumental goals focus on effectiveness measures. If Daniel's diet was to be instrumental in improving his countenance, then the evaluation must clearly examine changes in his countenance. Under the instrumental scenario the diet has no particular intrinsic worth; it is simply a means to the end of improved countenance. Similarly, if the reason for treating criminal offenders humanely is to reduce recidivism, then the evaluation appropriately measures recidivism.

The problem is that many policymakers want it both ways. They value racial integration intrinsically, but they also want integration to raise black achievement. Suppose then that integration does not raise black achievement scores; Is the policy of integration to be ended? That is the clear implication of an instrumental approach. On the other hand, if integration is simply right and good, then an evaluation of its effects on school achievement should not enter into decisions about continuation of the policy. Data about outcomes only become relevant as they permit implementation and process changes in the integration policy that might maintain the intrinsic commitment while also accomplishing instrumental objectives. But this game of trying to make *both* instrumental and intrinsic arguments in support of a policy at a single point in time can be quite dangerous. It is much harder to fall back on intrinsic worth when instrumental worth has failed than simply to refuse from the outset to even allow instrumental criteria (recidivism or school achievement) to enter the picture. Of course, taking the gamble that racial integration or humane treatment of offenders or whatever will be supported for *both* reasons of intrinsic worth and instrumental value is what leads to so many situations where negative outcomes (that is, failure to attain the desired instrumental results) are dismissed as irrelevant *after* the evaluation. At that point supporters of the program shift from instrumental arguments (the program is effective in attaining desired outcomes) to arguments that the program is intrinsically valuable—the evaluation results be damned. As with any gamble, in the game of evaluation the skilled players know the value of Kenny Rogers's advice about poker:

> You got to know when to hold them,
> Know when to fold them,
> Know when to walk away,
> And know when to run.

"The Gambler" (1979)

Whether to support a program, when to support a program, how to support a program, when to end a program, and how to end a program are all matters of calculation involving risks, skill, high stakes, and a chance that the evaluation results will deal program supporters a losing hand. The risks can be reduced by calculating *in advance* which evaluation game to play—whether to take an instrumental approach, an approach built on intrinsic worth, or chance looking at the program on both instrumental and intrinsic criteria. The evaluator's role in such discussions is to make clear the utilization implications and potential of different approaches in an attempt to minimize the risk of new or different criteria for judgment being introduced after the evaluation has been completed.

CREATIVE STORYTELLING

This chapter has attempted to illustrate how a good story can be used to make a number of different points. The story of Daniel and "History's First Evaluation" was used to (1) illustrate some of the major factors that influence utilization of evaluation findings; (2) show how evaluation methods flow from the evaluation question(s) being asked; and (3) explain and elucidate the distinction between instrumental and intrinsically valued goals.

Stories can be particularly effective for communicating with groups who are not familiar with evaluation terminology or are put off by jargon. As English professor and "underground grammarian" Richard Mitchell has observed:

> Our knowledge is made up of the stories we can tell, stories that must be told in the language that we know.... *Where we can tell no story, we have no knowledge.* (Mitchell, 1979, p. 34; emphasis added)

Mitchell goes on to confirm the point made by Bateson's thinking computer story at the beginning of this chapter: Telling stories is part of the unique and essential nature of being human. He even suggests that the ability to communicate through stories was a critical advantage in the evolutionary process of natural selection. He suggests that creatures who have language and can tell stories can survive "even if they have bad noses and short, stumpy legs." They can tell each other stories about the dangers they've faced, the successes they've experienced, and the lions they've encountered.

> We could tell ourselves the story of the last time we passed this way and lost Gbloog to a lion. Even more important, we could invent the story of the *next* time and either be prepared for a lion or decide to take the long way around. (Mitchell, 1979, p. 35)

There are lion stories and other survival tales to be told in evaluation. Stories can help us tell about the lion that was and anticipate the lion that will be, even invent a story about the lion that *might* be under conditions yet to be encountered. Creative storythinking, then, is part of the survival kit of evaluation explorers.

A concern that is sometimes raised against storythinking is that a selected story always represents a biased sample of events. For every story illustrating one point, there is a corresponding story illustrating another point. This argument confuses case sampling with storythinking. In using stories as case examples for *teaching purposes* one does not presume to have chosen a representative sample, a random sample, or even to be conducting an empirically based study. A story or case example should not be used to attempt to *prove* something. Certainly, when one enters the game of proofs, for each story that illustrates one point there is another that illustrates the opposite point. Stories do not constitute proofs of the way the world is; rather, they represent *illustrations* of points a teacher wants to communicate to students or others. The case of Daniel and "History's First Evaluation" does not prove that the factors identified as related to utilization do indeed explain why utilization of the findings occurred as they did. The purpose of telling the story is to illustrate empirical findings that have been verified in other research conducted for the purpose of verification. Thus it is important not to confuse the use of stories for illustrative purposes with the use of stories as logical or empirical proofs.

Storythinking and storytelling are learned competences. For those of you interested in further developing and refining these competences, I recommend studying some of the fine collected volumes of fables, tales, proverbs, and stories with special attention and openness to how such tales can be applied to evaluation and what these stories reveal about the nature of evaluative processes. I find that Sufi stories are superb in this regard. Having originated in the East, Sufi stories have been finding appreciative audiences in the West, particularly through the writings of one of the master storythinking Sufi teachers, Idries Shah. Sufi stories are used to bridge "the gap between the mundane life and a transmutation of consciousness in a manner which no other literary form yet has been able to attain"(Shah, 1964, p. 56). It is a literary form that is at once deductive and inductive, in harmony with both scientific ways of knowing and intuitive understandings of the world.

> The "inner dimensions" of teaching stories are held to make them capable of revealing, according to the stage of development of the student, more and more planes of significance.

> It is this theory that "one may work on different layers of the same material" which is unfamiliar to many people, who tend to prefer being told that a story has one message or one use only. (Shah, 1968, p. 197)

Idries Shah has worked for over 35 years in tracing, collecting, and studying the world's treasury of meaningful tales. He has published 16 volumes of Sufi stories and explications of Sufi storytelling/storythinking (Shah, 1964, 1968, 1971, 1972a, 1972b, 1973). In 1979 he published *World Tales*, which contains 65 stories that have persisted and endured through time and culture—tales representing "a certain basic fund of human fictions which recur, again and again, and never seem to lose their compelling attraction" (Shah, 1979, p. vii).

The point of this chapter is that the "compelling attraction" of fables and tales applies to evaluators and those with whom they work no less than with other people, both children and adults. *The multiple layers of stories can help reveal the multiple layers of evaluation.* In Shah's *Learning How to Learn* (1978), he examines the recurring themes of the Sufi literature and the ways in which storytelling brings the listener into intimate contact with the personal relevance of those themes. Many of the chapters could be from an evaluation text, and the stories in those chapters have immediate application to the world of evaluation:

Attaining Knowledge
When to Have Meetings
Conflicting Texts

Self-Deception
Secrecy
How Serious Is the Student?
Characteristics of Attention and Observation
Motivation of Transactions
Identification of Underlying Factors
Assumptions Behind Action
When Criticism Can Stop
Information and Experience
The Would-Be and Should-Be People
Real and Ostensible Self-Improvement
Confusion
Systems
The Vehicle and the Objective
Use, Misuse, and Disuse of Forms of Study
How Can One Method Be as Good as Another?
A Viable Unit
Intensely Standardized
Direct Contact with a Source of Knowledge
Latent Knowledge
Provoking Capacity
Systematic Study
Consistency and System
Illumination and Information
Habit of Judging
Higher-Level Work
Opinion and Fact
Learning and Nonlearning
Impartiality as a Point of View
Jumping to Conclusions
Explanation

This is but a sampling of the kinds of issues that Shah finds running through the world's treasury of fables, tales, and stories. He has found that there is a growing receptivity to storythinking in the West:

We have had to re-open the question of the possible value of tales, stories, jokes and narrative, and hold this door open in the face of a long-standing Western convention that such material is only of entertainment value. What has happened is that the equivalent of a technological infra-structure, or a basic literacy in this field, is being established in the West. (Shah, 1978, p. 101)

Basic literacy in storythinking is still limited, however. More than one reviewer of my evaluation writings has expressed annoyance at my frequent use of stories and proverbs in academic papers and texts. One external reviewer of a draft of this book wrote the publisher:

> Michael makes good use of anecdotes, examples, stories, etc., although he tends to include so many that I find them distracting and ultimately a nuisance.

My harshest critics in this regard are academic evaluation colleagues who want me to "get on to the point." Such critics, in my opinion, lack literacy in storythinking and have cut themselves off from a major source of wisdom about the world—a source of wisdom with multiple layers and multiple meanings demanding creative interpretation and application from the listener/reader. Perhaps that is the basis of their frustration, antipathy, and impatience, believing as they often seem to that there is some single point that one is supposed to get.

Finally, I find that there is a humanizing quality to storytelling that helps make evaluation less ominous, impersonal, and strictly *scientific*. The image of the evil, cold-hearted, and uncaring evaluator tends to evaporate with a reading from Dr. Seuss, Mother Goose, Hans Christian Andersen, the Brothers Grimm, or Aesop.

There are many sources one can turn to in seeking inspiration, or one may just playfully take up the challenge of looking for contemporary advice applicable to evaluation in stories written for other purposes. By selecting fables from a particular culture it is possible to help make the connection between that culture and the "culture" of evaluation. Courlander's *Treasury of Afro-American Folklore* (1976), Radin's *The Trickster* (1972), a collection of American Indian tales, and James's *Japanese Fairy Tales* (1980) are rich resources for making cultural connections in evaluation work. For those who prefer science fiction as their source of inspiration and/or wisdom, the collection by Silverberg and Greenberg (1980) is a place to start. Other materials I have found especially useful and stimulating are Pierre Delattre's *Tales of a Dalai Lama* (1978), *Beelzebub's Tales to His Grandson* (3 volumes) by Gurdjieff (1973), and standard collections of tales by Kingsley (1980), Kipling (1980), Steel (1980), and LaFontaine (1979), whose mid-seventeenth-century observation about tellers of tales is still apt:

> Art being our inheritance, we're in debt
> To ancient Greece for the fable-form; and yet

The field has not been harvested so clean
That late arrivers can't find ears to glean,
For the world of fiction's full of virgin spaces,
And every day our authors plant new places.

(La Fontaine, 1979, p. 63.)

Story Boarding

The "Story Board" is the centerpiece of creativity consultant Mike Vance's package for working with major corporation executives and managers to increase their creative thinking. Vance was part of the Walt Disney organization in the 1960s when the Story Board technique was developed.

The Story Board is a group creativity technique. A large wall or board is needed on which the group participants can turn their ideas into a story. As ideas for a project—or evaluation—unfold, they can be arranged in order on the wall or board until the complete story has been written from beginning to end. Tracing the coherence of the "story" helps to identify gaps where more detail is needed to make the story work.

> Story Boarding can be likened to taking your thoughts and the thoughts of others and spreading them out on a wall as you work on a project or attempt to solve a problem. When you put ideas up on Story Boards, you begin to see interconnections—you see how one idea relates to another, how all the pieces come together.
>
> Story Boarding demands a high level of participation on everyone's part. But undoubtedly, once the ideas start flowing, those working with the Story Board will become immersed in the problem, in finding its solution. And they will begin to "hitchhike on," or embellish, each other's ideas. (Vance, 1982, pp. 16-17)

Your Own Storythinking Patterns

Storythinking can be a powerful means of assisting understanding and creating new insights. Storythinking can be one of the options and tools in the repertoire of the creative and strategic evaluator. Is it an option you exercise as well and as often as you might? Is it a tool you use consciously and adeptly? Let me suggest that you take some time to examine your own storythinking and storytelling heuristics, patterns, and competencies. In what situations and under what conditions do you

A TALE OF SITUATIONAL ADAPTABILITY

While I was working on this chapter my 13-year-old son asked me what I was writing. I took his question as an opportunity to test the premise that once one has something to say, an appropriate story to illustrate the point can be adapted from existing fables. I briefly explained the idea of situational responsiveness and adaptability. I then asked him if any classic tales seemed to fit what I was trying to get at. Twenty minutes later he returned with the following story.

The Tortoise and the Hare:
A Fable About Situation Adaptability

by B.Q.T.P.

A hare was once born to very wealthy parents on an estate surrounded by lush forest. The mansion on the estate was equipped with an indoor gym. A special track ran around the boundary of the estate.

The young hare showed a flair for track and field. His parents hired the world's best hare coach who developed an intensive training schedule for the young hare. He soon knew every detail of the track—including every degree of each turn, the topography of its dips and hills, and even the cracks in the surface. He won all the major championships and boasted that he could beat anyone in the forest under any conditions whatsoever.

The only animal to come forth and accept the hare's challenge was an old tortoise. The hare was at first amused, then angry and insulted. The hare agreed to the challenge. The tortoise said simply, "Come what may, I shall do my best."

A huge outdoor course was created that stretched all the way around the forest. The two animals prepared themselves and then were signaled to start. The hare took off into the sunset flipping dust into the tortoise's eyes. The tortoise slowly meandered down the track.

Halfway through the race, clouds formed and it started to rain. The rabbit couldn't stand to see his $50.00 perm ruined, so he stopped for cover under a tree. The tortoise, on the other hand, decided that he needed to be flexible and adapt to getting a little wet by staying on track. "Come what may," he said, "I shall do my best."

After the rain lifted, the track was muddy, and the hare was again grounded for he refused to get his special $70.00 shoes muddy. For the tortoise, the mud made it hard to keep walking because of his short legs. "Come what may, I shall do my best." So he turned himself over and did the backstroke in the mud, and kept up his progress.

By and by, the tortoise passed the hare and won the race. The hare, who had given up, blamed his loss on "unfair conditions." But the tortoise had beaten the hare by adapting to the conditions as he found them. The hare, it turned out, was only a "good conditions" champion.

typically use stories? What are your resources for storyteaching? What are the strengths and weaknesses of your use of stories? Think back on the last time you used a story to illustrate a point you wanted to make, whether in a formal or informal setting. What heuristics did you employ? To what extent did you accomplish what you wanted to accomplish with the story? What might you have done differently? More effectively?

To further stimulate these reflections and to provide you with practice in using evaluation storythinking as part of your creative repertoire, I am closing this chapter with a parable from Halcolm about reducing uncertainty. It has many possible applications in thinking about program evaluation— or it may have none.

Reducing Uncertainty

A spirit appeared to a man walking along a narrow road. "You may know with certainty what has happened in the past, or you may know with certainty what will happen in the future, but you cannot know both. Which do you choose?"

The startled man sat down in the middle of the road to contemplate his choices. "If I know with certainty what will happen in the future," he reasoned to himself, "then the future will soon enough become the past and I will also know with certainty what has happened in the past. On the other hand, it is said that the past is prologue to the future so if I know with certainty what has happened in the past I will know much about what will happen in the future without losing the elements of surprise and spontaneity."

Deeply lost to the present in the reverie of his calculations about the past and future he was unaware of the sound of a truck approaching at great speed along the road. Just as he came out of his trance to tell the spirit that he had chosen to know with certainty the future, he looked up and saw the truck bearing down on him unable to stop its past momentum. (From Halcolm's *Evaluation Parables)*

CHAPTER 11: *Evaluation Alphabet Soup*

*There can be no acting or doing of any
kind, till it be recognized that there is a
thing to be done; the thing once
recognized, doing in a thousand shapes
becomes possible.*

Thomas Carlyle

Creativity does not typically flow from a vacuum. Some kind of stimulating structure or framework is often quite helpful. In attempting to help a group of students, workshop participants, or evaluation task force members generate options for evaluation a familiar framework may be useful to *force* thought. The organizing framework becomes a puzzle to which the participants provide the solutions. One of the most familiar of such organizing frameworks for forced brainstorming is the alphabet.

While discussing with Michael Scriven the origin of his ideas about "goal-free evaluation," he told me that his students had worked with him on a whole alphabet of ____-free evaluations:

> *A*nxiety-free evaluation
> *B*ias-free evaluation
> *C*ost-free evaluation
> etc.

The purpose of such an exercise is to get participants actively involved in generating options for themselves. The actual content and composition of an alphabet list is less important than the message being communicated to participants through the process: "We have the ability and knowledge to think up different evaluation approaches and create options for ourselves." This exercise also makes it clear that there are many, many different ways of thinking about and focusing an evaluation. There is no one, single right way to do an evaluation. Understanding that there are options and choices to be made is part of the foundation for actively involving stakeholders so that they know why their involvement is important—namely, that they are in the best position to decide what evaluation focus will best serve their interests. A suggestive alphabetical sample of 100 different evaluation emphases and options is listed at the end of this chapter.

Mnemonics and Acronyms

Another way of stimulating thinking, improving retention of evaluation ideas, and organizing training presentations is to devise evaluation mnemonics or acronyms. Instead of using the full alphabet to stimulate and force creative thinking, some particularly memorable word is identified, the letters of which stand for major evaluation concepts you wish to communicate.

One well-known mnemonic in evaluation is the "A VICTORY" model devised by Davis and Salasin (1975). This model identifies eight major factors that affect utilization of evaluations for program change. Salasin has called the A VICTORY model Howard Davis's "single greatest contribution" (Salasin, 1986, p. 216).

"A VICTORY" Model
of Factors Affecting
Evaluation Utilization
and Organizational Change

A—*Ability* to carry out the solution: staff, funds, space, sanctions
V—*Values* that give purpose, perceptions, and characteristics
I —*Idea* for proposed action step
C—*Circumstances* that prevail at the time
T—*Timing*
O—*Obligation*, the felt need or motivation
R—*Resistances* as they are relevant to the desired change
Y—*Yield*, or the rewards that the anticipated change may bring about

Howard Davis believed the A VICTORY model could be used for organizational diagnosis generally because of the generic nature of the model. In recently reviewing A VICTORY, Robert Rich concluded:

> The power of this tool is underappreciated. It can be used to diagnose and to predict change. It provides a framework of consultation within organizations. More important, it is helpful in identifying tractable versus intractable problems within organizations. (Rich, 1986, p. 205)

Making Up Your Own Acronyms

While mnemonics and acronyms can come across as overly contrived, experts on memory teach that these are powerful techniques for getting and holding our attention (see Anderson, 1980; Pollock, 1971; Silva, 1977). The "YCKE" story at the end of Chapter 8 is based on an acronym: *You Can't Know Everything.*

In introducing the idea of evaluation to new groups completely unfamiliar with the field, I will sometimes use the following mnemonic:

E	Evidence +
V	Values =
A	Action and
L	Long-term
U	Utilization
A	Aimed
T	Toward
E	Effectiveness

I once attended a combination feedback session/staff party that was billed as BYOB and BYOE (Bring Your Own Booze and Bring Your Own Excuses).

Still another approach is to build on a familiar framework, for example, the 3 Rs of education: readin', 'ritin', and 'rithmetic. But instead of three basics as in education, effective evaluations have six basics. The six basic Rs of effective evaluations are:

Responsive
Relevant
Realistic
Rigorous
Reliable
Readable

Metaphor Meets Mnemonic

As you become open to a variety of stimuli for thinking about evaluation, the spark of creativity may come from anywhere. On a consulting trip to Louisiana I became fascinated by the Bayou country and took a brief boat trip through part of the Bayou. Later, in the evaluation workshop I was doing in New Orleans, I found the Bayou had inspired my thinking about evaluation and allowed me to communicate with local people about utilization-focused evaluation with reference to their own geographical and cultural heritage. In response to a question about the effect of bias in evaluation, I responded:

> B   Bias
> A   Attenuates
> Y   Yield and
> O   Overturns
> U   Utilization

I then shared some thoughts about the difference between dissemination and utilization that were inspired by my trip through the Bayou.

BAYOU EVALUATIONS

The Bayou country of Louisiana is largely swampland and lowlands, much of it below sea level. It runs north of the Gulf some 200 miles in places. Folklore has it that the name comes from tidewater movements. Southern Louisiana folks would sit on their porches and watch the water rise past them, flowing north in the morning with the incoming tide and then flowing south again in the evening as the tide went out. As the old folks put it, "The water just goes *by you*," which, over the years, with the dialect of the area, became Bayou.

There is a similar phenomenon in evaluation. While the movements are less regular than the tides, and it would be the height of speculation to attribute the observed phenomenon to the effects of the moon, it is nevertheless clear that many evaluation reports flow back and forth across decision makers' desks without any of the contents ever settling into the consciousness of those decision makers or being translated into concrete actions on their parts.

A great many studies might well be called "Bayou Evaluations," caught in the ebb and flow of political and bureaucratic backwaters without ever catching a main current that is going somewhere.

APPENDIX

EVALUATION ALPHABET SOUP:
100 WAYS TO FOCUS AN EVALUATION

Specific Focus or Approach	Question Asked in this Type of Evaluation
1. Accessibility focus	To what extent and with what ease are clients able to actually obtain or gain access to program services?
2. Accreditation focus	Does the program meet the standards of the external accrediting organization?
3. Appropriateness focus	What services *should* clients be receiving? To what extent are current services *appropriate* to client needs?
4. Assets focus	What are the strengths of the program? What assets do clients bring to the program?
5. Attitude focus	What changes in attitudes, opinions, and thoughts occur as a result of participation in the program?
6. Audit focus	Is the program meeting accounting and contract obligations?
7. Awareness focus	Who knows about the program? What do they know?
8. Behaviors focus	What changes in client behaviors, actions, and observable performance occur as a result of the program?
9. Balance focus	What are the various viewpoints that exist about this program? What are strengths and weaknesses?
10. Causal focus	What variables explain and/or cause observed client outcomes?
11. Charitable focus	Are staff sincere in their efforts (regardless of whether or not they're actually doing anything worthwhile) (see Patton, 1986)?
12. Cognitive focus	What do participants *know* as a result of their program experiences?

13. Comparative focus	How does program A compare to program B?
14. Competency focus	What competencies are demonstrated by participants? Do participants meet minimal competency criteria?
15. Context focus	What contextual factors affect attainment of program goals?
16. Cost-benefit analysis	What is the relationship between program costs and program outcomes (benefits) expressed in dollars?
17. Cost-effectiveness evaluation	What is the relationship between program costs and outcomes (where outcomes are *not* measured in dollars)?
18. Criterion-referenced	To what extent has a specific objective been attained at the desired level of attainment (the criterion)?
19. Decision-focused	What information is needed to make a specific decision at a precise point in time?
20. Descriptive evaluation	What happens in the program? (No "why" questions or cause-effect analyses.)
21. Discrepancy evaluation	What differences are there between what we expect to be happening in the program and what is actually happening in the program?
22. Effectiveness evaluation	To what extent is the program effective in attaining its goals?
23. Efficiency focus	Can inputs be reduced and still obtain the same level of output or can greater output be obtained with no increase in inputs?
24. Effort focus	What are the inputs into the program in terms of number of personnel, staff-client ratios, and other descriptors of levels of activity and effort in the program?
25. Effortless evaluation 1 (staff/administration version)	What's the minimum we can do to meet requirements and still call what we've done an evaluation?
26. Effortless evaluation 2 (evaluator version)	What's the minimum amount of work the evaluator can do to fulfill the terms of the

	contract and make as much profit as possible?
27. Evaluability assessment	Is the program ready for a formal evaluation?
28. Extensiveness evaluation	To what extent is this program able to deal with the total problem? How does the present level of services compare to the needed level of services?
29. Extreme case focus	What has been the experience of clients who are unusually successful in the program? What has been the experience of clients who have failed in or dropped out of the program?
30. Experimental evaluation	How does the treatment group compare to a control (or comparison) group?
31. External evaluation	How can we get somebody else to do it?
32. Formative evaluation	How can the program be improved?
33. Goal attainment scaling	To what extent do individual clients attain individual goals on a standardized measurement scale of 1 (low attainment) to 5 (high attainment)?
34. Goals-based evaluation	To what extent have program goals been attained?
35. Goal-free evaluation	What are the *actual* effects of the program on clients (without regard to what staff say they want to accomplish)?
36. Hypothesis-testing focus	Is there a statistically significant difference between two groups on specific outcome dependent variables?
37. Impact evaluation	What are the direct and indirect program impacts on the larger community of which it is a part?
38. Internal evaluation	How can we do it ourselves?
39. Intimidation approach	How can we make sure that people are scared to death of evaluation and evaluators?
40. Jackass evaluation	Can we find a good Democrat to give this evaluation contract to?

41. Judgmental evaluation	Is the program ultimately good or bad, worthwhile or not worthwhile, effective or ineffective?
42. Judicial approach	What evidence is there that the program is worthwhile and effective (data presented by program advocates) and what evidence is there that the program is worthless and ineffective (data presented by program adversaries)?
43. Kill focus	What data can we collect to kill this program? How can we make the program look as bad as possible? (Have Gun, Will Travel)
44. Knight-errant approach	How can the evaluator save the program? (or) How can the evaluator save the clients from the program?
45. Knowledge focus	What do clients know as a result of participation in the program?
46. Licensure evaluation	Does the program meet licensing requirements?
47. Longitudinal focus	What happens to the program and to participants over time?
48. Management-focused evaluation	What data do managers need to manage and improve the program?
49. Meta-evaluation	Was the evaluation well done? Does the evaluation meet standards of excellence?
50. Monitoring approach	What ongoing data are needed to monitor program activities and outcomes on a continuous basis (management information system)?
51. Needs assessment	What do clients need and how can those needs be met?
52. Norm-referenced focus	How does this program population compare to some specific norm or reference group on selected variables?
53. Operations focus	What is happening in the day-to-day operations of the program? How can day-to-day operations be improved?

54. Outcomes evaluation

To what extent are desired client outcomes being attained? What are the effects of the program on clients?

55. Pachyderm approach

Can we find a good Republican to give this evaluation contract to?

56. Performance focus

What are participants actually able to do as a result of participation in the program?

57. Personality-focused evaluation

Would program staff make good Scouts? Are they warm, friendly, clean, neat, trustworthy..., and do they do their best to do their duty to God, country, and program?

58. Personnel evaluation

How effective are staff in carrying out their assigned tasks and in accomplishing their individual goals?

59. Pork-barrel evaluation

In whose vested interest is it that this program continue (or be killed) and what actions are they prepared to undertake to defend their interests?

60. Practical evaluation

How can evaluation be conducted cost-effectively, politically, and with minimal interference with the program?

61. Process evaluation

What are the strengths and weaknesses of the program? How are program processes perceived by staff, clients, and others? What are the basic program processes? How can these processes be improved?

62. Product evaluation

What are the characteristics of specific and concrete products produced by or used in a program? What are the costs, benefits, and effects of those products?

63. Public relations focus

How can we make the program look good to outsiders, especially funders?

64. Qualitative emphasis

How do program participants and staff describe program activities and effects in their own terms? What do firsthand observations of the program reveal?

65. Quality assurance

Are minimum and accepted standards of care being routinely and systematically provided to patients and clients? How can quality of care be monitored and demonstrated?

66. Quality-of-life focus

To what extent is client quality of life improved by the program? What are good quality-of-life indicators?

67. Quick-and-dirty evaluation

How can we do this as fast as possible at the lowest cost?

68. Reliability focus

To what extent can we collect reliable data on this program, data that are consistent and not subject to a great deal of measurement error?

69. Replication question

Can we and should we do the same evaluation again to be more sure of the results?

70. Reputation focus 1

What do key people in the community think of this program? What are community perceptions of the program, its strengths, and weaknesses?

71. Reputation focus 2

Who's the biggest-name evaluator we can get?

72. Reputation focus 3

How did I ever get involved in evaluating this mess and how can I get out of this disastrous design I proposed without destroying my reputation as an evaluator?

73. Reputation focus 4

How can we permit this program to be evaluated and still save our reputations as competent and caring administrators?

74. Responsive evaluation

What are the perceptions of different stakeholders and interest groups concerning evaluation issues and program effectiveness?

75. Rigor emphasis

What's the most methodologically rigorous approach we can use in evaluating this program?

76. Rigor mortis, avoidance of

How can we keep the evaluation data collection requirements from gradually stopping all other program activity?

77. Satisfaction focus

How satisfied with the program are staff and participants? What do they like? What do they dislike? What would they change?

78. Secondary data question

What data are available from other sources that would help us in evaluating this program and its impacts?

79. Self-study

What data do we want to gather on ourselves for our own enlightenment?

80. Social indicators approach

What routine social and economic data should be monitored to assess the impacts of this program (e.g., health statistics, crime statistics, housing statistics, employment statistics, and so on)?

81. Stakeholder-based evaluation

What do specific stakeholders in evaluation want to learn from the evaluation?

82. Summative evaluation

Should the program be continued? Should funding be substantially increased or decreased?

83. Systems analysis approach

What are the available alternatives and, given those alternatives, what is the *optimum* way to conduct this program?

84. Target group focus

Who is this program actually serving? Why the discrepancy, if any?

85. Treatment specification focus

What precisely is the treatment in this program and along what dimensions does the treatment vary?

86. Truth focus

How can we convince others we have *it*?

87. Unintended outcomes focus

What happens to clients or others that we didn't expect to happen? What are the consequences and effects of these unanticipated consequences?

88. Unobtrusive data question

How can evaluation data be gathered without interfering with the program or without participant awareness?

89. User focus

Who wants the evaluation conducted and what do they want to know?

90. Utilization-focused evaluation

What information is needed and wanted by primary intended information users

and stakeholders that will actually be
used for program improvement and to
make decisions about the program?

91. Validity focus   How can we get evaluation data that
actually measure what they are supposed
to measure and that actually tell us what
we want to know?

92. Values focus   *Whose* values are to be applied in evaluating the program and making judgments
about program effectiveness?

93. Watchdog evaluations   How can we make sure the program staff
doesn't get away with anything?

94. Weighty evaluation   How can we produce a thick evaluation
report?

95. Xenophobic evaluation   How can we make sure that no one from
outside gets a good look at our program?

96. Xenophobia-free
evaluation   How can we get as many people as
possible from the outside involved in this
evaluation so that they come to really
understand our program and what we're
doing?

97. Yeast approach   How can we engage in an evaluation
process that will create ferment in this
program?

98. Yield focus   What does the program really produce
that is worthwhile? (What will an evaluation produce that is worthwhile?)

99. Yin and Yang evaluation   What are the parallel but opposite motifs
that are necessary to identify if the program and its effects are to be fully understood? What are strengths and weaknesses, and how are they part of the same
whole?

100. Zounds focus   How can we really surprise people with
unexpected evaluation findings?

Continuing the List

Thomas Carlyle suggested at the opening of this chapter that once a
thing is recognized, "doing in a thousand shapes becomes possible."

This listing falls only 900 short of 1000, though I doubt *not* that there are over a thousand ways of thinking about and doing program evaluations. You will undoubtedly add your own ideas to the list as you adapt your evaluation approaches to new situations.

Let a thousand flowers bloom.

Mao Tse-Tung

CHAPTER 12: *Creative Methods*

> *At the end of my training I knew the*
> *six best designs for doing evaluations.*
> *After my first six evaluations I knew*
> *no best designs. I had a lot to unlearn.*
>
> *Halcolm*

There can be no list of creative designs. Such a list would be a contradiction in terms. Creative designs are those that are situationally responsive, appropriate, credible, and useful. While I cannot present a table of creative methods, I can share some of the methods I've used that are rather different from those I studied in the classic methods texts. The examples in this chapter were originally included in *Practical Evaluation* (Patton, 1982).

The design and measurement ideas presented in this chapter are all deviations from standard practice. Each idea is subject to misuse and abuse if applied without regard for ways in which the quality of data collected can be affected because of threats to reliability and validity. I have not discussed such threats and possible errors at any length because I believe it is impossible to identify *in the abstract and in advance* all the trade-offs involved in balancing concerns for accuracy, utility, feasibility, and propriety. For example, having program staff do client interviews in an outcomes evaluation *could* (a) seriously reduce the validity and reliability of the data, (b) substantially increase the validity and reliability of the data, or (c) have no measurable effect on data quality. The nature and degree of effect would depend on staff relationships with clients, how staff were assigned to clients for interviewing, the kinds of questions being asked, the training of the interviewers, attitudes of clients toward the program, and so on. Program staff might make better or worse interviewers than external evaluation researchers depending on these and other factors. An evaluator must grapple with these kinds of data quality questions for all designs, particularly the kinds of nontraditional designs discussed in this chapter.

Practical but creative data collection consists of using whatever resources are available to do the best job possible. There are many constraints. Our ability to think of alternatives is limited. Resources are always limited. This means that data collection will be imperfect, so dissenters from evaluation findings who want to attack a study's methods can always find some grounds for doing so. A major reason for actively involving decision makers and information users in making methods decisions is to deal with weaknesses in the design, and consider trade-off threats to data quality, *before* data are generated. By strategically calculating threats to utility, as well as threats to validity and reliability, it is possible to make practical decisions about the strengths of creative and nonconventional data collection procedures. It is also necessary at the design stage to consider threats to feasibility: Can the proposed evaluation design actually be implemented?

It is important to review critically the evaluation designs presented in this chapter. Anderson (1980), in work on problem-solving approaches, has reported that "critical" thinking and "creative" thinking are seldom found operating simultaneously. The critical thinker assumes a stance of doubt and skepticism; things have to be proven; faulty logic, slippery linkages, tautological theories, and unsupported deductions are the targets of the critical mind. Evaluators are trained to be rigorous and unyielding in critically thinking about research methods. Therein lies the adherence to the "accuracy" part of the standards of evaluation. Creativity is no justification for research findings that lead to incorrect, unjustified, and inaccurate findings. The creative designs reviewed in this chapter are subject to the same careful scrutiny that would be applied to conventional designs. Readers are urged to pay particular attention to potential problems of subject reactivity, ways of checking for data quality, and limitations on generalizability.

PARTICIPANT INTERVIEW CHAIN

As a participant-observer in a wilderness training program for adult educators, I was involved in (1) documenting the kinds of experiences program participants were having and (2) collecting information about the effects of those experiences on their regular work situations. In short, the purpose of evaluation was to provide formative insights that could be used to help understand the personal, professional, and institutional outcomes of intense wilderness experiences for these adult educators.

Sufficient resources were not available to permit much data collection by the two of us doing the evaluation. Therefore, we began discussing with the program staff ways that the participants might become involved in the data collection effort to meet *both* program *and* evaluation needs. The staff liked the idea of involving participants thereby introducing them to observation and interviewing as ways of expanding their own horizons and deepening their perceptions.

The participants' backpacking field experience was organized in two groups of 10 participants each. We used this fact to design a data collection approach that would fit with the programmatic needs for sharing of information between the two groups. Participants were paired for interviewing each other. At the very beginning of the first trip, before people knew each other, all of the participants were given a short, open-ended interview of 10 questions. They were told that each of them, as part of their project participation, was to have responsibility for documenting the experience of their pair-mate throughout the year. They were given a little bit of interview training, a lot of encouragement about probing, and told to record responses fully thereby taking responsibility for helping to build this community record of individual experiences. They were then sent off in pairs and given two hours to complete the interviews with each other, recording the responses by hand.

At the end of the 10-day experience when the separate groups came back together the same pairs of participants, consisting of one person from each group, were again given an interview outline and sent off to interview each other about their respective experiences. This served the program need for sharing of information and an evaluation need for the collection of information. The trade-off, of course, was that with the minimal interview training given the participants and the impossibility of carefully supervising, controlling, and standardizing the data collection, the resulting information would be of variable quality. On the other hand, there were not sufficient evaluation resources for the two evaluators to conduct 20 in-depth interviews with all of the participants, nor was there time at either the beginning or the end of the experiences to allow such data collection to occur. This mode of data collection also meant that confidentiality was minimal and certain kinds of information might not be shared.

On the subsequent two wilderness field experiences the same people were again paired to interview each other, although the nature of the questions changed somewhat to fit the new circumstances and timing of data collection. Most of the participants reported enjoying the interviewing, though they weren't all enthusiastic about the work of taking notes; yet most did quite a conscientious job of recording verbatim quotes and capturing details. A few became very interested in applying similar types of data collection in their home educational setting. The data proved quite useful in documenting and understanding the experiences participants were having and the effects of those experiences on their personal and professional situations. The costs of collecting the information were minimal, and far from interfering with the program, the evaluation became integrated into program activities increasing both the usefulness of the evaluation process and its credibility to participants and staff.

A plan to have the participants write up case studies of their pairmates fell through because the participants were simply not willing to spend the time and make the effort to write up detailed case studies. There are limitations to how far one can push client involvement in data collection and analysis. But before those limits are reached, there is a great deal of useful information that can be collected by involving participants in a program in the actual data collection process.

I have since used similiar participant interview pairs in a number of training program evaluations with good results. The trick is to integrate the data collection into the program.

DATA COLLECTION BY PROGRAM STAFF

Another resource for data collection that is often overlooked is the program staff. Raising the possibility of involving program staff in data collection immediately raises objections about staff subjectivity, data contamination, losses of confidentiality, the vested interests of staff in particular kinds of outcomes, and the threat that staff can pose to clients or students from whom they are collecting the data. Balancing these objections are the things that can be gained from staff involvement in data collection: greater staff commitment to the evaluation; greater staff understanding of the data collection process; training staff in data collection procedures; increased understanding by staff of program participants' perceptions; increased data validity because of staff rapport with participants; and cost savings in data collection.

One of my first evaluation experiences was studying a program to train teachers in open education at the University of North Dakota. Faculty were interested in evaluating that program, but there were almost no resources available for a formal evaluation. There certainly was not enough money available to bring in an external evaluation team to design the study, collect data, and analyze the results. The main data collection consisted of in-depth interviews with student teachers in 24 different schools and classrooms throughout North Dakota, and structured interviews with 300 parents who had children in those classrooms. The only evaluation monies available would barely pay for the transportation and the actual mechanical costs of data collection. The interviewers were the staff and students at the university. Structured interview forms were developed for both the teacher and parent interviews; a full day of training was given to all of the interviewers; and a highly structured system of assigning interviewers to geographical areas was worked out so that no staff were collecting data from their own student teachers. The in-depth interviews with student teachers were tape recorded and transcribed. The parent interviews involved a precoded, structured instrument. I did follow up interviews with a 5% sample of the parents as a check on the validity and reliability of the student and staff data.

After data collection, seminars were organized for staff and students to share their personal perceptions based on their interview experiences. It was clear that the interviewing had had an enormous impact on both staff and students. One major outcome was the increased respect both staff and students had for the parents. They found the parents to be perceptive, caring, and deeply interested in the education of their children. Prior to the interviewing many of the interviewers had held quite negative and derogatory images of North Dakota parents. The systematic interviewing had put them in a situation where they were forced to listen to what parents had to say rather than tell parents what they (as educators) thought about things, and through that listening it was clear that they had learned a great deal. The formal analysis of the data yielded some interesting findings about the program; the evaluation was used to make some changes in the program; and the data provided a source of case materials used in training future program participants. But it is very likely that the major and most lasting impact of the evaluation was the actual experiences of students and staff who learned a great deal by participating in the data collection. That experiential impact was more powerful than the formal findings of the study.

By the way, had the interviewers been paid at the going commercial rate the data collection would have cost at least $10,000 just in personnel costs. As it was, there were no personnel costs in data collection and a considerable human contribution was made to the university program by both students and staff.

INTERACTIVE RESEARCH

The involvement of program staff or clients as colleagues in program evaluation changes the relationship between evaluators and staff. The relationship becomes interactive and cooperative, rather than one-sided and antagonistic. William Tikunoff (1980) has used this "interactive research" approach in educational research and development projects. He found that putting teachers, researchers, and trainer/developers together as a team increased both the meaningfulness and the validity of the findings because teacher cooperation and understanding of the research made the research less intrusive, thus reducing rather than increasing reactivity.

The problem of how research subjects or program clients will react to staff involvement in an evaluation, particularly involvement in data collection, needs careful scrutiny and consideration in each situation in which it is attempted. Reactivity is a potential problem in both conventional and nonconventional designs. Breaches of confidence and/or reactivity-biased data cannot be justified in the name of creativity. On the other hand, as Tikunoff's experiences indicate, interactive designs may increase the validity of data and reduce reactivity by making evaluations less intrusive, and making subjects or clients less resistant or suspicious.

The previous two examples of nontraditional data collection approaches have focused on who collects the evaluation data. By contrast, the next section is one solution to the problem of locating a good, but inexpensive sample of people from whom data can be collected.

A READY AND WILLING COMMUNITY SAMPLE

There is great interest these days in community surveys. Health programs, criminal justice programs, education programs, and community planning efforts of all kinds are attempting to conduct community surveys as parts of needs assessments, evaluations, and planning efforts. Such surveys can be quite costly because of the difficulties of constructing a reasonable sampling frame, drawing a random sample, and getting interviewers out and about the community to collect the data. In addition to being expensive, the organization of such projects usually involves fairly lengthy time horizons of several months, often a year or more.

In considering the time and cost involved in community surveys, one county planning department in Minnesota came up with a quite creative solution. It occurred to them that there is a ready and willing sample of people who represent a broad cross section of the community and who, because they happen to have a considerable amount of time on their hands, they are likely to be quite willing interview respondents. *This sample consists of people who have been called for jury duty and are waiting for an actual jury assignment.*

Jury participants are drawn from voter lists. While the resulting sample is not entirely random because many people get out of jury duty for one reason or another, it represents a not altogether unattractive proxy for a random sample with the advantages that no expensive sampling procedures are necessary and the interview respondents are all gathered together at one place in time so that they are easily accessible to interviewers. Moreover, the length of time needed to plan such a study is fairly minimal because no time has to be devoted to the lengthy process of identifying and constructing a sampling frame, drawing the sample, and matching interviews to sample respondents.

All you have to do is write your instrument and go down to the courthouse to conduct the interviews. My experience has been that people awaiting jury duty are quite willing to be interviewed because they have nothing else to do while they are waiting. Relatively large samples can be obtained in this way at low expense, allowing the planning department to get some basic ideas about how the more active citizens in the county (registered voters) are thinking about major issues of the day.

Of course, one has to get the approval of relevant county officials and judges to do such interviewing, but our experience has been that the judges know how boring it is to be waiting for jury duty so they are quite happy to have prospective jurors entertained, and even providing a useful public service while they are standing by to perform the public service that has brought them to the courthouse. Even if one were not to use this sample for a full study it represents an excellent group for doing pilot studies, for testing out instruments, and for carrying out exploratory research.

TEACHING INSTEAD OF DOING

Many demonstration projects in education, chemical dependency, health, criminal justice, and other areas of human service programming are so small that their evaluation budgets, even if they consist of as much as 5% of program funds, allow the purchase of no more than a few days of an evaluator's time. For example, many of the Title I and Title IV-C programs in schools involve evaluation budgets of $500, $1000, or sometimes as much as $2000. Because of the limited funds involved, many of these evaluations end up consisting entirely of a one- or two-day site visit by an evaluator at one or two times in the course of the project year, resulting in a fairly minimal description of what is happening in the program.

One way of making use of these limited evaluation funds, particularly in the early formative years of the project before the full credibility of an external evaluator is needed for summative purposes, is to have the evaluator train people in the program to collect evaluative data and to work with them in setting up their own evaluation system rather than collecting the data directly. This strategy follows the ancient proverb, "Give a man a fish and he eats for a day; teach him to fish and he eats for a lifetime."

In a number of instances we have found that it is possible to integrate evaluation into the program in such a way that the evaluation becomes part of the learning experience of program participants. Perhaps the best example in this regard was an evaluation of a "school service" project. The purpose of the project was to develop new approaches to creating student learning experiences that contributed to the school and the community. These "school service" projects thus served a dual role; they allowed the students to (1) get practical experience while they were learning something and (2) provide a needed service as part of their learning experience. The evaluation design called for doing some case studies of actual school service projects. If the evaluation monies were spent for professional evaluator time to collect data for the case studies, it would have been possible to look at no more than three school service projects. As an alternative, we suggested creating a school service experience through the evaluation project. A group of students would be trained by the evaluator to conduct case studies and the students, as their school service learning, would actually collect the data and write the case studies. In this way it was possible to construct a much larger number of case studies while providing some practical benefits to the program as part of the evaluation. The quality of the resulting case studies was considerably lower than would have resulted had the professional evaluators constructed the cases based on their own data collection. However, the quality was sufficient to serve the minimal purposes for which data were collected and the much larger number of cases made it possible to understand a greater variety of school service experiences than would have been possible with two or three cases done solely by the evaluator.

AN *N* OF ONE

Sampling trade-offs can be one of the most difficult issues to deal with in an evaluation particularly where resources are quite limited. It is worth remembering that some of the major breakthroughs in knowledge have come from studies with small sample sizes. Freud's work was based on a few clinical cases. Piaget significantly changed educational thinking about how children learn with an in-depth study of two children—his own.

In *Qualitative Evaluation Methods* (Patton, 1980) I discussed a number of "purposeful" sampling approaches that involve small samples selected for their high information payoff. One type of purposeful sampling—"the critical case"—involves an *n* of one.

Critical cases are those that can make a point quite dramatically or are, for some reason, particularly important in the scheme of things. A clue to the existence of a critical case is a statement by a decision maker to the effect that "if the program doesn't make it there, it won't make it anywhere." Perhaps, then, the focus of the evaluation should be on understanding what is happening in *that* critical program. Another kind of clue would be a statement to the effect that "if that program is having problems, then we can be sure all the programs are having problems." Looking for the critical case is particularly important where resources may limit evaluation to the study of only a single site. Under such conditions it makes strategic sense to pick the site that would yield the most information and have the greatest impact on decision-maker actions and understanding.

While studying one or a few critical cases does not technically permit broad generalizations to all possible cases, logical generalizations can often be made from the weight of evidence produced in studying a single, critical case. Physics provides a good example of such a critical case. In Galileo's study of gravity he wanted to find out if the weight of an object affected the rate of speed at which it would fall. Rather than randomly sampling objects of different weights in order to generalize to all objects in the world, he selected a critical case—the feather. If in a vacuum, as he demonstrated, a feather fell at the same rate as some heavier object (a coin) then he could logically generalize from this one critical case to all objects. His findings were enormously useful and credible.

There are many comparable critical cases in social action programming—if one is creative in looking for them. For example, suppose national policymakers want to get local communities involved in making decisions about how their local program will be run, but they are not sure that the communities will understand the complex regulations governing their involvement. The first critical case is to evaluate the regulations in a community of well-educated citizens; if they cannot understand them less educated folks are certain to find the regulations incomprehensible. Or conversely, one might consider the critical case to be a community consisting of people with quite low levels of education: "If *they* can understand the regulations, anyone can."

A variation of the critical case strategy involves selecting (or sometimes avoiding) a politically sensitive site or unit of analysis. For example, a statewide program may have a local site in the district of a state legislator who is particularly influential. By carefully studying the program in that district, evaluation data may be more likely to attract attention and get used. This does not mean that the evaluator then undertakes to make that site look either good or bad, depending on the politics of the moment. This is simply an additional sampling strategy for trying to increase the usefulness and utilization of information where resources permit the study of only a limited number of cases.

Identification of critical cases depends on recognition of the key dimensions that make for a critical case. As noted in the last paragraph, the critical dimension may be political sensitivity or visibility. A critical case might be indicated by the financial state of a program; a program with particularly high or particularly low cost-per-client ratios might suggest a critical case. A critical case might come from a particularly difficult program location. If the funders of a new program are worried about recruiting clients or participants into a program it may make sense to study the site where resistance to the program is expected to be greater to provide the most rigorous test of the possibility of program recruitment. If the program works in that site, "it could work anywhere."

INSTRUMENT VALIDATION
à la MOTHER MEASUREMENT

Critical case sampling is a technique for making logical generalizations. Evaluators are more often involved with and concerned about making empirical generalizations. The extent to which one can have confidence in empirical generalizations depends partly on the validity and reliability of the data collected in the evaluation. This section reproduces a creative solution to the validity and reliability problem. The solution is from *Discrepancy Digest* (February 1980), The Evaluation Training Consortium Newsletter from the Evaluation Center, Western Michigan University.

Dear Mother Measurement:

I have a question regarding the assessment of validity and reliability of instruments which I presently use to evaluate participant satisfaction with inservice workshops. The real problem is that the content and format of each workshop is different. Consequently, I must use a new and completely different instrument for each workshop. This means I am never able to re-use instruments to get data concerning validity and reliability. I realize that instrument validation can be complex, but is there something easy I can do that will solve my problem?

I. M. Unsatisfied

Dear Unsatisfied:

Yes, there are a number of procedures that can be used for instrument validation that range from simple procedures to a major evaluation effort. The procedure I will describe is ideal for your situation, and it can also be used if you are planning to use an instrument more than once and want an indication of its validity before you actually begin using it at workshops.

You will need a small group of individuals that you can administer your instrument to prior to each workshop. Here is the procedure you should follow. Generate three different short scenarios concerning how participants might react to your workshop. For example, the first scenario might read something like this; "The workshop you just attended was tremendous, met all of your needs and was extremely beneficial, etc. . . . " The second would read something like this: "The workshop you attended was alright. You learned some new information, but felt lukewarm about the experience, etc. . . . " The third scenario: "The workshop you just attended was a disaster, poorly organized and boring; you got nothing from attending, etc. . . . "

Using the small group of individuals you have selected, randomly assign them to three groups, each group being given a different scenario. They will be instructed to assume that they are participants in a just completed inservice workshop and the printed scenario they have been given is how they actually felt about the workshop experience. The subjects are then given your workshop evaluation form, and told to mark at the top the number of the scenario card they have. They are then told to complete the instrument using only the scenario card to guide their responses to the questions.

The overall scores on the completed instruments should fall into three distinct groups congruent with the scenario the individual had. A high positive correlation between scores on the instrument and assigned scenarios would indicate your instrument was sensitive in differentiating among these three possible outcomes to your workshop. Additionally, you can evaluate responses to individual items to determine those questions that do or do not differentiate among the three possible workshop outcomes.

Love,
Mother

DATA COLLECTION TRADE-OFFS

Each of the examples in this chapter involves an attempt to optimize the use of limited resources while serving both the program and the need for evaluation. Each example also involves trade-offs between data quality, data credibility, varying roles for the evaluator, different threats to validity and reliability, and evaluation costs. By discussing the options with the relevant decision makers in each case it was possible to arrive at designs and data collection procedures that served more than one purpose and built a constructive foundation for future evaluation efforts.

Every evaluation situation presents options. The evaluator's task is creatively to identify those options, assess the strengths and weaknesses of each approach, and work with decison makers to come up with a design that is appropriate to the situation at hand. Far from being a deterrent, the fact that you come up with a design or approach that, to the best of your knowledge, has never been tried before, may be as good a reason as any to try it.

Thinking along the lines suggested in the preceding sections assumes a creative commitment to conduct cost-effective evaluations. Cost-effective evaluations are those where the benefits to the program are worth the cost of conducting the evaluation. Michael Scriven (1976) has referred to such evaluations as "cost-free" evaluations. They involve no cost to the program, in the long run, because what is added to the program exceeds the cost of the evaluation, or, in many cases, the savings to the program or to program funders exceeds the cost of doing the evaluation. Given increasingly limited resources for the development of programs and the conduct of evaluations there is every likelihood that evaluators will be called on more and more to demonstrate the cost-effectiveness of their work. Evaluators can expect to be held accountable both for utilization and for showing that the evaluation results were justified in terms of the cost expended on research.

Scriven's concerns about cost-effective evaluations are reflected in his recent work on what he has called "responsibility evaluation," as exemplified in the "school evaluation profile." A number of principles of cost-effective evaluation are illustrated in Scriven's description of responsibility evaluation:

1. In responsibility evaluation you start by asking: If we ignore all the variance of all factors over which there is no manipulable control, is there enough variance left to be worth fooling around with? You identify the factors over which there is no control and ignore them.
2. For whatever remains, can we identify the actor(s) who have control over these factors?
3. Third, can we get measures of these factors?
4. Then, can these measures be obtained cheaply? As we all know schools are pressed for funds. The economy issue is important.
5. Finally, will the measures be interpretable? We must avoid using measures or indicators that are so complex or esoteric that they are not comprehensible by school personnel. (Scriven, 1979a, p. 50)

Cost-effectiveness analysis is not simply something to be undertaken after an evaluation has been completed. Indeed, if an evaluation is to be cost-effective, a careful assessment of potential benefits and expected costs should be carried out *before* data collection, and such discussions should take place in the context of a real consideration of creative alternatives, *including the alternative of not doing the evaluation at all.* The next section provides a concrete example of how cost-benefit criteria can affect an evaluation approach.

INTERNAL-EXTERNAL EVALUATION COMBINATIONS

Internal evaluations, where people in the program collect the data themselves, are typically less expensive than evaluations conducted by external evaluators. External evaluation, however, tends to have more credibility and legitimacy than internal evaluation. In workshops I am often asked to compare the trade-offs between internal and external evaluation, or what are euphemistically called "in-house" evaluations and "out-house" evaluations.

The problem in the way in which the question is typically posed to me is that it sets up an artificial dichotomy. The question usually concerns the advantages and disadvantages of internal *versus* external evaluation. Actually, there are a good many possible combinations of internal *and* external evaluations that may be more desirable and more cost-effective than either a purely internal *or* purely external evaluation.

Accreditation processes are a good example of an internal-external combination. The internal group collects the data and arranges it so that the external group can come in, inspect the data collected by the internal group, sometimes collect additional information on their own, and pass judgment on the program. There are many ways in which an evaluation can be set up so that some external group of respected professionals and evaluators guarantees the validity and fairness of the evaluation process while the people internal to the program actually collect and/or analyze the evaluation data. The cost savings of such an approach can be substantial while still allowing the evaluation to have basic credibility and legitimacy through the blessing of the external review committee.

I worked for several years with one of the leading chemical dependency programs in the country, the Hazelden Foundation of Minnesota. They have established a quite rigorous evaluation process that involves data collection at the point of entry into the program and then follow-up questionnaires 6 months, 12 months, and 18 months after leaving the program. Hazelden's own research and evaluation department collects all of the data. My responsibility as an external evaluator is to monitor that data collection periodically to make sure that the established procedures are being followed correctly. I then work with the program decision makers to identify the kind of data analysis that is desirable. They perform the data analysis with their own computer resources. They send the data to me and I write the annual evaluation report. They participate in analyzing, interpreting, and making judgments about the data, but for purposes of legitimacy and credibility the actual writing of the final report is done by me. This internal/external combination is sometimes extended one step futher by having still another layer of external professionals and evaluators pass judgment on the quality and accuracy of the final report through a *meta-evaluation* process—evaluating the evaluation.

There are limitations to this kind of process. One of the limitations is that the external group may impose unmanageable and overwhelming data collection procedures on the internal people. I saw this happening in an internal-external model with a group of school districts in Canada. The external committee was asking for a "comprehensive" data collection effort by the local schools that included data on learning outcomes, staff morale, facilities, curriculum, the school lunch program, the library, parent reactions, the perceptions of local businesspeople, analysis of the school bus system, and so on. After listening to all of the things the external committee thought the internal people should do, the internal folks renamed the evaluation approach. They suggested that the model should not be called the "Internal-External Model" of evaluation but rather the "Internal-External-Eternal Model" of evaluation.

THREATS TO DATA QUALITY

This chapter has presented some alternative and nonconventional approaches to data collection. The first example illustrated one approach to interactive research, as exemplified by the participant interview chain. The subsequent suggestions for actively involving program staff in data collection provided yet another perspective on interactive research. I then discussed the potential of using people who are awaiting jury duty as a ready, willing, inexpensive, and easily accessible sample for pilot and exploratory studies, or for community surveys. Purposeful and small samples were considered as alternatives to random sampling. There was also a section on teaching people to do their own data collection for evaluation purposes. The chapter included a selection from "Mother Measurement" on a creative instrument validation approach. Data collection trade-offs, cost-effective evaluation, and responsibility evaluation à la Scriven were discussed. Finally, I presented some alternative ways of structuring and organizing data collection and analysis: internal-external evaluation combinations.

The purpose of presenting this diverse range of data collection alternatives has been to illustrate the possibilities for creative solutions to all kinds of practical design and measurement problems. These examples have been offered in the hope that they will stimulate thinking about creative but practical methods options.

This chapter only scratches the surface in relation to the full range of creative designs that are possible in evaluation. In the last several years my evaluation work and consulting have brought me into contact with hundreds of evaluators. While much of the tone of this book may come across as critical of standard evaluation practice, I know from direct observation that there is a great deal of creative work being done by evaluators in all kinds of difficult and challenging situations. My observations suggest that what these evaluators have in common is a commitment to do the most and best they can with the resources available, the short time lines they face, and the intense political pressures they feel—all of which constitute the context for their work. They share a belief that *doing something is better than doing nothing, so long as one is realistic and honest in assessing and presenting the limitations of what is done.*

This last caveat is important. I have not attempted to delineate all the possible threats to validity and reliability that may be posed by the design alternatives in this chapter. This is not a methods, measurement, and design text. My purpose has been to stimulate thinking about creative methods options. Moreover, as I noted in the introduction to this chapter, I believe it is impossible to identify *in the abstract and in advance* all the trade-offs involved in balancing concerns for validity, reliability, utility, feasibility, propriety, and accuracy that will need to be considered in any particular situation. Even when faced with the reality of particular circumstances and specific evaluation problems, it often is not possible to determine in advance precisely how a creative design or measurement approach will affect the quality of the data collected. Both "truth tests" (whether data are believable and accurate) and "utility tests" (whether data are useful) are important to decision makers, information users, and stakeholders (Weiss & Bucuvalas, 1980). One is obligated to think about and deal with threats to validity that may reduce the utility of data, just as one is obligated to consider threats to utility that may result from overly elaborate and too-sophisticated designs aimed at reducing threats to validity. One is obligated to take validity and reliability constraints into consideration in data analysis, as those constraints become known in the process of data collection and analysis. One is obligated to be forthright in reporting on the quality of data in an evaluation. But, what one is *not* obligated to do is return the technical, validity-reliability-accuracy criteria to a position of predominance and ascendancy as the primary standards against which an evaluation is judged. As the standards of evaluation make clear (Stufflebeam, 1980), technical concerns for data accuracy should be made in conjunction with concerns for utility, feasibility, and propriety. There is a lot of room for creative data collection approaches to meet the spirit and challenge of these standards. Indeed, there is a substantial need for creative evaluation approaches to evaluation to meet the spirit and challenge of these standards. It is in that spirit, and in the face of the challenge represented by the new standards, that the ideas in this chapter have been presented.

A CLOSING PERSPECTIVE

Designing practical but creative evaluations means not forcing new situations into old molds—in this case, traditional research designs. To do so is to make the error of the traveler who came across a peacock for the first time, as told in a story from Halcolm:

> A traveler to a new land came across a peacock. Having never seen this kind of bird before, he took it for a genetic freak. Taking pity on the poor bird, which he was sure could not survive for long in such deviant form, he set about to correct nature's error. He trimmed the long, colorful feathers, cut back the beak, and dyed the bird black. "There now," he said, with pride in a job well done. "You look more like a standard guinea hen."

CHAPTER 13: *Evaluation Humor*

> *Professions, like nations, are civilized*
> *to the degree to which they can satirize*
> *themselves.*
>
> *Peter DeVries*

This chapter is devoted to humor in evaluation. The original outline for this book did not include a separate chapter on humor. Humor is something that seems to work best when it is woven in and out of the whole fabric of a presentation rather than concentrated in one spot. Like the other techniques and approaches offered in this book, humor must emerge from and be adapted to fit individual style. I have attempted to offer occasional humorous diversions and illustrations throughout the book. But because *humor can have such a powerful effect in breaking through the barriers of fear and tension that imprison creativity,* it seemed to me that humor in evaluation deserved discussion in a separate chapter, if for no other reason than to call attention to its importance as another available option in the repertoire of the creative evaluation professional.

THE EVALUATION HALL OF FAME

When beginning to work with people on an evaluation I often begin with a group session where we can lay the groundwork and develop a shared framework. At such sessions I like to begin with something light. The selection that follows is ideal for such purposes. I introduce the reading with a few words of context.

Today we'll be doing some evaluation work together. Some of you may find that you actually resonate to evaluation work. Indeed, some of you may want to consider becoming an evaluator. In the interest of helping you think through that possibility today I want to begin by sharing with you at least one image of what it means to be an evaluator. What follows are the impressions of a Midwestern newspaper columnist, Donald Kaul, after his first chance encounter with an evaluator at a party.

Impression of an Evaluator

by Donald Kaul[1]

I met a fellow the other day who made me weep. It was at a party. He was a good-looking chap, well dressed with the look of eagles about him. He stood in a careless pose, laughing and talking with the prettiest girls in the room. I hated him immediately.

Yet I found it difficult to maintain this hostility once I had met him, for he was an utterly charming person. Not only was he a mine of amusing stories, but he possessed that rare ability to listen attentively to your stories and respond properly.

In sum total, he had that singular quality of grace that adheres to a certain class of persons—People Who Have It Made. He absolutely radiated the good cheer that is the natural product of being absolutely certain of one's station in life and confident of one's ability to occupy it.

"What," I asked him after a time, "do you do?"

"I'm an evaluator," he said.

"Pardon me?"

"An evaluator," he repeated. "Surely you know what an evaluator is?"

"Not, I'm afraid, in this context. What do you evaluate?"

"Federal programs. It's the newest thing, dear boy. Each federal program—and there are thousands of them—has an evaluation clause written into its budget. Thus one not only has a program to help the Hopi Indians or to improve the court system of South Dakota, one has a program to find out if the original programs are working. That's where evaluators come in. We travel around a lot."

"How did you get to be an evaluator?"

"I answered an ad. I got tired of being a leather craftsman in an abandoned mining town in Colorado. I'd become that after I gave up being an underground radical. Before that I was in the Harvard Business School. I didn't know what the ad meant, to tell you the truth. I thought it might be for the CIA. As it turned out, it was even better."

I left the room then, my face scalded by bitter tears. I knew the anguish of one who, in a moment, realizes that he has wasted his life. An evaluator! That's what I should have been. My talent, my training, my very genes cried out my fitness for the profession, had I but known earlier. Even as a child I was always evaluating things—my parents, my playmates, games. If there was a problem and the group members put their heads together to solve it, I always was the one who stood at the side, evaluating the solution.

It wasn't really my fault. When I was a kid there weren't such things as evaluators. A foreman at the auto plant, that as about as close as you could get. I remember, when I was a senior in high school on the near-west side of Detroit, going to my counselor and saying: "I don't know what I want to be when I grow up."

"You like horses?" he said. "You could be a cowboy, maybe. Or, if you're more mechanically inclined, you could be a fireman and sit in the back of the ladder truck and steer the rear wheels."

We finally settled on engineering, after we determined that I did not have the manual dexterity necessary for taxidermy. I washed out of several schools before setting my life's course on journalism.

While I have enjoyed my career, I must confess that I do not feel that natural affinity for journalism that I do for evaluation. I think I could have become one of the greatest evaluators of all time. Enshrined in the Evaluators' Hall of Fame.

I might have gone on to become that brother to evaluation, a consultant. Oh well, it does no good to pine over what might have been. Still, I wish I'd aimed higher.

SCRIVEN'S IDEAL EVALUATOR

To be enshrined in the Evaluator's Hall of Fame presumably one would have to approach some ideal of evaluator performance. Michael Scriven has designed an examination to help any future such Hall of Fame make its selections. Unfortunately, he hasn't supplied the answer to the exam question, so if you're aiming for the ideal you'll still have to decide for yourself which of the three Scriven models will get you a Hall of Fame nomination.

THE THREE UMPIRES TEST: (TUT) It's time for another in our series of professional selection tests, and since the Early Egyptian Follies has just opened in San Francisco, we are fortunate to be able to present a test with the appropriate acronym. (Uttered once, the acronym refers to the test; uttered twice in quick succession, it refers to individuals who have failed to pass the test.) The test reads as follows:

In the following story, which of the participants should be regarded as coming closest to the ideal evaluator? If more than one answer is appropriate, please identify the evaluators to whom you feel each of the role models would be most appropriate. "Three baseball umpires gathered together at a favorite bar during the off-season, and took to philosophical speculation about the nature of their task. In particular, about the epistemological status (validity) of their calls. Rather well along in the evening, they summed up their positions as follows; The first umpire, "I calls them as I sees them." The second umpire, "I calls them as they is." The third umpire, "They ain't nothing till I calls them." (Scriven, 1979, p. 37)

A Matter of Perspective

Utilization-focused evaluation begins with the premise that different stakeholders will have different perspectives on a program. It is critical for an evaluator to take those different perspectives into account in designing the evaluation. I had an experience as a Peace Corps volunteer that deeply impressed me with how different people can have quite different perspectives.

The local agricultural director with whom I worked invited me to his village of birth, a very small village deep in the bush of eastern Burkina Faso (then Upper Volta) in West Africa. When we arrived he took me to his grandmother's hut. Since he was a man in his fifties, his grandmother figured to have seen a lot of years—and a lot of changes in Africa: the coming of the first white men to eastern Upper Volta; the French military raids on Gourmanche villages to conscript young men for military service in World Wars I and II; the smallpox and measles epidemics of the 1950s caused by the testing of live vaccines in West Africa; the construction of the Ouagadougou-Niamey road; and Upper Volta's independence in 1963.

In the evening she served us millet beer as I sat with the director talking about the upcoming first manned space flight to the moon, a subject in which he was greatly interested. As she filled my calabash he said to her, "Grandmother, the Americans are going to the moon."

She smiled at me and politely replied, "A tienupuni.... Have a good trip." Then she went on about her preparations for the night, no more impressed than if I were setting off for Fada N'Gourma, the main town of the region, 45 kilometers away.

HUMORIZATIONS SYSTEMATIZING COGNITIVE
AND CONCEPTUAL CLARITY AND COMMUNICATIONS
REGARDING SATIRISTIC HEURISTICS

Perhaps nothing is an easier target for humor than academic jargon. In the first chapter I suggested that the proliferation of a specialized jargon in evaluation was evidence that the field is ready for designation as a discipline. To help participants in an evaluation process feel like they have some expertise in the discipline I usually introduce a certain amount of evaluation jargon "to be used at your next cocktail party to impress friends and lovers with your newfound stature as an evaluation expert." While some of my colleagues recommend avoiding all jargon in working with laypersons, I find that participants in an evaluation process enjoy becoming facile with a limited number of new terms (such as *formative, summative, operationalize, standard deviation*—which many people turn into "standard deviates," an interesting contradiction in terms).

One way of introducing—and poking fun at—jargon is to describe all the advantages of speaking administratease, academese, or educatorese, especially the advantage of being able to sound terribly intellectual while disguising the fact that you have nothing to say. I then offer to teach the audience the secret of speaking in jargonese.

The secret is revealed in a jargon guide developed by Barbara Stover and Ilva Walker, two rhetoric and speech teachers at Danville, Illinois, Junior College. They've passed the guide on to students in mimeograph form to prepare them for entry into the worlds of government, education, and human service agencies. The content of the guide is shown as Table 13.1. The table is made up of five columns: A,B,C,D, and E. To construct a magical mystical sentence in superbly elegant jargon one simply makes a random or nonrandom selection from each column, adding connecting words and appropriate verb tense as necessary. For example, the first five digits of the serial number on my tape recorder are 94471. The ninth word from column A is "conceptual"; the fourth words from columns B and C, respectively, are "ontological" and "balance"; the seventh word from column D is "facilitate"; and the first phrase from column E is "total modular exchange." This now can be made to read:

Conceptual and ontological
balance facilitates
total modular exchange

TABLE 13.1
Guide to Jargon-Ease

A	B	C	D	E
Comprehensive	cognitive	nuclei	indicates	total modular exchange
Flexible	reciprocal	focus	terminate	in-depth discussion
Adaptable	stylistic	balance	geared	multipurpose framework and goals
Culturally	ontological	chain of command	compile	serial communication
Perceptual	prime	productivity	articulate	serial transmission of applicable code
Evaluative	supportive	conformance	verbalize	tools and instruments
Innovative	workable	panacea	facilitate	postsecondary education enrichment
Interdisciplinary	resultant	input	implement	changing needs of society
Conceptual	behavioral	throughput	incur	motivational serial communications
Ideological	judgmental	accountability	sensitize	high potential for assessing failure
Optimal	ethnic	feedback	synthesize	control group and experimental group
Minimal	attitudinal	objective	integrate	student-faculty relationships
Categorically	multicultural	resources	fragment	identifiable decision-making process
Unequivocally	encounter	perspective	maximize	sophisticated resource systems analyses
Intrapersonal	counterproductive	curricula	minimize	vertical team structure
Interpersonal	generative	priorities	energize	translation in depth
	cognate	diversity	individualize	classroom context
		environment	encapsulate	individual horizons
		overview	orientate	
		strategies		
		posture		
		methodologies		
		introversion		
		posits		
		concept		

SOURCE: Developed by Barabara Stover and Ilva Walker, Danville Junior College, Illinois. Select one item from each line and adapt the connecting words and parts of speech as necessary to make a jargon-ease sentence.

This doesn't make any sense, but who would dare show their ignorance by questioning it? Of course, if it does make sense to you, you may want to ask yourself whether you've been reading (or writing) too many administrative memoranda, or sitting in on too many high-level briefings from expensive consultants. If so, you may want to look more closely at (A) categorically (B) generative (C) throughput to (D) encapsulate your (E) individual horizons and (E) motivational serial communications. I recommend this because (A) evaluative (B) stylistic (C) introversion can (D) synthesize your (E) sophisticated resource systems analyses (D) integrated with (E) the changing needs of society and a (F) multipurpose framework and goals. I hope we understand each other now.

I like to hand out the Guide to Jargon-Ease to nonscientists with whom I'm working. I tell them, "I may slip in a few jargon samples now and then just to see if you're listening. Let me know if you catch me." This legitimizes the humorous asking of questions about concepts and ideas that don't make sense to participants.

REVOLUTIONARY EVALUATION

The selection that follows is one of my favorites. Written by Edward Schwartz (1974) as a reflection on the process of submitting a program proposal to a government funding agency, the sentiments here expressed find instant recognition and commiseration by anyone who has ever written a grant proposal. I typically use this piece at the end of the day, or after a particularly intensive and serious working session, for example, after a morning of goals clarification or data analysis. I would usually introduce this selection with the recognition that

> we've been working extremely hard. I appreciate the seriousness with which you've undertaken these evaluation tasks. After an intensive session like this I sometimes find it refreshing to get a perspective on what we've been doing.
>
> During the bicentennial year of America's Independence celebrations I happened upon a bit of writing that, I think, helps put some perspective on the processes of planning and evaluation. I'd like to share with you Edward Schwartz's vision of what the American Revolution might have been caught up in if some of our current approaches had existed then.

July 20, 1776

Mr. Thomas Jefferson
Continental Congress
Independence Hall
Philadelphia, Pa.

Dear Mr. Jefferson:

We have read your "Declaration of Independence" with great interest. Certainly, it represents a considerable undertaking, and many of your statements do merit serious consideration. Unfortunately, the Declaration as a whole fails to meet recently adopted specifications for proposals to the Crown, so we must return the document to you for further refinement. The questions which follow might assist you in your process of revision.

1. In your opening paragraph you use the phrase "the Laws of Nature and Nature's God." What are these laws? In what way are they the criteria on which you base your central arguments? Please document with citations from the recent literature.

2. In the same paragraph you refer to the "opinions of mankind." Whose polling data are you using? Without specific evidence, it seems to us, the "opinions of mankind" are a matter of opinion.

3. You hold certain truths to be "self-evident." Could you please elaborate. If they are as evident as you claim, then it should not be difficult for you to locate the appropriate supporting statistics.

4. "Life, liberty, and the pursuit of happiness" seem to be the goals of your proposal. These are not measurable goals. If you were to say that "among these is the ability to sustain an average life expectancy in six of the 13 colonies of at least 55 years, and to enable all newspapers in the colonies to print news without outside interference, and to raise the average income of the colonists by 10 percent in the next 10 years," these would be measurable goals. Please clarify.

5. You state that "whenever any Form of Government becomes destructive of these ends, it is the Right of the People to alter or to abolish it, and to institute a new Government. . . . " Have you weighed this assertion against all the alternatives? Or is it predicated solely on the baser instincts?

6. Your description of the existing situation is quite extensive. Such a long list of grievances should precede the statement of goals, not follow it.

7. Your strategy for achieving your goal is not developed at all. You state that the colonies "ought to be Free and Independent States," and that they are "Absolved from All Allegiance to the British Crown." Who or what must change to achieve this objective? In what way must they change? What resistance must you overcome to achieve the change? What specific steps will you take to overcome the resistance? How long will it take? We have found that a little foresight in these areas helps to prevent careless errors later on.

8. Who among the list of signatories will be responsible for implementing your strategy? Who conceived it? Who provided the theoretical research? Who will constitute the advisory committee? Please submit on organizational chart.

9. You must include an evaluation design. We have been requiring this since Queen Anne's War.

10. What impact will your program have? Your failure to include any assessment of this inspires little confidence in the long range prospects of your undertaking.

11. Please submit a PERT diagram, an activity chart, and an itemized budget.

We hope that these comments prove useful in revising your "Declaration of Independence."

Best Wishes,

Lord North[2]

SERENDIPITOUS EVALUATION

When considering creative designs there is necessarily concern about the rigor of such designs. Sometimes there are trade-offs between rigor and creativity. To facilitate discussions about what rigor means, I sometimes introduce the ultimate in rigor—the triple blind experiment.

With a little creativity it is possible to improve on the double blind experiment and create a "triple blind experiment." This design has been recommended as the best hope for achieving scientific breakthroughs in medicine because the triple blind experiments are "so completely unbiased and randomized that an accidental discovery of great importance may turn up" (R.F., 1977, p. 20). The triple blind experiment relies heavily on the principle of serendipity, a principle articulated most succinctly by mathematician Sir Arthur Stanley Eddington:

> We need a super-mathematics in which the operations are as unknown as the quantities they operate on and a supermathematician who does not know what he is doing when he performs these operations.

Applying the serendipity principle to evaluation leads to the triple blind design for program evaluation: The program participants do not know what they are getting; the program staff do not know what they are providing; and the evaluators do not know what they are evaluating. Here is the best of all possible worlds where goal-free evaluation meets the goal-free program in a design that is completely free of values, bias, and vested interests. The integrity of the design is further enhanced if halfway through the experiment one introduces a rigorous element of role reversal: The program participants provide the unidentified service to the evaluators, and the results are evaluated by the scientifically untrained program staff.

Original credit for this creative evaluation design goes to Christopher Columbus. In Columbus's original version of serendipitous research, you start out with the best of intentions and high hopes for success but immediately head in the wrong direction. Throughout the project you don't know where you are, and after the project you don't know where you've been. This permits maximum operation of the serendipity principle and, as Columbus demonstrated, increases enormously the likelihood of making a great discovery.

Lewis Carroll introduced his own terminology for evaluations built on the serendipity principle. He called it the Jabberwocky approach to evaluation: "Unknowable actors executing unknowable actions." The first final report produced by evaluator Carroll using the Jabberwocky approach created great excitement among the stakeholders of the time and contributed in no small way to his later eminence. That report concluded:

> Twas brillig, and the slithy toves did gyre and gimble in the wabe; all mimsy were the borogoves, and the mome raths outrabe.

R. F. (writing anonymously to avoid interruption of his serendipitous experiments in a major government bureaucracy concerned about mental health) has estimated the likely impact of using triple blind experiments in scientific (that is, value-free, bias-free, interest-free) studies:

> The chance that triple-blind testing will produce something of consequence is calculated to be at least as great as that of spontaneous mutation. This probability is about one times 10 to the minus sixth power per generation. But considering the large number of chaotic investigations now in progress, the chance of a significant breakthrough in the next few thousand years is not improbable. (R. F., 1970, p. 20)

You see, then, the kind of utilization enhancement that can result from a little creativity in evaluation designs.

BEHOLD, MY CHILD, THE QUESTIONNAIRE

Many evaluations involve some survey data. Poor quality questionnaires—and there is no shortage of these in evaluation—create problems in analysis, interpretation, and response rate. In working with a group to design a questionnaire I urge them to imagine being on the receiving end of the survey. To assist them in taking the stance of the poor, beleaguered survey respondent, I'll read the following poem. It was submitted anonymously to N. J. Demerach III and Kenneth G. Lutterman in lieu of a response to an anonymous questionnaire they sent out in their study of student values and campus religion at the University of Wisconsin.

A NOTE FROM THE UNDERGROUND
BY RESPONDENT No. 5542

The little men in untold legions
Descend upon the private regions.
Behold, my child, the questionnaire,
And be as honest as you dare.

As briefly as possible, kindly state
Age and income, height and weight.
Sex (M or F); sex of spouse
(or spouses—list).

Do you own your house?
How much of your income goes for rent?
Give racial background, by percent.
Have you had, or are you now having
Orgasm? Or thereunto a craving?
Will Christ return? If so, when?
(kindly fill this out in pen)
Do you masturbate? In what style?
(fill and return the enclosed vial)
Feces? Whose?

And were you beaten?
Was your mother? Sister? Dog?
(attach descriptive catalogue.)
Have you mystic inspiration?
Our thanks for your co-operation."

Distended now with new-got lore,
Our plump and pleasant men-of-war

Torture whimsey into fact,
And then, to sanctify the act.
Cast in gleaming, ponderous rows,
Ingots of insipid prose
A classic paper: Soon to be,
Rammed down the throats of such as we.

EVALUATION CONSULTING COSTUMES

Humor can be an effective way of presenting information about one's self, one's profession, one's perspective, and one's concerns. Humor can also be an effective way of learning about the perceptions and concerns of others. It is said that people show their character in nothing so much as in what they find laughable. In the following example humor helped me present information about myself while learning a great deal about the people with whom I was working.

I was asked to work with the staff of an agency renowned for its disorganization, incompetence, and ineffectiveness. This staff group, I was told, had been counseled by a host of management and communications consultants—all to no avail. Now the board wanted an evaluation with recommendations for "whipping the office into shape." I was told that I could expect the staff to be hostile. One previous consultant I knew told me that they had erected an almost impenetrable façade to protect themselves from outside attack—or help. From all that I had heard about the staff and their history (I made a number of discrete inquiries), it was clear that I needed to elicit their interest and cooperation or they would sabotage the evaluation (à la Machiavelli, Chapter 7). If I came on too strong they'd surely rebel. So I decided to try a light introduction aimed at letting them know that I was aware of their (justified?) antagonism to consultants. Then I hoped to carve out a role for myself that would (it was hoped) distinguish me from my predecessors while giving them an invitation (see Chapter 2) to participate actively in the evaluation process. The idea was to start off by laughing at myself (and my consultant colleagues) with a bit of satire. If successful, the satire would gradually expand to encompass the group.

> Satire concerns itself with logically extending a premise to its totally insane conclusion, thus forcing onto an audience certain unwelcome awareness.
>
> Jules Feiffer

I adapted the satire I used from a chapter on consultant posturing by Steele (1975). It is worth keeping in mind, as you read this transcript, that here we have one of those situations where you probably had to be there. Nevertheless, try to hear the words as they would be presented in a hyped-up, exaggerated, hyperbolic style, self-mocking, and at least enough timing in the delivery to give the impression that maybe there's a bit of tongue-in-cheek in what is being said.

"Good morning, I'm Michael Patton, the latest consultant to be sacrificed to this group. I understand that you folks are quite knowledgeable about and experienced with consultants. When I found out that you were a sophisticated group in dealing with—and from what I hear confounding—consultants, I thought I'd better check back with the pros at consulting school for a quick refresher course on the latest consulting techniques.

"I apparently contacted them at just the right time because they've introduced into the curriculum some new material that I think you'll find interesting. It comes from a book by Fritz Steele (1975) on *Consulting for Organizational Change*. In this book Fritz unveils 'the compleat consultant's costume catelogue.' He begins by presenting absolutely irrefutable evidence (in other words, he gives his opinion) that most encounters between client and consultant are massive examples of double presentation-of-self exercises being carried out under the handicap of having to pretend that some sort of task is being done at the same time (p. 85). Since appearances are critical in presentation-of-self, Fritz set out to systematically study the effects on client groups of the style of clothing worn by a consultant. After much data collection and detailed analysis he arrived at a mathematical representation of this phenomenon, which has become the core curriculum in the very best evaluation training programs."

I then gave them the following hand-out, which we went over together.

> The important measure of success (in a consulting exchange) is not whether an interpersonal event led to change, or to greater understanding, but rather whether it led to the client seeing the consultant in the manner in which the consultant wanted to be seen. Not to be overly technical, it could be expressed by the following equation: $(Ia = Id (.25Ip + .15V + .60CL) + Y)$, where Ia is the actual image of the consultant in client's eyes; Id is the image which the consultant desires to create; Ip is the previous image, which the client carries into the present encounter with the consultant; V is the verbal propaganda which the consultant spews out; CL is the impact of the clothes the consultant is wearing; and Y is a general correction factor, roughly standing for "You never can tell for sure. . . . "
>
> From the equation, it becomes immediately obvious which factor is the important one if you want to systematically increase a consultant's ability to manage his image in the eyes of the client. Unfortunately, that factor is Y, about which we still know nothing to speak of. (Steele, 1975, pp. 85-86)

There was more puzzlement than amusement in their reaction to the handout. They weren't yet prepared to let themselves be entertained. It was a hard group, heavy with body language of passive aggression—but they appeared curious. This wasn't quite what they had expected. They seemed to be still evaluating, collecting data about what I was up to before making a judgment. It wasn't just the Fritz material that I wanted them to find amusing. I wanted them to see the funny side of the situation we mutually found ourselves in—they the "client," me the "consultant." If we could laugh together at our situation we might be able to work together. I continued. "Based on this formula Fritz has created and field tested a catalogue of costumes for consultants. There is the New York Yankees baseball uniform that is especially effective for letting the group you're working with know that you are *really going to be a member of the team.* There is the suit of mirrors for letting others see you as a mirror-image of themselves (for use only when working with people who love themselves; with low self-esteem types the mirror suit can be a disaster). There is the astronaut suit for working with technically oriented organizations where people value being up on the latest and most sophisticated equipment. There is the Knight's suit of armor to be worn when giving negative feedback to clients. There is a full line of military uniforms for use when you want to speak with authority and give people commands to follow. There is the magician's outfit for 'that one consultant in four who aspires to a higher standard and wishes to continually amaze and confound the client with his feats of magic' (p. 103). Then there is the ghost costume—a white sheet. Fritz explains that this costume, and I quote:

> was designed to give the client as little data as possible, about the consultant or anything else. Its main feature is a large wraparound sheet and a pair of clog shoes (so that no feature of the consultant can actually be seen by the client). This is technically known as *visibility inscrutability* (vi). . . . In field testing this model we had several instances where the client forgot that the consultant was there at all. But the goal is to infuse the relationship with that air of mystery and mystique that can be so handy at certain key moments in a consultation, such as when a client resists what you are suggesting. (Steele, 1975, p. 102)

"Now, of course, the Fritz work was all done on costumes for general management and communications consultants. Evaluators, however, have developed their own special wardrobes. There's the Attila the Hun costume for pillaging programs. There's a very lovely and enticing costume for prostitution gigs where the evaluation consultant just lays down and collects a lot of money for a few minutes work. (*This brought the first real outburst of laughter—a very knowing kind of laughter letting me know that they recognized the type and had not yet excluded me from that category.*) There's a calculator costume—very uncomfortable to wear I am told—for generating lots of numbers about a program. Of course, there's the traditional line—the judge's robe for deciding the guilt or innocence of a program; the Sherlock Holmes garb for sniffing out the dirt on a program; and the beautifully tranquil Angel of Mercy costume for escorting dead programs to their eternal resting place in that big Agency in the sky.

"I can tell from your reactions (*there had been growing laughter and a few side comments—particularly in recognition of the prostitution costume*) that you're already familiar with this full line. I was afraid of that, so I've spent the last week trying to come up with an original costume just for this group. I didn't want to wear an outfit you'd already seen and grown tired of. I decided to come to this costume party—we'll discuss your costumes in a moment—I decided to come today as the Wizard of Oz . . . [Pause]. You don't seem to recognize the costume [I turned around modeling my quite ordinary suit]. I'm dressed as the Wizard appeared *after* Dorothy's dog Toto exposed him behind the curtain—an ordinary man in ordinary clothes. You'll remember that the Wizard had been trying to help Dorothy and her companions realize their high hopes while somehow coping with their profound skepticism and disappointment. 'Why you're no wizard at all!' she exclaimed. You'll recall also that the Wizard (before his exposure) gave Dorothy and her friends a task to complete: bringing him the broom of the Wicked Witch of the West. By working together on that assignment they each discovered what they were looking for, though it remained for the Wizard to help them analyze their experience, help them interpret the data, and give formal recognition to their newfound knowledge, as much for legitimacy in the eyes of others as for themselves. All the Wizard did was lay out a process for them to follow that permitted them to find out for themselves what they needed to know [Pause].

"The reputation and public image of your office is not a very favorable one. In fact, the word on the streets is that you're lost—maybe not in the land of Oz—but lost in any case. The purpose of an evaluation process is to help people in a program find out where they are. In my experience, when folks take that process seriously and work at completing the necessary tasks, more often than not they learn some things about themselves along the way.

"That's what I have to offer you—a process and a set of tasks that may, upon completion, tell you where you are and a little bit about how to get where you want to go. I invite you, then, to put on your costumes and start down the yellow brick evaluation road:

Some of you look like Dorothys—skeptical but determined—and, being lost, pretty short on options.

Some of you may be like the tin man—rusted, immobile, and thinking you're incapable of any longer caring, grown heartless from too many storms and too little shelter.

Some of you may come along as the lion—afraid, indeed scared to death if you'd admit it, but hiding the fear and perhaps willing to go along and see if maybe, just maybe, there's something there for you.

And then there's the scarecrow—all the appearance of being brainless and vulnerable (not even the crows respected him any longer), but wanting badly to find self-respect and feeling incomplete without a really functioning brain. Can you even remember when you stopped thinking?

"I don't know if any of those costumes feel like they fit. I can tell you that that's how you appear to the public. A tragi-comic agency of characters. Lost, Heartless, Brainless, Defensive (scared to death).

"So much for my presentation of self. I've been abrupt and pretty hard on you, but I wanted to be straight. What I have to offer you is a process and some tasks to be undertaken. I can't guarantee the outcome. Often it works; sometimes it doesn't work. A lot depends on the people in the process and how they complete the tasks.

"The first step in the process is finding out whether or not you're willing to undertake the required tasks. I'm going to stop talking now and ask for your assessment of the situation. Do you know where you are as a program and as an office? Do you know where you want to go? Do you know how to get there?"

What followed was an intense, open, and sometimes angry discussion. They did know how they appeared to the public. Many of them didn't like how they appeared, to which a stonefaced man in the corner responded, "Ye shall know the truth and the truth shall make you ill. . . . Let's do it."

The discussion lasted an hour and ended with a commitment from most (but not all) of those present to seriously undertake a rigorous evaluation. It was a stormy venture, but the resulting evaluation led to some major personnel and substantive program changes. The costume motif was sustained throughout the evaluation process as people joked about which role they were playing at different points in time. Various costume images provided a mechanism for release of tension and the raising of sensitive issues. There were lots of nominations, for example, for the Wicked Witches of the East and West.

At times I think that humor may have been the cement that held the process together. The joking in no way seemed to interfere with the seriousness of the actual evaluation tasks undertaken. Maybe that's because as Mark Van Doren observed, "Humorists are serious. They're the only people who are."

There's Always a Lesson

One of the questions I often get from evaluation students and others who've heard me use various humorous bits with groups is, "What do you do if you're trying to be funny and nobody laughs?"

Judging from the comments of all kinds of entertainers, including professional comics, it is natural to be nervous before an audience. I get very nervous when I'm trying out new material—whether it's humorous or serious material. I don't enjoy making a fool of myself any more than anyone else. Before I did the presentation in the preceding section I had a terrible night. I didn't sleep. I couldn't eat breakfast in the morning. And at the last minute I almost talked myself out of doing it. But the tension is not just from fear of appearing foolish. I find it's a process of energizing myself to do the very best job I can to make contact with a group of people, contact that will make it possible for us to work together effectively.

Failure is a matter of definition. The audience never completely knows what you are trying to do, so it's often possible to define an apparent failure (nobody cracked a smile) as a success. I'm convinced that no matter what happens in a workshop, consulting session, or task force meeting, there's always some way of using what happens to make a point. *There's always a lesson.* Any outcome (laughter or silence) is data. As an evaluation facilitator working with a group you can help shape the interpretation of that data (laughter or silence).

I once used some supposedly hysterical material laced with sexual innuendo in speaking to a university women's group. The material, given to me by a friend, poked fun at male hang-ups about evaluating sexual performance. Wrong approach! I couldn't have used worse judgment. It was the wrong group, wrong material, wrong night. At the end of the bit (which I shortened considerably), I looked at the cold, hostile stares and knew that my only hope was to put a lot of distance between myself and the sexist material I had used. In so doing I could use the audience reaction as an example of the nature of evaluation research. *There's always a lesson.* I closed the presentation as follows:

"Now you've heard this material and, judging by the looks on your faces, I don't think you much cared for it. Do you know that the guy who wrote that material thought it would be hysterically funny, especially to women? On paper he thought the stuff looked great. But in the actual test before a live audience—yourselves—the stuff turned out to be disastrous: insulting, inappropriate, insensitive.

"In effect, what we've just done is carry out an evaluation. The treatment is the material. The evaluation data consist of your reactions to the material. The judgment is clearly negative.

"This illustrates why an *empirical*—and I emphasize the word "empirical"—approach is so important in evaluation. A lot of program plans look good on paper to the people who write the plans. But the real test comes when those plans are used in the field. The purpose of an evaluation is to find out the real effects of a program on participants. It's clear from our experience tonight that no matter how good something may look to someone, on paper, the real evaluation comes in observing what happens in actual implementation."

We then had an excellent discussion analyzing the characteristics of the offending material. On what dimensions should the material be rated? We designed an experiment that would permit testing the material with different audiences under different conditions. What I had expected to be a ten-minute introductory piece became the focus for two hours of animated discussion from which emerged all the points I had wanted to make.

There is always a lesson to be learned and used in observing audience reaction to humor, games, simulations, handouts, or any other aspect of a presentation. All you have to do is watch what is happening—and use it. There are no failures as long as there are data. There is always a lesson.

A TECHNOLOGY OF FOOLISHNESS

For God's sake give me the man who has brains enough to make a fool of himself.

Adlai Stevenson

The ideal of evaluation explicitly stating goals and empirically monitoring achievement of those goals is an exemplar of human reason and rationality. Whatever modifications may be made, whatever competing models may emerge, evaluation research will remain in essence an expression and manifestation of the rationality of *Homo sapiens*—the distinguishing characteristic of our species. Yet the practice and politics of evaluation reveal our shortcomings in trying to attain rational ideals. The realities of evaluation practice are often exemplars of the less-than-rational sides of human nature. Laughter, seeing the funny side of things, and self-mocking satire are ways of understanding and managing the discrepancies between our professional ideals and the realities of evaluation practice.

James March (1972) has written insightfully on the need for a "technology of foolishness" to balance purely rational views dominant in planning, evaluation, and social science.

> If we had a good technology of foolishness, it might (in combination with the technology of reason) help in a small way to develop the unusual combination of attitudes and behaviors that describe interesting people, interesting organizations, and interesting societies of the world. (March, 1972, p. 428)

In creative evaluation the use of humor is part of the technology of foolishness.

Humor has many functions (Goldstein & McGhee, 1972; Foss, 1961). Research shows that humor can turn away anger and inhibit aggression (Baron & Ball, 1974). Humor can facilitate human communication (Bateson, 1953). It can reduce anxiety (Doris & Fierman, 1956; Laffal, Levine, & Redlich, 1953); contribute to general mental health (Klein, 1974; Levine, 1963; Shaw, 1960); and grease the wheels of social interaction (Martineau, 1972). Humor also is a powerful stimulant to and correlate of creativity (Fry & Allen, 1976; Schoel & Busse, 1971; Treadwell, 1970). Indeed, there is an enormous body of research on humor and its effects (see Chapman & Foot, 1976, for a representative collection).

Not everyone is comfortable using humor. Certainly not everyone is effective with every kind of humor. Like other elements in the repertoire of the creative evaluator, humor must be adapted to individual style and program/workshop circumstances. On the issue of developing an individual approach to the effective use of humor, evaluation sage Halcolm has some advice. With his wise counsel, this chapter on evaluation humor will be brought to a close.

The Experienced Humorist

An apprentice came to Halcolm to solicit guidance on how to entertain people and make them laugh. As a Sufi apprentice he had often been enlightened by the subtle humor and satire in many Nasrudin stories, but he felt inadequate in his own delivery of these stories—and completely unable to create his own humorous material. Halcolm reminded him that humor is a matter of individual taste and style, but he was touched by the sincerity and enthusiasm of the apprentice so he decided to try to help him. Halcolm then gave the apprentice some of his best one-liners.

That night the apprentice went to the local teahouse where he knew his fellow apprentices would be gathered. He managed to work himself into the center of a large group and at an opportune moment he began repeating the one-liners Halcolm had given him. His compatriots listened attentively, then regarded him curiously, but nary a laugh. The apprentice was devastated.

The next day he told Halcolm about his disastrous performance. Halcolm kindly suggested that perhaps one-liners were not his cup of tea, so to speak, so he gave him some humorous stories to try at the next teahouse gathering. Again hopeful, the apprentice approached the evening with high expectations. This time his performance created quite a reaction. Rather than the curious silence of the first night, his storytelling was met with jeers and boos. The apprentice was crushed.

Halcolm heard about the performance and pondered what comfort he might give the dejected apprentice. But the young man was too ashamed and despondent to even seek an audience with Halcolm. By evening Halcolm knew the apprentice lacked the courage to seek further counsel, so Halcolm went off in search of the would-be humorist. He found him sitting alone under a tree outside the compound wall. As Halcolm approached he heard the gentle and beautiful refrain of a song accompanied by the mandolin. Halcolm had forgotten that the apprentice was an accomplished musician and singer. The wise old sage listened until the music ended, then called the young man's name. Halcolm told him that different gifts were given to different people. Perhaps the young man had overlooked his superb talent of song. Might he not be satisfied to entertain with music?

The apprentice became suddenly animated, his eyes twinkling with insight. "You're right, of course, honored Master," the apprentice said. "I can sing funny songs to make people laugh."

Halcolm was distressed at the interpretation the apprentice gave to his encouragement. He gently suggested that serious ballads and hymns seemed more in keeping with the young man's gift and temperament, but the apprentice was determined to become a humorist. He begged Halcolm to give him some amusing songs he could sing at the teahouse. Seeing the young man's determination, Halcolm relented and taught the apprentice three humorous tunes. He also counseled him to begin with the more serious material that the musician performed so beautifully. Halcolm also agreed to be personally present at the teahouse to lend support during the performance.

When they arrived at the teahouse a large crowd had gathered. Word had leaked out that there was to be a special event that evening, and that Halcolm would be making one of his rare appearances at the teahouse. Halcolm led the nervous young man to the center of the assembly and introduced him as a gifted musician. The crowd responded enthusiastically to the opening ballads, which allowed the young artist to display his full range of voice and his inspired mandolin playing. The young man then launched into his humorous material. The first tune brought polite applause; on the second song the audience began to show annoyance; and by the middle of the third song even Halcolm's presence was insufficient to stop the jeers and insults.

Hurt and angry, he stopped singing and began talking. He told the audience of his great desire to entertain them, how he wanted to make them laugh. With great feeling and in considerable detail he related his experiences of the last three days. He told of the one-liners and the stories Halcolm had given him. He reminded them of his humiliation and great suffering. He was so caught up in the intensity of his feelings that he only gradually became aware that the entire assembly was laughing uproariously. Unconsciously and unintentionally the apprentice had fallen into a self-mocking rendition of his experiences that was more comic than tragic. He had discovered the classic "I don't get no respect," self-deprecating style of humor, and encouraged by the reactions of the audience, he played it to the hilt. He was an enormous success describing in comic style everyman's experience of failure. He finished with an unusually serious ballad of failure in love, but sung in a self-mocking style, he brought the teahouse down. He had discovered his own style of humor.

It remained for Halcolm to explain the nature and reasons for his success. Talking the next day, the young man was still in a quandary about how to develop his craft and enlarge his repertoire of material. "I suppose," counseled Halcolm, "you'll have to get more experience in humiliation. Given the nature of the human experience, I expect you'll have no difficulty finding new material. Learn to laugh at your tragedies and share that laughter with others. In so doing, you will have discovered not only a craft, but a way of life."

NOTES

1. Used by permission of Donald Kaul.
2. From Schwartz (1974). Used by permission of Social Policy Corporation, copyright 1974.

CHAPTER 14: Creative Evaluation Themes

Creativity will dominate our time after the concepts of work and fun have been blurred by technology.

Issac Asimov (1983, p. 42)

The Center for Creative Leadership has reported that more than half of the *Fortune* 500 Corporations have instigated formal creativity training for key managers and executives (DeWitt, 1986, p. 1B). While different companies and training courses use varying techniques, there are common themes that provide guidance for creative thinking.

(1) *Be open.* Creativity begins with openness to the possibility that what is does not have to be what will be.

(2) *Generate options.* There is always more than one way to think about or do something.

(3) *Divergence before convergence.* Begin by exploring a variety of directions and possibilities before focusing on the details. Branch out, go on mental excursions and brainstorm multiple perspectives before converging on the most promising.

(4) *Use multiple stimuli.* Creativity training often includes exposure to many different avenues of expression: drawing, music, role-playing, story boarding, metaphors, improvisation, playing with toys, and constructing futuristic scenarios.

(5) *Side-track, zig-zag, and circumnavigate.* Creativity is seldom a result of purely linear and logical deduction. The creative person explores back and forth, round and about, in the out, over and under. . . .

(6) *Change patterns.* Habits, standard operating procedures, and heuristics are barriers to creativity. Become aware of and change your patterned ways of thinking and behaving.

(7) *Make linkages.* Many creative exercises include practice in learning how to connect the seemingly unconnected.

(8) *Trust yourself.* Self-doubt short-circuits creative impulses. If you say to yourself, "I'm not creative," you won't be.

(9) *Work at it.* Creativity is not all fun. It takes hard work, background research, and mental preparation.

(10) *Play at it.* Creativity is not all work. It can and should be play and fun.

These are some of the common themes that cut across various approaches to creativity. With these larger themes as context, I turn now to a review of the major themes of creative evaluation practice in this book.

MAJOR THEMES

Taking the Professional Standards Seriously

An important sign of the coming of age of a profession is the development of professional standards of practice. Evaluation now has such a set of standards indicating what constitutes excellence and acceptable behavior. The first chapter discussed the nature, origin, and importance of the standards. Before about 1975 the premises and standards of evaluation research could scarcely be differentiated from those of basic researchers in the traditional social and behavioral sciences. Technical quality and methodological rigor were not only primary, but were about all that counted. The emergent standards of evaluation research broadened the responsibilities of social and behavioral scientists engaged in the professional practice of evaluation. The new standards focus on four criteria: utility, feasibility, propriety, amd accuracy. These are our standards of excellence.

Taking the standards seriously means consciously and deliberately integrating attention to the standards into each evaluation one conducts. Taking the standards seriously means that, as an evaluator, one is part of a profession, and one is accountable to one's professional colleagues to uphold professional standards of excellence. The corollary to this professional accountability is that decision makers and information users have a right to expect evaluators with whom they contract to uphold professional standards in the conduct of their work. Taking the standards seriously means translating them from abstract values into concrete patterns of practice. The point here is that the standards have real, practical implications for how an evaluation is conducted. They are also the source for the creative mandate in evaluation.

Situational Responsiveness

These new standards recognize that there is no one best way to conduct evaluations routinely. Every evaluation situation is unique. A successful evaluation—one that is useful, practical, ethical, and accurate—emerges from the special characteristics and conditions of a particular situation: a mixture of people, politics, history, context, resources, constraints, values, needs, interest, and chance. This constitutes a major shift in perspective from evaluation judged by a single, standard, and universal set of criteria (methodological rigor as defined by the hypothetic-deductive paradigm) to situational evaluation where judgment criteria are multiple, flexible, and diverse.

Situational evaluation means that evaluators have to be prepared to deal with many different people and situations. Judgments about the relative creativity of a particular evaluation process or evaluation finding can only be made with reference to a particular situation involving specific people, a specific program, and specific constraints. The standards of evaluation are not absolute behavioral guidelines. They require adaptation and interpretation in the context of specific circumstances and constraints.

Situational responsiveness is the challenge to which creative evaluation thinking is the response. Situational responsiveness is a challenge because the evidence from behavioral science is that in most areas of decision making and judgment, when faced with complex choices and multiple possibilities, we fall back on a set of deeply embedded rules and standard operating procedures that predetermine what we do, thereby effectively short-circuiting situational adaptability. This may help explain why so many evaluators who have genuinely embraced the ideology of situational evaluation find that the approaches in which they are trained and with which they are most comfortable just happen to be particularly appropriate in each new evaluation they confront — time after time after time. The first chapter reviewed the research findings from studies of human heuristics that support this claim that most of the time evaluators, and the decision makers with whom they work, are running — and thinking — according to preprogrammed tapes. It turns out that most of the time, in order to make even trivial decisions, we rely on routine heuristics, rules of thumb, standard operating procedures, tricks of the trade, and scientific paradigms.

A major difficulty posed by the human reliance on paradigms and heuristics for problem solving and decision making is not just their existence, but our general lack of awareness of their existence. Autonomic thinking systems and conditioned reflexes are barriers to creative evaluation thinking. It is difficult to be attuned and responsive to the uniqueness of each new situation when our programmed heuristics and paradigms are controlling the analytical process, screening unfamiliar data, anchoring the new situation within the narrow parameters of our past experiences, and making available to us primarily those definitions and approaches we have used most often in the past. Yet there is also evidence that, while it is neither easy nor unusual, it is possible to become aware of our paradigms and heuristics, and in that awareness take control of our decision processes, thereby releasing our creative potential and enhancing our ability to be truly situationally responsive and adaptive. This book has aimed at increasing heuristic awareness and enhancing the potential for creative evaluation by enlarging the evaluator's capacity to respond situationally.

Training Evaluation Users for Use

Another basic theme of this book has been that situationally responsive and active-reactive-adaptive evaluators will find opportunities in virtually any evaluation to train decision makers, funders, information users, staff, and stakeholders of all kinds in the basics of evaluation. Training is not something to be restricted to traditional classroom settings. When working with a group of people in an evaluation process, the situation can be defined as partly a training exercise aimed at empowering participants to assert greater control over program implementation and outcomes through their increased knowledge about and understanding of both program and evaluation processes. When a program evaluation is defined as a learning opportunity for participants—learning about program evaluation as well as learning about the program being evaluated — the evaluator is helping build an increasingly sophisticated group of consumers able to better use information for program improvement. My premise has been that all effective evaluators are trainers, and as trainers all evaluators can enhance their professional practice by actively involving decision makers and information users in all stages of the evaluation process. Thus a recurring theme in every chapter has been the importance of and ways to involve stakeholders, thereby increasing their understanding of the evaluation and their commitment to use evaluation findings.

Simplicity and Focus

Another common theme of previous chapters has been the importance of simplicity and focus in making manageable the complex realities we encounter, and in facilitating communications about those complex realities. Metaphorical communications, conceptual thinking, and flowchart construction are all tools for simplifying and focusing evaluation problems and processes. Much of the creative imperative of the profession is a search for ways to simplify the enormous complexities of real-world programs and bring focus to what often appear to be diffuse, all-encompassing, haphazard, and/or multifaceted processes, many of which seem specially designed to keep evaluators (and decision makers) confused and off balance.

Multiple Evaluator Roles and Responsibilities

Yet another theme that runs throughout this book is the diversity inherent in the role of the creative utilization-focused evaluator. Evaluators are called on to be scientists, program consultants, group facilitators, keen observers, statisticians, project administrators, diplomats, politicians, writers, and trainers. In order to be truly situationally responsive, the evaluator needs to be able to draw on a large repertoire of techniques, approaches, models, and methods. The image of the professional evaluator that I hope has emerged in these pages is of a flexible, adaptable generalist. Since graduate schools are designed to produce subject matter and methods specialists, it is not easy to become a generalist — a person able to use a variety of methods and approaches. Kipling advised us to "love all men, but none too much." The evaluation corollary is to love all methods and models, but none too much.

A Sufi story tells of a musician who sat in the town plaza every day strumming over and over the same string on his lute. Whenever one of the townspeople would ask why he played only one string, he responded that he was a specialist, and he did not intend to take up the study of another string until he completely mastered his first specialty. I am reminded of this story when evaluators explain to me that they're satisfied doing only one type of evaluation in which they feel confident and well trained. Specialists are not renowned for their situational adaptability, except for their skill in adapting situations to fit their specialty. Practical evaluators who take seriously the charge to adapt themselves and their methods to the needs of specific situations and decision makers may find that they can make good use of specialists, thereby securing the depth that they may need in a particular instance, without becoming a specialist.

Communications and Group Facilitation

At the heart of the multiple roles the creative evaluator plays is the role of communications facilitator. Whether acting as an information broker, a data manager, a storyteller, an artist, a humorist, or a scientist, the evaluator is facilitating communications. Helping people communicate about their information needs; helping them interpret data; helping them translate data into decisions and program improvements; and helping them develop realistic goals for both programs and evaluation of programs — these are processes that involve skilled communications facilitation.

Skillful communications and information brokering require a keen sensitivity to the needs and interests of those with whom one is working. This is important in working one-to-one with a client and is essential when facilitating a group. Every chapter in this book deals with ways of enhancing communication and mutual understanding in an evaluation process.

Negotiation

The two-way flow of communications between evaluators and stakeholders includes negotiation. The notion of being active-reactive-adaptive implies the evaluator's negotiating stance by placing the mandate to be "active" first in this consulting trinity: active-reactive-adaptive. Responsiveness does not mean rolling over and playing dead (or passive) in the face of stakeholders' interests or perceived needs. Just as the evaluator in utilization-focused evaluation does not unilaterally impose focus and methods on an evaluation, so too stakeholders should not be allowed unilaterally to impose their initial perceptions or preconceptions on the evaluation. *It is a negotiated process.* This allows the concerns and perspectives of both stakeholders and evaluators to merge and intermingle with the host of other factors that affect an evaluation, thereby giving uniqueness and relevance to the final negotiated design and product.

Individual Style

Just as evaluation situations and program decision makers are unique, so too individual evaluators are unique. Evaluators bring to evaluation situations their own style, personal history, and professional experience. All of the techniques and ideas presented in this book must be adapted to the style of the individual using them. This is clear in the imagery of the evaluator as humorist, artist, and storyteller, but it is also true for the evaluator who uses metaphors, matrices, flowcharts, experiential games, simulation exercises, and original conceptual distinctions. I have urged creative evaluators throughout this book to make the most of their own personal and professional resources: thus the importance — and inevitability — of individual style.

Self-Evaluation and Ongoing Professional Development

The second chapter examined the personal and professional commitments necessary for evaluation repertoire expansion, self-analysis, and skills development. Opening with the premise that creative evaluation requires creative evaluators, Chapters 2 and 3 examined some of the reasons for striving to be more creative: the "calling" of the profession; personal engagement as one who takes an active rather than passive stance toward the world; the effectiveness that comes from situational flexibility; and the personal satisfaction of creative responsiveness. After inviting readers to conduct a baseline assessment of their evaluation skills, thinking, ideology, and feelings, I explored some of the dilemmas of evaluation practice; performing well while still learning; being open without being empty; finding a balance between time for reflection and the rewards of action and being busy; and being responsive to one's own needs and the needs of one's clients. These dilemmas are not so much to be resolved as managed, and managing them is likely to require its own bits of creativity now and then.

Chapter 2 offered five prerequisites for creative development as a professional: (1) recognition that there is something to be learned; (2) recognizing a need for and the importance of creative evaluation approaches; (3) believing that learning to be more creative is possible; (4) commitment to put time, energy, and resources into the creative process; and (5) a willingness to take risks. Finally, the chapter considered the problem of defining creativity, and offered the materials in this book as resources for the reader to use in developing his or her own definition and standards of creativity as applied to evaluation.

Creative evaluators pay attention to what influences them. Creative evaluators are keen observers of their own actions as part of the ongoing process of observing and studying the entire evaluation endeavor. These observations are used to keep creative evaluators situationally responsive, open to new possibilities, and capable of reaching into their large repertoire of techniques, methods, and approaches to find or adapt a technique, method, or approach that is appropriate to the situation at hand.

Building a Repertoire

"Repertoire" traditionally refers to the stock of plays, roles, or songs that a company, actor, or singer is familiar with and ready to perform. I have suggested throughout this book that evaluators need a broad repertoire of methods, communication approaches, group facilitation techniques, conceptual options, and ways of explaining evaluation. The repertoire in this book includes new conceptual distinctions, metaphors, flowcharts, matrices, simulations, games, experiential exercises, alphabet soup, storythinking, picturethinking, creative designs, humor, and at the end of this chapter—song. Of what does your evaluation repertoire consist? What are you familiar with and ready to use in your evaluation performance?

Utilization-Focused Evaluation

The overarching premise of this book is that the driving force in an evaluation should be a concern for how decision makers, information users, and stakeholders will use evaluation processes and findings. The utility criterion is the first priority in creative evaluation. Situational responsiveness is important because in such responsiveness lies the hope of making findings appropriate, relevant, accessible, understandable, interesting, timely, important, attention-getting — all of which is to say, in a word, useful.

Utilization-focused evaluation is not a formal model or recipe for how to conduct evaluations. Rather, it is a creative and responsive set of options. The active-reactive-adaptive evaluator chooses from among these options as he or she works with decision makers and information users throughout the evaluation process. There is no formula guaranteeing success in this approach—indeed, the criteria for success are variable. Utilization means different things to different people in different settings, and is an issue subject to negotiation between evaluators and intended users.

There are only two fundamental requirements in this approach; everything else is a matter for negotiation, adaptation, selection, and matching. First, the intended evaluation users must be identified — real, visible, specific, and caring human beings, not ephemeral, general, and abstract "audiences," organizations, or agencies. Second, evaluators must work actively, reactively, and adaptively with these specific stakeholders to make all other decisions about the evaluation— decisions about focus, design, methods, analysis, interpretation, and dissemination. The essence of utilization-focused evaluation is, quite simply, the focus on users and utility. The techniques in this book have all been aimed at actively involving primary intended users in a meaningful and useful evaluation process.

This book closes, then, with the focus on use. The purpose of creative evaluation is to make a difference: to improve programs and decision making about programs. To that end I close with the words to Halcolm's *Utilization Anthem*. This song was performed for the first time in public at the annual awards banquet of the joint meeting of the Evaluation Research Society and the Evaluation Network in San Francisco in 1984. This song is meant to be sung by evaluators to intended users as the evaluator rides off into the sunset to do good in yet another new program.

Halcolm's Utilization Chorus
(sung to the tune of *Auld Lang Syne*)

May all the data *not* be forgot
And simply left to rot;
Oh, sneak a look every now and then,
And see what you have got.

(Chorus)

Yes, see what you have got,
Oh, see what you have not,
We'll drink a cup of kindness then
And see what the program has wrought.

References

Abt, Clark S. *Games for learning*. Social Studies Curriculum Project, Occasional Paper No. 7. Cambridge, MA: Education Services, 1966.

Abt, Clark C. *Serious games*. New York: Viking, 1974.

Adams, James L. *Conceptual blockbusting*. San Francisco: San Francisco Book Company, 1976.

Alexander, H. A. Eisner's aesthetic theory of evaluation. *Educational Theory*, 1986, Summer, 36, 259-270.

Alkin, Marvin C., Daillak, Richard, & White, Peter. *Using evaluations: Does evaluation make a difference?* Beverly Hills, CA: Sage, 1979

Ames, F. H., Jr. RATTLE. In J. Ertel (Ed.), *Selected papers, The Journal of Irreproducible Results*. Chicago: Journal of Irreproducible Results Publishers, 1977.

Anderson, Barry F. *The complete thinker*. Englewood Cliffs, NJ: Prentice-Hall, 1980.

Andrews, F. M., Davidson, T., Klein, L., O'Malley, P., & Rodgers, W. *A guide for selecting statistical techniques for analyzing social science data*. Ann Arbor: Survey Research Center, Institute for Social Research, University of Michigan, 1974.

Asimov, Isaac. Creativity will dominate our time after the concepts of work and fun have been blurred by technology. *Personnel Administrator*, 1983, 28(2), 42-46.

Bandler, Richard, & Grinder, John. *Patterns of the hypnotic techniques of Milton H. Erikson, M.D., vol. 1*. Cupertino, CA: Meta Publications, 1975.

Barkdoll, Gerald L. Type III evaluations: Consultation and consensus. *Public Administration Review*, 1980, March/April 174-179.

Baron, R. A., & Ball, R. L. The aggression-inhibiting influence of nonhostile humor. *Journal of Experimental Social Psychology,* 1974, 10, 23-33.

Bateson, Gregory. The role of human communication. In H. Von Forester (Ed.), *Cybernetics*. New York: Macey Foundation, 1953.

Bateson, Gregory. The pattern which connects. Speech for the Lindisfarne Association, October 17, 1977, at the Cathedral of St. John the Divine, Manhattan.

Bateson, Gregory. Introduction. In *Mind and nature: A necessary unity*. New York: E. P. Dutton, 1978.

Bavelas, Alex. Communication patterns in task-oriented groups. In D. Cartwright & A. Zander (Eds.), *Group dynamics: Research and theory*. New York: Harper & Row, 1960.

Beardsley, P. L. *Redefining rigor*. Beverly Hills, CA: Sage, 1980.

Becker, Howard. Preface. In J. Wagner (Ed.), *Images of information: Still photography in the social sciences.* Beverly Hills, CA: Sage, 1979.

Berman, Paul. A new perspective on implementation design: Adaptive implementation. In P. D. Hood (Ed.), *New perspectives on planning, management, and evaluation in school improvement: A report of the 1979 Far West Laboratory summer workshop on educational dissemination and school improvement.* San Francisco: Far West Laboratory for Educational Research and Development, 1979.

Bernstein, Ilene, & Freeman, Howard E. *Academic and entrepreneurial research.* New York: Russell Sage, 1975.

Bertcher, Harvey J. *Group participation: Techniques for leaders and members.* Beverly Hills, CA: Sage, 1979.

Black, M. *Models and metaphors.* Ithaca, NY: Cornell University Press, 1962.

Bogen, J. E. The other side of the brain. *Bulletin of the Los Angeles Neurological Societies,* 1969, 34, 73-105.

Braskamp, L. A., & Brown, R. D. (Eds.). *Utilization of evaluative information.* San Francisco: Jossey-Bass, 1980.

Brightman, Harvey, & Noble, Carl. On the ineffective education of decision scientists. *Decision Sciences,* 1979, 10, 151-157.

Bruner, Jerome. *The process of education.* Cambridge, MA: Harvard University Press, 1960.

Bruner, Jerome. *Towards a theory of instruction.* Cambridge, MA: Harvard University Press, 1967.

Bruner, Jerome. Nature and uses of immaturity. *American Psychologist,* 1972, 27, 681-708.

Bryson, John M., & Delbecq, Andre L. A contingent approach to strategy and tactics in project planning. *Journal of the American Planning Association,* 1979, 45, April.

Buzan, T. *Use both sides of your brain.* New York: E. P. Dutton, 1976.

Campbell, Jeanne. Factors and conditions influencing utilization of information by schools: The cases of Minnesota's planning evaluation and reporting legislation. Ph.D. dissertation, University of Minnesota, 1983.

Chapman, A. D., & Foot, H. C. (Eds.), *Humor and laughter: Theory, research and applications.* London: John Wiley, 1976.

Clark, David. The configurational perspective and goal-free planning. In P. D. Hood (Ed.), *New perspectives on planning, management, and evaluation in school improvement:* A report of the 1979 Far West Laboratory Summer Workshop on Educational Dissemination and School Improvement. San Francisco: Far West Laboratory for Educational Research and Development, 1979.

Comtois, Joseph. The unifying framework of evaluation. *Bureaucrat,* 1981, 3(3).

Connolly, W. E. *The terms of political discourse.* Lexington, MA: D. C. Heath, 1974.

Couper, John. Imaginaction: everyone's genius. *Human Potential,* 1984, 1, 3-11.

Courlander, Harold. *A treasury of Afro-American folklore.* New York: Crown, 1976.

CYDR (Center for Youth Development and Research). *Self-evaluation method.* St. Paul, MN: CYDR, University of Minnesota, 1974.

Davis, Howard R., & Salasin, Susan E. The utilization of evaluation. In E. L. Struening & M. Guttentag (Eds.), *Handbook of evaluation research, vol. 1.* Beverly Hills, CA: Sage, 1975.

DeGroot, A. Perception and memory versus thought: Some old ideas and recent findings. In B. Kleinmuntz (Ed.), *Problem solving.* New York: John Wiley, 1966.

Delattre, Pierre. *Tales of a Dalai Lama*. London: Penguin, 1978.
Dewar, Thomas. The professionalization of the client. *Social Policy,* 1977, September-October.
DeWitt, Karen. Employees being taught new thoughts. *USA Today,* 1983, November 5, B1-2
Doris, S., & Fierman, E. Humor and anxiety. *Journal of Abnormal and Social Psychology,* 1956, 53, 59-62.
Duke, Paul, & Greenblat, Cathy. *Game-generating games.* Beverly Hills, CA: Sage, 1979.
Edwards, Betty. *Drawing on the right side of the brain.* Los Angeles: J. P. Tarcher, 1979.
Eisner, Elliot. *The educational imagination.* New York: Macmillan, 1979.
Etheredge, Lloyd S. Government learning: An overview. In S. Long (Ed.), *Handbook of political behavior.* New York: Plenum, 1980. (Page citations refer to prepublication mimeograph.)
Evaluation Standards Committee (Joint Committee on Standards for Educational Evaluation). *The standards for evaluation of educational programs, projects, and materials.* New York: McGraw-Hill, 1981.
F., R. The triple blind test. In J. Ertel (Ed.), *Selected Papers: The Journal of Irreproducible Results.* Chicago: Journal of Irreproducible Results Publishers, 1977.
Far West Laboratory for Educational Research and Development. *Proceedings: Educational evaluation and public policy. A conference.* San Francisco, CA: Author, 1976.
Ferguson, M. *The brain revolution.* New York: Taplinger, 1973.
Fluegelman, A. (Ed.). *The new games book.* Garden City, NY: Headlands Press, 1976.
Foss, B. The functions of laugher. *New Scientist,* 1961,11, 20-22.
Frank, Frederick. *The zen of seeing.* New York: Vintage, 1973.
Frank, Frederick. *The awakened eye.* New York: Vintage, 1979.
Fry, W. F., & Allen, M. Humor and creativity. In A. S. Chapman & H. C. Foot (Eds.), *Humor and laughter: Theory, research and applications.* London: John Wiley, 1976.
Geertsen, Reed (Ed.). *Eighty-one techniques for teaching sociological concepts.* Washington, DC: American Sociological Association, 1979.
Gephart, William. The president's corner. *Evaluation Network Newsletter,* 1979, Spring.
Gephart, William. Speech delivered in plenary session at the 6th Annual Meeting of the Evaluation Network, Memphis, Tennessee, 1980.
Ghiselin, B. *The creative process.* New York: Mentor, 1955.
Goldstein, J. H., & McGhee, P. E. (Eds.). *The psychology of humor.* New York: Academic Press, 1972.
Grinder, John, & Bandler, Richard. *The structure of magic, vols. 1 & 2.* Palo Alto, CA: Science and Behavior Books, 1976.
Grinder, John, & Bandler, Richard. *Frogs into PRINCES: Neuro linguistic programming.* Moab, UT: Real People Press, 1979.
Guba, E. G. *The use of metaphors in constructing theory.* Paper and Report Series No. 3. Portland, OR: Northwest Regional Educational Laboratory, 1978.
Gurdjieff, G. I. *Beelzebub's tales to his grandson.* New York: E. P. Dutton, 1973.
Guttentag, Marcia, & Elmer Struening. *Handbook of evaluation research, vols. 1 and 2.* Newbury Park, CA: Sage, 1975.
Hage, Jerald. *Techniques and problems of theory construction in sociology.* New York: John Wiley, 1972.
Henri, Robert. *The art spirit.* Philadelphia: J. B. Lippincott, 1923.

Hoopes, David S., Pederson, Paul B., & Renwick, George. (Eds.). *Overview of intercultural education, training and research, vol. 1: Research; vol. 2: Training and education; vol. 3: Special research areas.* Society for Intercultural Education, Training, and Research (SIETAR). LaGrange Park, IL: Intercultural Network, 1978.

Hoopes, David S., & Ventura, Paul (Eds.). *Intercultural sourcebook: cross-cultural training methodologies.* LaGrange Park, IL: Intercultural Network, 1979.

Horn, Robert E., & Cleaves, Anne. *The guide to simulations/games for education and training.* Beverly Hills, CA: Sage, 1980.

House, Ernest. Assumptions underlying evaluation models. *Educational Researcher,* 1978, 7, 4-12.

House, Ernest. *Evaluating with validity.* Beverly Hills, CA: Sage, 1980.

Hurty, Kathleen. Report by women's caucus. *Proceedings: Educational evaluation and public policy, a conference.* San Francisco: Far West Laboratory for Educational Research and Development, 1976.

Inbar, Michael. *Routine decision-making: The future of bureaucracy.* Beverly Hills, CA: Sage, 1979.

International Livestock Center for Africa. *International livestock center for Africa: the first years.* Addis Ababa, Ethiopia: ILCA, 1980.

James, Grace. *Japanese fairy tales.* New York: Mayflower Books, 1980.

Janowitz, Morris. Where is the cutting edge of sociology? *Sociological Quarterly,* 1979, 20, 591-593.

Jaynes, J. *The origin of consciousness in the breakdown of the bicameral mind.* Boston: Houghton Mifflin, 1976.

Johnson, David. *Reaching out.* Englewood Cliffs, NJ: Prentice-Hall, 1972.

Kelly, E. F. Evaluating and metaphor: A terrible beauty. Paper presented at the annual meeting of the American Educational Research Association, Washington, D.C., 1975.

Kingsley, Charles. *The heroes, or Greek fairy tales for my children.* New York: Mayflower Books, 1980.

Kipling, Rudyard. *Just so stories.* New York: Mayflower Books, 1980.

Klein, S. P. On the use of humor in counseling. *Canadian Counselor,* 1974, 8, 233-239.

Kleinmuntz, B. (Ed.). *Problem solving.* New York: John Wiley, 1966.

Kleinmuntz, B. (Ed.). *Formal representations of human judgment.* New York: John Wiley, 1968.

Koestler, A. *The act of creation.* London: Hutchinson, 1964.

Kolhoff, Kathleen. *Canyon walls/smokefilled bars.* Murray, KY: Kolhoff copyright, 1980.

Krenkle, Noele, & Saretsky, Gary. Evaluation a la Machiavelli. *Phil Delta Kappan.* 1973, December.

Krishnamurti, J. *Think on these things.* New York: Harper & Row, 1964.

Kuhn, Thomas. *The structure of scientific revolutions.* Chicago: University of Chicago Press, 1970.

Laffal, S., Levine, S., & Redlich, F. C. An anxiety reduction theory of humor. *American Psychologist,* 1953, 8, 383-393.

LaFontaine, J. *Selected fables* (J. Michie, trans.). New York: Viking, 1979.

Levine, S. Humor and mental health. In A. Deutsch & H. Fishman (Eds.), *Encyclopedia of mental health, III.* Metuchen, NJ: Scarecrow Press, 1963.

Lieberman, Anne. Two school improvement cases studies. In P. D. Hood (Ed.), *New perspectives on planning, management, and evaluation in school improvement: A report on the 1979 Far West Laboratory summer workshop on educational dissemination and school improvement.* San Francisco: Far West Laboratory for Educational Research and Development, 1979.

Lincoln, Yvonna S., & Guba, E. G. The distinction between merit and worth in evaluation. *Educational Evaluation and Policy Analysis,* 1980, 2, 61-71.

Lynn, Laurence E. Crafting policy analysis for decision makers. Interview conducted by Michael Kirst in *Educational Evaluation and Policy Analysis,* 1980, 2, 85-90. (a)

Lynn, Laurence E. *Designing public policies, a casebook on the role of policy analysis.* Santa Monica, CA: Goodyear, 1980. (b)

McGulgan, F. L., & Schoonover, R.A. (Eds.). *The psychophysiology of thinking.* New York: Academic Press, 1973.

McKenzie, R. A. *The time trap.* New York: AMACOM, 1972.

McKnight, John. Professionalized service and disabling help. Paper presented at the First Annual Symposium on Bioethics of the Clinical Research Institute of Montreal, October 8, 1976.

McLellan, J. *The question of play.* Oxford, England: Pergamon, 1970.

March, J. G. Model bias in social action. *Review of Educational Research,* 1972, 42, 413-429.

Martineau, W. H. A model of the social functions of humor. In J. H. Goldstein & P. E. McGhee (Eds.), *The psychology of humor.* New York: Academic Press, 1972.

Mazia, Donald. Comment on cell numbers. *AIBS Bulletin.* Berkeley: University of California, February 1962.

Millar, S. *Psychology of play.* Baltimore: Penguin, 1968.

Mitchell, Richard. *Less than words can say.* Boston: Little, Brown, 1979.

Mitroff, Ian. Systemic problem solving. Pp. 129-143 in Morgan W. McCall, Jr., & Michael M. Lombardo (Eds.), *Leadership: Where else can we go?* Durham, NC: Duke University Press, 1978.

Newell, A., & Simon, H. A. *Human problem-solving.* Englewood Cliffs, NJ: Prentice-Hall, 1972.

Ortony, A. Why metaphors are necessary and not just nice. *Educational Theory,* 1975, 25, 45-53.

Patton, Michael Q. Structure and diffusion of open education. Ph.D. dissertation. Madison: University of Wisconsin, 1973.

Patton, Michael Q. *Utilization-focused evaluation.* Beverly Hills, CA: Sage, 1978. 2nd edition, 1986.

Patton, Michael Q. *Qualitative evaluation methods.* Beverly Hills, CA: Sage, 1980.

Patton, Michael Q. Making methods choices. *Program Evaluation and Planning,* 1981, 3(4).

Patton, Michael Q. *Practical evaluation.* Beverly Hills, CA: Sage, 1982.

Patton, Michael Q., Ippel, David, & Lekowitz, Steve. Role-playing as a cross-cultural training technique. In A. Wright & A. Hammons (Eds.), *Cross-cultural handbook.* Estes Park, CO: Estes Park Center for Research and Education, 1969.

Perrow, Charles. *Organizational analysis.* Belmont, CA: Wadsworth, 1970.

Pollock, Ted. *Managing yourself creatively.* New York: Hawthorn Books, 1971.

Radin, Paul. *The trickster: A study in American Indian mythology.* New York: Schocken, 1972.

Raudsepp, Eugene. How creative are you? *Writer's Digest*, 1981, February, 26-28 (from Princeton Creative Research, Princeton, New Jersey).

Rayder, Nicholas. Methodological and ethical problems of research in early childhood education. In *Proceedings: Educational evaluation and public policy, a conference.* San Francisco: Far West Laboratory for Educational Research and Development, 1977.

Reilly, Mary (Ed.). *Play as exploratory learning.* Beverly Hills, CA: Sage, 1974.

Rich, Robert F. Howard Davis's writings. *Knowledge: Creation, Diffusion, Utilization*, 1986, 8, 197-216.

Rogers, J. *Adult learning.* Milton Keynes: Open University Press, 1977.

Rossiter, Charles. Four steps to creative insight. *Human Potential*, 1984, 1, 8-9.

Rothenberg, Albert. Creative contradictions. *Psychology Today*, 1979, 13, 54-62.

Rouff, L. L. Creativity and sense of humor. *Psychological Reports*, 1975, 57, 1022.

Rutman, Len. *Planning useful evaluations: Evaluability assessments.* Beverly Hills, CA: Sage, 1980.

Salasian, Susan E. A will and a way to make life better. *Knowledge: Creation, Diffusion, Utilization*, 1986, 210-221.

Schoel, D. R., & Busse, T. V. Humor and creative abilities. *Psychological Reports*, 1971, 29, 34.

Schwartz, Edward. Dear Mr. Jefferson. *Social Policy*, 1974, 5, 10-11.

Scriven, Michael. Prose and cons about goal-free evaluation. *Evaluation Comment: The Journal of Educational Evaluation*, 1972, 3, 1-7.

Scriven, Michael. A perspective on evaluation. Videotape interview. Minneapolis, MN: Program Evaluation Resource Center, 1976.

Scriven, Michael. Merit vs. value. *Evaluation News*, 1978, 8, 20-29.

Scriven, Michael. Snapshots by Scriven. *Evaluation Network Newsletter*, 1979, 11, 35-37.

Seefeldt, Michael. The evaluator as artist: The problem of explicit definition. Paper presented at the 6th Annual Meeting of the Evaluation Network, Memphis, Tennessee, 1980.

Shah, Idries. *The Sufis.* Garden City, NY: Doubleday, 1964.

Shah, Idries. *The way of the Sufi.* London: Jonathan Cape, 1968.

Shah, Idries. *The pleasantries of the incredible Mulla Nasrudin.* New York: E. P. Dutton, 1971.

Shah, Idries. *The magic monastery.* New York: E. P. Dutton, 1972. (a)

Shah, Idries. *The exploits of the incomparable Mulla Nasrudin.* New York: E. P. Dutton, 1972. (b)

Shah, Idries. *The subtleties of the inimitable Mulla Nasrudin.* New York: E. P. Dutton, 1973.

Shah, Idries. *Learning how to learn.* London: Octagon Press, 1978.

Shah, Idries. *World tales.* New York: Harcourt Brace Jovanovich, 1979.

Shaw, F. S. Laughter: Paradigm of growth. *Journal of Individual Psychology*, 1960, 16, 151-157.

Silva, Jose. *The mind control method.* London: Grenada Publishing, 1977.

Silverberg, Robert & Greenberg, Martin H. (Eds.). *Treasury of modern science fiction.* New York: Arbor House, 1980.

Simon, Herbert. *Administrative behavior.* New York: Macmillan, 1957.

Simon, Herbert. On how to decide what to do. *Bell Journal of Economics*, 1978, 9, 494-507.

Smith, M. Brewster. Foreword. In M. Reilly (Ed.), *Play as exploratory learning.* Beverly Hills, CA: Sage, 1974.

Smith, Nich. *The development of new evaluation methodologies.* Paper and Report Series No. 6. Portland, OR: Northwest Regional Educational Laboratory, 1978.

Smith, Nick. Evaluation utilization: Some needed distinctions. *Evaluation Network Newsletter,* 1980, 16, 24-25.

Smith, Nick L. *Metaphors for evaluation: sources of new methods.* Newbury Park, CA: Sage, 1981.

Sperry, Roger W. Lateral specialization of cerebral function in the surgically separated hemispheres. In F. J. McGulgan & R. A. Schoonover (Eds.), *The psychophysiology of thinking.* New York: Academic Press, 1973.

Steel, Flora Annie. *English fairy tales.* New York: Mayflower Books, 1980.

Steele, Fritz. *Consulting for organizational change.* Amherst: University of Massachusetts Press, 1975.

Stadsklev, R. (Ed.). *Handbook of simulation gaming in social education, part I. Text.* Alabama: Institute of Higher Education Research and Services, 1974.

Stadsklev, R. (Ed.). *Handbook of simulation gaming in social education, part II. Directory:* Alabama: Institute of Higher Education Research and Services, 1975.

Stufflebeam, Daniel. An interview with Daniel L. Stufflebeam. *Educational Evaluation and Policy Analysis,* 1980, 2, 90.

Sutton-Smith, B. Child's play, very serious business. *Psychology Today,* 1971, December.

Tansey, P. J., & Unwin, D. *Simulation and gaming in education.* London: Methuen, 1969.

Taylor, John, & Walford, Rex. *Learning and the simulation game.* Beverly Hills, CA: Sage, 1978.

Templin, Patricia. Photography in evaluation. *Research on Evaluation Program Newsletter,* 1979, 2. (Portland, OR: Northwest Regional Educational Labortory).

Templin, Patricia. Photography in evaluation: Revisited. *Research on Evaluation Program Newsletter,* 1980, 2. (Portland, OR: Northwest Regional Educational Laboratory.)

Tikunoff, William, with Ward, B. *Interactive research and development on teaching.* San Francisco: Far West Laboratory for Educational Research and Development, 1980.

Treadwell, Y. Humor and creativity. *Psychological Reports,* 1970, 26, 55-58.

Tversky, A., & Kahneman, D. Judgement under uncertainty: Heuristics and biases. *Science,* 1974, 185, 1124-1131.

Vance, Mike. *Creative thinking.* Chicago: Nightingale-Conant Corporation, 1982.

Wagner, Jon (Ed.). *Images of information: Still photography in the social sciences.* Beverly Hills, CA: Sage, 1979.

Weiss, Carol H. (Ed.). *Using social research in policy making.* Lexington, MA: D. C. Heath, 1977.

Weiss, Carol H., & Bucuvalas, Michael J. Truth tests and utility tests: Decisionmakers' frames of reference for social science research. *American Sociological Review,* 1980, 45, 302-313.

Wright, Albert, & Nammons, Mary Anne. *Guidelines for Peace Corps cross-cultural training.* Estes Park, CO: Center for Research and Education, 1970.

Wright, Gene. *Masters of magic.* New York: Pyramid, 1976.

Worthen, B. Metaphors and methodologies for evaluation. Paper presented at the annual meeting of the American Educational Research Association, Toronto, 1978.

von Oech, Roger. *A whack on the side of the head: How to unlock your mind for innovation.* New York: Warner Books, 1983.

Young, Carlotta Joiner, & Comtois, Joseph. Increasing congressional utilization of evaluation. In F. M. Zweig (Ed.), *Evaluation in legislation.* Beverly Hills, CA: Sage, 1979.

About The Author

Michael Quinn Patton is on the faculty of the University of Minnesota, where he served as Director of the Minnesota Center for Social Research (1975-1980) and where he was named outstanding teacher of the year (in 1976) for his innovative evaluation teaching. Dr. Patton has served as an evaluation consultant to a wide range of human services projects, including programs in agricultural extension, education, criminal justice, health, energy conservation, and community development. He has participated in evaluations at the local, county, state, national, and international levels, including a two-year project at the University of the West Indies (Trinidad).

Dr. Patton is the author of four immensely popular books on evaluation (*Utilization-Focused Evaluation*, now in its second edition; *Qualitative Evaluation Methods; Practical Evaluation*; and the present volume). He has also recently completed work on a volume entitled *How to Use Qualitative Methods in Evaluation* for the second edition of the *Program Evaluation Kit* (in press). He is the author of numerous articles, reports, and conference papers on evaluation and is in considerable demand as a lecturer and workshop leader on this subject—both in the U.S. and overseas. Dr. Patton was recently elected to serve as President of the American Evaluation Association for 1987-1988. In 1984, he was the recipient of the Evaluation Research Society's Myrdal Award for "outstanding contributions to evaluation use and practice."